THE FRANK FAMILY THAT SURVIVED

Gordon F. Sander is an American journalist and historian who until recently was based in London, where he contributed to a variety of papers, including the *Financial Times*, as well as BBC Radio 4, for which he wrote and narrated the acclaimed documentary which inspired this book. He was most recently writer-in-residence at Risley College, Cornell University, and is the author of *Serling* (1992), which was nominated for the Pulitzer Prize.

Further praise for *The Frank Family That Survived*:

'A remarkable wartime story' *Mail on Sunday*

'*The Frank Family That Survived* is an absorbing account of their ordeal, written by none other than the son of the survivors, grounded in a larger socio-political reality, and filtered through the perspective of a distinguished historian-journalist . . . His book is also likely to linger in the memory because of certain vital questions it raises.' *The Statesman (India)*

'Gordon Sander's book will appeal to anyone who was moved by Anne's diary, answering as it does the oft-asked question of what might have become of Anne Frank had she survived. It also is beautifully written. It deserves to be widely read.'
Carol Ann Lee, author of *Anne Frank: A Biography*

'This is the remarkable story of a Jewish family called Frank . . . It isn't often that one reads about the Jews who survived the Occupation. It is a joy to read of a family who outsmarted their Nazi tormentors.'
Glasgow Evening News

By the same author

SERLING

THE FRANK FAMILY THAT SURVIVED

A Twentieth-Century Odyssey

Gordon F. Sander

arrow books

Published by Arrow Books in 2005

1 3 5 7 9 10 8 6 4 2

Copyright © Gordon F. Sander 2004

Introduction © John Keegan 2004

The right of Gordon F. Sander to be identified as the author of this work has been
asserted by him in accordance with the Copyright, Designs and Patents Act, 1988

First published by Hutchinson in 2004

Arrow Books
The Random House Group Limited
20 Vauxhall Bridge Road, London, SW1V 2SA

Random House Australia (Pty) Limited
20 Alfred Street, Milsons Point, Sydney
New South Wales 2061, Australia

Random House New Zealand Limited
18 Poland Road, Glenfield
Auckland 10, New Zealand

Random House (Pty) Limited
Endulini, 5a Jubilee Road
Parktown 2193, South Africa

The Random House Group Limited Reg. No. 954009

www.randomhouse.co.uk

A CIP catalogue record for this book is available from the British Library

Papers used by Random House are natural, recyclable products made from
wood grown in sustainable forests. The manufacturing processes conform to the
environmental regulations of the country of origin

Printed and bound by CPI Antony Rowe, Eastbourne

ISBN 0 09 944329 5

To the memory of Anne Frank and her family, my great-grandmother, Leontine Marburger, Edgar Reich, and the 102,000 Dutch Jews who did not survive.

Contents

Illustrations

Myrtil and mother (*Dorrit Sander*)
Breitenheim youths (*Gustav Ahlers*)
Fred in Holland (*Dorrit Sander*)
Sybil and Jeanne (*Dorrit Sander*)
Evening Standard headline (*Evening Standard*)

Second section

Wilhelmina, Gerbrandy and Bernhard (*Netherlands Institute for War Documentation*)
Seyss-Inquart with schoolchildren (*Netherlands Institute for War Documentation*)
Myrtil and Dorrit in Scheveningen (*Dorrit Sander*)
Dorrit, Sybil and friends (*Dorrit Sander*)
Sketch of Dorrit and Edgar dancing (*Dorrit Sander*)
Sketch of Dorrit and Edgar in the snow (*Dorrit Sander*)
Westerbork list (*Netherlands Institute for War Documentation*)
Edgar at Westerbork (*Dorrit Sander*)
Pieter van den Zandestraat in 1965 (*Gordon F. Sander*)
Round-up of Amsterdam Jews (*Netherlands Institute for War Documentation*)
Rauter and disciple (*Netherlands Institute for War Documentation*)
Annie van der Sluijs and friend (*Dorrit Sander*)
Number 14 Pieter van den Zandestraat (*Gordon F. Sander*)
Aftermath of Haagse labour raid (*Netherlands Photo Archives*)
V-2 missile
Starving Dutch children (*Netherlands Institute for War Documentation*)
Results of misdirected bombing raid (*Royal Air Force*)
Hagenaars greet 'food bombers' (*Netherlands Institute for War Documentation*)
V-E day headline (*The New York Times*)
The Franks after liberation (*Dorrit Sander*)
Myrtil and Julius in Israel (*Dorrit Sander*)
Anne Frank (*Getty Images*)
Sybil and Dorrit in New York (*Dorrit Sander*)
Flory on ship (*Dorrit Sander*)
Newlywed Dorrit and Kurt Sander (*Dorrit Sander*)
Flory at *vernissage* (*Dorrit Sander*)
Three generations of Franks (*Dorrit Sander*)
Dorrit revisits Number 14 (*Dorrit Sander*)

Maps

INTRODUCTION

John Keegan

The story of *The Frank Family That Survived* is as arresting as that of the Frank family – Anne Frank's family – that did not. With this difference: it is a story of triumphant overcoming of circumstances rather than tragic submission to them.

There are so many tragedies associated with the Second World War and its aftermath that the tragedy of the Dutch Jews could be easily overlooked. It might, but for the accident of the survival of Anne Frank's diary, be generally unknown. Yet, smaller in scale though it was than the tragedy of the Polish Jews, it deserves to be remembered. The native Dutch Jewish community was exceptionally talented, as well as being fully integrated into Dutch society. It had been joined during the Thirties by a large contingent of German Jews, fleeing persecution in Hitler's Reich. It was to this émigré community that the Franks of Gordon Sander's story belonged.

Ironically German Jews fled to Holland because they believed that they would be safe there. Holland proclaimed its neutrality which had been respected by all combatants during the First World War. In 1940, however, Hitler decided to violate Dutch territory in his *blitzkrieg* through Belgium into France. The Netherlands in the aftermath of his triumph therefore became part of German-occupied Europe and the Dutch Jews hostage to Hitler's racial policies.

Until 1942 the Dutch Jews survived by German tolerance. Then it became clear that the German occupiers intended to move against them by deporting them to the East. Some, anticipating a ghastly outcome to deportation, went into hiding. Both Frank families did so, in Amsterdam and The Hague respectively.

The Amsterdam Franks were eventually betrayed and fell into German hands. The Hague Franks were protected and supplied by good Dutch friends, until in 1945 Canadian troops of the Liberation Army at last appeared and they could leave their place of hiding and emerge into freedom.

I am privileged to know Dorrit Frank, now Sander, who survived the war in hiding in The Hague. She appears quite unmarked by her experience, indeed looks back on their years as 'an adventure'. It was an adventure that could have ended for her in the gas chamber. Her courage and resilience alone make her story worth telling. Her son, Gordon Sander, has transformed it from a personal saga into a moving and important account of the occupation of the Netherlands and their liberation. *The Frank Family That Survived* is a major contribution to our understanding of the Second World War in all its complexity.

Acknowledgements

First and foremost I must thank my mother, Dorrit, my aunt, Sybil, and my late grandmother, Flory, the three members of the Frank family who were good enough to let me interview them in 1979, when I first tried to write some of their story for a magazine article; and again in 2001, when I was working on the BBC radio series, *The Frank Family That Survived*, by which time Flory had passed away; and then again last year when I was working on this book. This is, indeed, a family-woven tapestry.

How am I to properly thank my mother? In addition to allowing me to interview her yet again for several dozen hours for this book, once it finally became a book, she did dozens of other things to help me, and to help it, along. This long list includes, but is not limited to: flying to London to meet with Tony Whittome, my editor at Random House, and Anthea Morton-Saner, my agent at Curtis Brown; rummaging through her albums to find photos for me – all of the family photos come from her; translating sections of Dutch and German source books for me (she is still fluent in both languages); making calls to Sybil or her friend Jeanne Guthschmidt, née Houtepen, the surviving member of the four Dutchwomen who aided the Franks of 14 Pieter van den Zandestraat, with whom she is still close; to answer lingering questions about aspects of the Franks' experiences while in hiding; reading the entire manuscript several times; and providing home-cooked meals and encouragement during my regular sorties home from London and Ithaca – all this when she is at an age when many of her contemporaries are in their dotage. For all these things and more, as well as for giving me permission to write about the Frank family in the first place, thanks, Mom!

I am also deeply grateful to my Aunt Sybil for her less extensive, but still very crucial cooperation. Less the raconteur and perhaps even more deeply scarred by her war experiences than her sister, Sybil initially co-operated with me in 1979 but was unhappy about going back *there*, i.e. to 14 Pieter van den Zandestraat, in 2001, when I decided to do my radio broadcast. The notes from our original interviews were sufficient for the two short fourteen-minute programmes I wrote at that time.

However, I felt, Sybil's cooperation, as well as her blessing, were imperative for the book. Thankfully she granted me both, including sitting down and writing out a twelve-page letter that filled in many of the remaining holes in my account of the Frank family saga, as well as taking several later fact-checking calls from my assistants. Although I was not able to spend as much time with Sybil as I would have liked, I have tried to credit her version of events, in the minor ways they differ from my mother's as well as to include her voice in this account. This book is hers too.

I am also deeply grateful to my late grandmother, Flory, whom I interviewed at great length in 1979 for the original magazine article. I am very glad that something finally came of all those hours we spent in her apartment on Riverside Drive discussing the war. My late grandfather Myrtil's formidable spirit also permeates this book, and his memory helped me see it to completion.

Various other members of the Frank diaspora also provided vital information and documentation. Prominent amongst these is my mother's cousin, Lotte, whose parents, Lisbeth and Ernst, moved to Palestine in the 1930s and made a new life there with Lisbeth's mother, Johanna (my great-grandmother). As family genealogist, Lotte helped me trace the Frank family tree back to the eighteenth century, when the first Frank, David Frank, ambled into Breitenheim. In addition, Lotte provided me with a wealth of information about the Frank family's Rhenish period, including the original vineyard, right down to a copy of Max Frank's letterhead, which is reproduced herein. Although I have never been to Breitenheim, thanks to Lotte I feel that I have. I look forward to meeting her someday, and extending my heartfelt thanks to her, in person. In the meantime, these words have to make do.

I am indebted to my English cousin Celia, the daughter of my great-uncle Julius, Myrtil's brother, who was a virtual sister to me during my London years, and who, with her husband, Martin, has encouraged me throughout. There is, unquestionably, a little piece of her in this book, as well as, by extension, of Julius. I am also indebted to Celia's mother, Louise, who took the time to answer a lengthy questionnaire from me about her colourful ex-husband and his early days.

While I am on the subject of the Frank family, I must also extend heartfelt thanks to my brother Lee for supplying me with several key pieces of information about the Franks and their underground landlord and helper, the late Annie van der Sluijs whom he met during a pilgrimage of his own to Holland with my cousin Gerald in 1981, as well as for his general support of my family historical endeavours. Likewise, I am grateful to Sybil's daughter, Vicki, for her backing.

The process of researching and writing this book has, I believe, brought us as a family a little closer together.

Moving away from the Franks, and back to England, I must thank Sir John Keegan, whom I am privileged to call my friend and mentor, and who, along with his dear wife, Susanne, catalysed and presided over both the broadcast and literary forms of this tale, and who bolstered me in every conceivable kind of way – including feeding and sheltering me! And is there a better cook, or host, in all of England than Susanne Keegan? It would not be too much of an exaggeration to say that this book is a flower of Kilmington.

Speaking of flowers, particularly of the English variety, I would be remiss if I did not proffer profuse thanks to Rose Keegan, daughter of John and Susanne, for her love and support of my various English projects, including this one, as well as for correcting my English pronunciation. Certainly one of the most memorable moments of my life was at Kilmington Manor one evening in September 2001, when I listened along with John and Rose to the first segment of *The Frank Family That Survived* which I had nervously recorded several weeks before at Broadcasting House and saw how moved they were. It was then, I think, that I decided that I must do something more with this. And thanks, too, to my honorary English brother, Matthew, for his staunch backing (and numerous beers!).

While we are in the vicinity of Broadcasting House, I must, too, offer my profound thanks to Richard Bannerman, my producer at Radio 4, for guiding *The Frank Family That Survived* through the labyrinthine corridors of the BBC, and out through the microphone. If it wasn't for Richard's original confidence in this project, neither the series nor the book would have happened.

I would also like to acknowledge Gillian Walnes of the Anne Frank

Trust, who has devoted her life to maintaining the memory and ideals of Anne Frank and who has been a great support.

On to Holland.

One of the best dividends of a project such as this is the friends you make along the way – friends like Dienke Hondius, the historian at the Anne Frank House. For countless insights into the Dutch Holocaust; for welcoming me into, as well as letting me use, her home in Amsterdam as a temporary base for my researches; for providing me with introductions to other key members of the Dutch historical profession (a very closed club); as well as numerous other favours and kindnesses, she and her husband, Jan Erik, also of the Anne Frank Foundation, have my deepest gratitude. In November 2003 I was pleased partly to repay Dienke's help by inviting her to join me for a presentation about the Dutch Holocaust that we delivered at the Society of the Humanities at Cornell. That was certainly a fine moment, as well.

I am also grateful to the other distinguished Dutch historians who helped me better to understand the context for this story. High on this list is Bart van der Boom, the chronicler of The Hague during World War II, who is responsible for much of the 'local colour', such as it is, in this book, and who went to considerable trouble for me, including, on one memorable spring Amsterdam afternoon, poring over the map of The Hague with me in his canalside apartment overlooking the Prinsengracht not far from the *Anne Frank Huis*. I am also indebted to Bert Jan Flim, another Dutch Holocaust expert, who also provided valuable data.

I am grateful to the staff of the Netherlands Institute for War Documentation, the superlative Dutch war archive, where I found numerous key documents relating to the Franks, including the original 1941 Dutch–Jewish census – what a moment that was when Myrtil's name flew up at me in the microfilm reader there – and the dreadful ones confirming when Edgar Reich, my mother's fiancé, and Leontine, her grandmother, were dispatched to Auschwitz and Sobibor, respectively. I am thankful to Johannes Houwink ten Cate, the chief Holocaust expert there, for his time and good offices. Ditto his fellow archivist Rene Kok and Peter Romijn, Head of Research and a Holocaust scholar in his own right, who answered many of my questions, as well as did everything they could to make a foreign researcher feel at home in their special institution. Two other Dutch facilities and their staff greatly assisted me: Memorial Camp Westerbork, the moving museum on the site of the former transit camp from where Leontine, Edgar, and 102,000 others were dispatched to the East; and Bibliotheca Rosenthalia, the Judaica library of Amsterdam University.

Very high on my Dutch honour roll are Ernst Sittig, the nephew of Annie van der Sluijs and his wife, Sylvia, who were my hosts during my various sorties to The Hague and who, remarkably enough, tracked *me* down after hearing my BBC broadcast. Ernst, who lived at 14 Pieter van den Zandestraat after the Franks moved out, was able to draw an exact blueprint of the flat for me, as well as fill me in on many other things, including the tragic fate of the Schnells, the German-Jewish émigrés who lived at number 14 before the Franks. In a very real sense, they took both me and my project to their hearts, and I will always love them for it. I am also extremely thankful to Leo Ullman, another Dutch Jew who 'dived under' in Amsterdam in 1942 and who survived, thanks to a sympathetic Dutch policeman, for generously sharing his memories and observations with me.

Dank je wel!, as well, to my Dutch friends Jacky Voncken and Theresa Norris, who took it upon themselves to act as my co-hosts during my stays in Amsterdam, supplying me with lots of *jonge jenever* and sympathy, and checking my Dutch spelling to boot. Thank you all, and thank you, Holland!

Two Germans made a significant contribution to this book. I am particularly indebted to Nina Senger, a Berlin-based art historian, who, after getting in touch with me to answer a question she had about my grandfather's art dealings, repaid the favour many times over by agreeing to help me find material *I* needed about the Franks' early days, including a crucial book about Breitenheim that I would never have obtained otherwise. I am also deeply thankful to my old friend and colleague, Matthias Matussek, the London bureau chief of *Der Spiegel*, who kindly reviewed the German section of the book, and whose friendship, along with that of his wife, Ulrike, helped me outgrow my inherited Germanophobia.

Finally, to America, and to my alma mater, Cornell University. Perhaps the wisest decision I made during the course of this project was to bring it back to Cornell, where my career as a writer and historian began thirty years ago. I wrote the manuscript itself as an artist in residence at Cornell's Risley Residential College for the Creative and Performing Arts.

I am deeply indebted to the students and staff of Risley for giving me, and this book, a home for the past two years, as well as a virtual family to boot. I am not sure how I would have completed it if not for Risley, and in particular the three gung-ho Risleyites – Sarah Ruth Jacobs, David Schoonover and Erin Geld – who were consecutively my chief assistants and researchers here.

Each brought something special to this project. Sarah, a brilliant English major from Maine who was my aide-de-camp during the 2002–03 academic year, brought her persistence and her deep research skills, as well as her knowledge of German. David, the future lawyer to whom Sarah passed the research torch, and who powered me through the first few chapters of the book, brought his uncanny analytical ability, as well as his knack for unearthing amazing source material.

Next we come to Erin Geld, the precocious freshman who took up the baton from David, and invested the greater part of her freshman year in this project, as well as, cumulatively, the most time in it. For sacrificing her Saturday nights, as well as quite a few Sunday mornings; for putting up with my handwriting; for her unfailing good humour and steadfast faith in me and this project, and much much more I shall forever be in her debt. I am not sure whether, given the chance, she would do it again, nor am I sure I would ask her, but I sure am glad she did all she did when she did, without which I am not sure what I would have done!

Thanks, too, to the three Cornell history professors who helped imbue me with my love of history, as well as my historiographical standards, as a student at Cornell thirty years ago, and who returned as my advisers upon my return to the Hill – Michael Kammen, Laurence Moore and Dominick LaCapra. I also thank James McConkey, Professor of English Emeritus, my mentor as a memoirist, for his navigational assistance.

Thanks, as well, to the Cornell Fine Arts Library, under whose magical dome I wrote the bulk of this book, and where I hope to write many more. Thank you, Cornell!

Other friends on both sides of the Atlantic to whom I am indebted for information, food, encouragement, or other forms of support include: Bryan Alexander, Jesse Braverman, Eric Goldstein, Urs Jakob, Ami Hasan, Claire Lauruol, Christian Moustgaard, David Owen, Ron Simon, Bob Stein, Louise Tornehave and Suzanne Tremblay.

In New York I would like to acknowledge the support of David Harris, executive director of the American Jewish Committee, who has been a backer of this project since its inception a quarter of a century ago. The Center for Jewish History of the Leo Baeck Institute has also been a tremendous resource.

Acknowledgements

Last but certainly not least, profound thanks to Tony Whittome, of Random House and his colleague, James Nightingale.

I am also extremely grateful to Anthea Morton-Saner, my agent at Curtis Brown Limited, for being amongst the first to believe, and much else, as well. Ditto her American counterpart, Kirsten Manges, who, as a Dutch national, took especial interest in this project.

Finally we come to the part where I, the author, give thanks to my wife or partner. In the event, I did not have a wife or partner during this project. Frankly, I fear to think of anyone having to put up with me during the darker passages of this particular literary odyssey, and so, in the end, I got through them myself. Perhaps, I hope, I will not be quite so alone on the next trip. However, if I was alone this time I think this book was the beneficiary. And I thank God for giving me the strength to complete it.

Ithaca, New York
20 April 2004

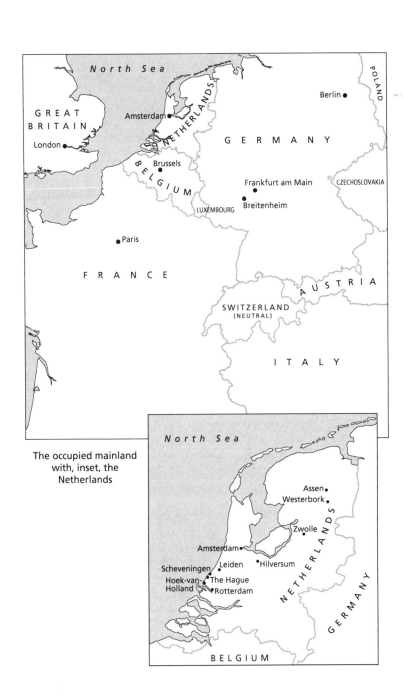

North Sea

GREAT
BRITAIN

London ●

Amsterdam ●

NETHERLANDS

BELGIUM

Brussels ●

POLAND

Berlin ●

GERMANY

Frankfurt am Main ●

Breitenheim ●

LUXEMBOURG

CZECHOSLOVAKIA

● Paris

FRANCE

SWITZERLAND
(NEUTRAL)

AUSTRIA

ITALY

The occupied mainland
with, inset, the
Netherlands

North Sea

Assen ●

Westerbork ●

Zwolle ●

Amsterdam ●

NETHERLANDS

Leiden ●

Scheveningen

Hoek-van-
Holland

The Hague

● Hilversum

Rotterdam ●

GERMANY

BELGIUM

PROLOGUE

14 July 1942

Now we must disappear . . .
What Myrtil Frank said to his family at
9 Eendrachtstraat, Amsterdam, the evening
before the Franks 'dived under'

Tuesday 14 July 1942 was the longest day in the lives of Myrtil and Flory
Frank and their daughters, Dorrit and Sybil, four German-Jewish émigrés
trapped in occupied Holland. Dorrit recalled that it was at about ten in
the morning that she, her mother and sister emerged from their latest
and last 'legal' residence at 9 Eendrachtstraat, a small, nondescript street
in the *Rivierenbuurt* or River Quarter district of Amsterdam *Zuid*, and
began walking north in the direction of the city's main train station,
Centraal Station. They were accompanied by Annie van der Sluijs, Dorrit's
Dutch teacher and the family's close friend, who had agreed to let the
Franks go to ground in a small apartment she maintained in The Hague.
Walking determinedly in pairs, but not so determinedly as to draw attention to themselves, the four casually dressed women were focused on one
thing and one thing only that sweltering July morning: getting safely to
The Hague. 'It was very hot and we were very frightened,' said Dorrit.
The Hague, normally a fifty-minute train ride from Amsterdam, 'seemed
a million miles away'. And for all practical purposes, given the minefield
they had to negotiate before they got there, it was.

As the Frank women left 9 Eendrachtstraat and took their first steps
into the broad daylight of occupied Holland, the pulsing terror they had
all felt on 10 May 1940, the day the Germans invaded – the feeling that
they were again quarry for the Nazis, the same Nazis they had already

successfully escaped seven years before – came flooding back, leading the three *onderduikers* – or 'people who dive under', as the increasing numbers of Jews and other people who were going into hiding were dubbed – to feel faint and unsteady of gait. From this moment, the Franks, now without their obligatory yellow *sterren*, considered a criminal offence in itself, were taking their lives in their hands. But there was no turning back.

Years later, Dorrit and Sybil would remember few details of their long, perilous walk to the train terminus in the faraway centre of town. 'We were in a trance,' Dorrit said. However, by examining a street map of Amsterdam, it is possible to divine the probable route the four women – as well as Myrtil, who decided to join them later (a group of five would look too suspicious, he felt) – took that morning. As the map indicates, there are only so many ways to traverse the approximately two-mile distance from south to north from Eendrachtstraat to Centraal Station, and it is fairly certain that the women would have taken the most direct path.

First, the four would have taken a short zigzag out of the small, maze-like portion of the *Rivierenbuurt* in which Eendrachtstraat was located: right several hundred feet on Grevelingenstraat, left on to Volkerakstraat, then right again on to Deurloostraat. This would have brought them to Scheldestraat, a major north–south thoroughfare which, after Amstelkanaal becomes Ferdinand Bolstraat, is one of the main streets leading out of the Amsterdam South area.

In the crowded lanes of what had become a large pen for the bulk of Holland's Jewish population, Flory, Dorrit, Sybil and Annie would first have encountered significant pedestrian traffic. Here, as they passed crowds of Jews still wearing their stars, along with the usual admixture of non-Jewish Amsterdammers who journeyed to the Ferdinand Bolstraat and its surrounding streets to bargain-hunt, their composure would first have been put to the test.

The reality of the German occupation would not have been more apparent that day than on most of the seven hundred and ninety-odd days that had transpired since 16 May 1940, when the victorious *Wehrmacht* marched into Amsterdam, trundling its equipment, including a blaring marching band, followed by the Gestapo and other units of the new 'civil' administration, as thousands of weeping Dutchmen looked on.

The Germans, hoping not to further alienate the local populace, whom they still wished to win over to the Nazi cause, had been considerably less conspicuous since then, preferring to leave most of the day-to-day administration of the ancient city of 800,000 to their orderly minded Dutch 'cousins'. This pleasant co-arrangement had worked so well that the Germans had rarely found it necessary to station more than a hundred of their police in the city at any one time.

The principal and memorable exception to this rule had occurred during the *Februaristaking* – or 'February strike' – of the previous year, when large sections of the populace rose up in protest at the increasing anti-Jewish measures, shutting down transportation and throwing the city into chaos. The strike (which at least one Dutch historian has called the only known anti-pogrom strike in history) wrong-footed the Germans, who had begun to think that they had won the battle for Dutch hearts and minds. The near-insurrection was quickly suppressed with the armed aid of several hundred additional German policemen with instructions to shoot at will; which they did, killing nine strikers and sympathisers and wounding a score of others.

Things had quietened down considerably since then and they had remained quiet, allowing German forces to return to their preferred low profile and to leave the policing of Amsterdam in the hands of the local constabulary. If Flory, Dorrit, Sybil and Annie saw any policemen as they strode up Ferdinand Bolstraat, looking as debonair as they could under the circumstances, the chances are they would have been Dutch police. No doubt, if they were looking, they would have seen a German military vehicle or staff car pass. However, at least from a distance, everything would have seemed quite normal: just the usual blur of shoppers, cars, lorries and, of course, because this was Holland, a myriad of bicycles.

If the women had been looking – but of course, they really weren't. At that moment they were interested in getting to the station and getting on that train. Their eyes were focused straight ahead.

By the same token, the women could doubtless have glimpsed press posters proclaiming the latest victory of Hitler's armies in Russia, then steadily approaching Moscow; or of the German U-boats, who were having a field day sinking Allied freighters in the Atlantic; as well as other assorted manifestations of Nazi rule. Of course, they didn't need press posters to be reminded of the fact that, all the brave (and illicit) talk about a so-called Second Front in Europe notwithstanding, any plausible hope of an Allied invasion of *Festung Europa* lay years in the future. They knew that. That was one of the reasons they were 'diving under'.

Nor did they need any additional reminder of the principal reason they had decided to take cover: the fast-escalating and increasingly visible repression of the Jewish population. They would have been able to discern this in the haunted looks of the properly bestarred Jews they passed on the street, many of whom would have been wondering when the 'authorities', in tandem with the *Joodsche Raad* or Jewish Council – the 'community organisation' the Germans had established in order to better deal with 'Jewish affairs' in the wake of the *Februaristaking* – would make their next move. Already under intense pressure from Berlin to meet the stipulated Dutch contribution to the recently mapped-out *Endlösung* (Final Solution), Ferdinand Aus der Fünten – the Austrian majordomo of the *Zentralstelle*, or Central Office for Jewish Emigration, as the *Endlösung*-expediting organisation was euphemistically called – had already communicated to the Council his extreme displeasure at the poor response to the first official call-up of Jews for 'labour deployment' in the East ten days earlier, when less than half of those summoned had responded.

For the past week Amsterdam had buzzed with rumours that Aus der Fünten and his Austrian Nazi colleague, Hans Albin Rauter, the head of the local SS, were preparing some sort of mass raid on the three semighetto Jewish districts of the city, including the *Rivierenbuurt*. Evidently a number of the summoned Jews had begun to suspect what 'labour deployment' really meant. Something had to be done, Aus der Fünten and Rauter had confidentially agreed.

In the event, just now, as the women walked north on Ferdinand Bolstraat, Rauter's men were preparing to carry out a lightning *razzia* (raid) on Jewish Amsterdam in order to help expedite matters, the first of the dozens of raids that would all but clear the city of its above-ground Jewish population. After two years of playing cat and mouse with the Jewish community (if the cowed and divided indigenous Jewish population of 140,000 could still be called that), the Nazi *Maus* trap was about to snap shut.

No doubt, if they had been looking, Flory, Dorrit, Sybil and Annie would have seen evidence of this increasing tension that morning in Amsterdam. If not, they would have sensed it.

Onward the three Jewesses and their Gentile friend walked, past the famed flea market on Albert Cuypstraat, filled as usual with bargain-hunters and stalls stretching into the distance; past the towering Heineken brewery, with the big golden letters 'HEINEKEN BROUWERIJ' proudly embossed on the side; over the Stadhouderskade and into the heart of the centrum; up and over Prinsengracht, the first of the four canalised 'rings' comprising

Amsterdam proper; over the next, the Keizergracht, past the fortress-like headquarters of the collaborationist-run state bank, the *Nederlandse Handelsmaatschappij*. The frieze of three stolid workmen carved into the bank's granite façade stared down at the fugitives, indifferent to their fate.

Onward, into the bustling heart of the occupied city – there would have been more suits now, as well as more German uniforms – bracing themselves for the yet more dangerous and illegal train ride to The Hague which loomed ahead. The fugitive party continued to walk, up the crowded Rokin and across the vast Dam Square, past the empty palace of the Dutch queen, Wilhelmina, who, following the German invasion, had fled to England in 1940, whence the exiled *Moeder des Vaderlands* – or the 'Nation's Mother', as she had been affectionately called before the war – broadcast stirring speeches of resistance over the illegal British radio. Some of Wilhelmina's subjects listened; some, resigned to the inevitability of German victory, did not. In any event, there probably would have been a German armoured car stationed here, if only as a further reminder of who really ruled the land of William the Silent. That would have been hard to avoid.

Onward they went, eyes straight ahead, as they had agreed the night before, when Myrtil had first revealed to the family his preparations for 'diving under' in The Hague. 'Now we must disappear,' he had told his wide-eyed daughters (his wife, of course, already knew). Past the restricted, Jews-only, café, where Dorrit and her fiancé Edgar, then 'interned' (as it was called) at Kamp Westerbork, the still publicly accessible German work camp in the north-east, had met in March. (Unbeknownst to Dorrit, Edgar was about to be selected for the first train to the East, scheduled to leave for Auschwitz the following morning.)

At the time, Edgar had been released from Westerbork for the day so that he could go through the motions of registering for the latest census. The Germans were still trying to keep up appearances then. The owner had at first tried to bar his way into the restricted café because in his opinion, the blue-eyed, blond-haired young man did not look Jewish enough! To think: *Not Jewish enough!* And they couldn't help but laugh, despite themselves. *Not Jewish enough!*

Perhaps Dorrit recalled this as she walked by.

Onward, up the pedestrian-filled Damrak, closer, closer, quickly but not too quickly, onward to freedom, or whatever awaited the newly committed *onderduikers* at 14 Pieter van den Zandestraat, the address of Annie's apartment.

Finally, at 11.30, about an hour and a half after setting out from Eendrachtstraat, the four women entered the cavernous Centraal Station.

The first leg of the 'dive' was over.

Now came the second and most dangerous part, the fifty-minute train ride to *Den Haag*. Departing shortly after noon, the ten-car, three-*Klasse* train was scheduled to make one stop, in Leiden, before continuing on to The Hague, where the Franks had lived during the first seven years of their Dutch exile. During the halcyon years before the war and the German invasion, when the family were domiciled in a large three-storey house in Scheveningen, the beachside annexe of The Hague, they had taken this same route back and forth many times.

But, of course, that had been when Jews were free to travel, before the cat-and-mouse game with the Nazis had begun. In their case this had included an intervening move to Hilversum (after the Germans made all German-Jewish refugees move away from the coast, on the dubious pretext that they might abet a future Allied counter-invasion), and a subsequent forced move to Amsterdam and Eendrachtstraat, as part of the further concentration of the Jewish population.

The women entered a car marked '*2nd Klasse*'. Myrtil and Annie, during their planning for this day, had agreed that it would be best if they travelled second class, although every class of the train was essentially as dangerous as any other. Silently the four filed into one of the vacant upholstered booths, Flory and Dorrit seated opposite Annie and Sybil, deliberately avoiding eye contact with each other, each playing their role.

The star-less trio of Jewish women had boarded the train as criminals and their Gentile friend as a criminal conspirator. Now they really were past the point of no return. Before they embarked, if they had been caught without their *sterren* and had been stopped by a Dutch policeman, particularly a sympathetic one, the prospective *onderduikers* might have got away with a simple reprimand. But taking a train – any train – was different. Flory and the girls, in express defiance of the widely promulgated ban of 15 June on Jews taking trains, or any kind of public transport, as well as the edict of 29 April requiring them to wear *sterren*, and thus, now, presumably fugitives, would not have got away with a reprimand any more: they would have been arrested. As Flory waited for the train to get going, she later recalled, she couldn't help but think back to the last time the Franks had taken a train, to

flee the Nazis in March 1933, after the original decision to seek Dutch
sanctuary. But that had been different: at least they had known what
was ahead of them – or at least they had *thought* they knew.

But again, there was little time for retrospect. The only thing that
mattered now was *getting there*, to 14 Pieter van den Zandestraat.

After what seemed an eternity, the old steam-powered train finally
snaked out of Centraal Station, bound for The Hague. The personnel
on the train were all Dutch: Arthur Seyss-Inquart, the German
Reichskommissar and head of the Nazis' so-called 'Austrian Mafia' in
Holland, had agreed to allow the Dutch to run their own trains,
provided they fulfilled German transport requests. Right on time, the
efficient Dutch conductor entered the Franks' compartment, politely
asked them and the equally deadpan Annie for their tickets, and left.
Now the women were alone with their thoughts and their fears.

At any moment, one of the German soldiers regularly assigned to
guard trains in order to apprehend law-breakers – a broadening category including downed Allied pilots and escaping Jews – might appear
in the compartment door and demand everyone's papers.

None appeared. The train continued its scheduled passage . . .

. . . '*STATION LEIDEN . . . LEIDEN*,' the conductor announced
from the head of the car a very long forty minutes later, as the train
slowly pulled into the famous town. Its celebrated university, which
became an early centre of the resistance, had already been closed down.
'*LEIDEN . . . LEIDEN*.'

A middle-aged couple approached the car during the seven-minute
wait. The woman had come to see her husband off. Because of the
heat, the windows of the car were open, and in spite of themselves,
the party of fugitives found themselves listening to the couple's placid
goodbyes.

'Will you be back by six?' the wife called out as the train departed.
While the Franks, ensconced in their parallel universe, listened on, the
dutiful Dutch husband, standing in the aisle next to their compartment, pantomimed his assent. Yes, he would be back by six. 'Then I'll
put the potatoes on!'

The women suppressed smiles: if only we had such concerns, they
thought to themselves.

Another nerve-racking twenty minutes later, the train from
Amsterdam bearing the three Franks and their gentile guardian arrived
at Station Hollandse Spoor. Myrtil had instructed them to take the

train there, rather than the one that went to The Hague's main station, Station Staatspoor (today's Central Station), even though the latter was actually closer to their ultimate destination, on the hunch that the former, smaller one, would have less security.

And so that was what they did. The second leg of the dangerous trip was over. Father had been right: still no sign of police or soldiers (or at least none that they could later recall, but then again, perhaps they weren't looking).

Silently, the four women paired off and, following Annie's lead, walked through the somewhat unfamiliar streets to her flat and their designated hiding place. Having once lived there for seven years, the Franks already knew most parts of The Hague, but they were not as familiar with the twisting streets of this lower-class area of town, which lay between the station and the city centre. Pieter van den Zandestraat was a minuscule street lined with two rows of modest two-storey attached apartments. It was not far from the Binnenhof, the ancient site of the former Dutch legislature and now the nerve centre of the German occupation.

After their second running of the Nazi gauntlet, the three fugitive German Jews and their Dutch accomplice arrived at the modest wooden door of number 14. It was adorned only with a small brass knocker and a decorative pane of *de Stijl*-style coloured glass on the top. They walked in.

Years before, Dorrit had met Annie for her Dutch lessons in this warren-like flat. It hadn't seemed small then. It did now, as the three took a first, wary look around. That space – that blessed, cursed space – would continue to shrink in size for the next thirty-four months, the term of the Franks' self-incarceration.

Of course, they did not know that then. Above all, they had made it.

But where was Father?

Flory and the girls waited; Annie thought it best to leave. Finally, around six, while it was still light, as Dorrit later recalled, her father opened the door, flashed his ever-ready, ebullient smile and embraced his family. He had just made it out of Amsterdam, he said. Everything was closed down. Search parties were pulling people out of their homes in the River Quarter. The *razzias* had begun.

The Franks had got out just in time. They had successfully disappeared. But *what* had they got into? How long would they have to stay here, in this modestly furnished pied-à-terre, crammed with the supplies with which Myrtil and Annie had stocked their not especially secure hiding place?

'If we had known that we would be there for nearly three years,' Flory recalled, 'I'm not sure we would have undertaken it.'

PART ONE

FATHERLAND
GERMANY, 1866–1933

CHAPTER I

Breitenheim

We Jews are Germans and nothing else.
Israelit, German-Jewish newspaper

Like her husband, Myrtil, Flory Frank belonged to both the most and the least fortunate generation of German Jews: the most fortunate because theirs, the generation that was born at the end of the nineteenth century and came of age around the time of the First World War, was the first to enjoy the fruits of full emancipation, including success in business and public life; the least because that emancipation coincided with the rise of Adolf Hitler.

Nearly half a century after the Franks fled Germany for Dutch exile in 1933, Flory still looked pained when she described how she felt after she arrived in Holland. 'I felt as if I had lost my fatherland,' she said one sunny afternoon in 1979 at her rooftop apartment on Riverside Drive in Manhattan, where she and Myrtil (who had died in 1968) were able to re-create a simulacrum of the good life they had once enjoyed in Berlin.

But it was only a simulacrum. Nothing could replace the feeling of belonging, of acceptance, that the Franks and their peers had enjoyed as Jews – as *German* Jews – before the Nazi blight.

Flory was then an octogenarian with a razor-sharp memory. 'I was proud to be Jewish,' she said as, surrounded by her fine art collection, she recalled those long-lost days. Her paintings included at least one work which the Franks were able to take with them when they fled Germany and had managed to hold on to after they fled the Nazis again in 1942 and went into hiding: it was a survivor, like Flory herself. 'I was proud to be Jewish,' she said again, as the sun set behind her, 'but I was also proud to be a German.' There was no bitterness in Flory's voice, only sadness.

And for a few wonderful years, when Weimar was at its apogee, what a world that was, as the fun-filled photographs from the Franks' Berlin days showed.

'Of course,' she added, as an afterthought, 'I knew there were weaknesses in the German character. Too much false pride, for one . . .'

'If we are not German we have no homeland,' the German-Jewish politician Gabriel Riesser said in 1867, expressing much the same sentiment as Flory. Like Myrtil and her, as well as their parents, he saw no contradiction in being German and being Jewish. Or, as Riesser's contemporary, the poet Erich Muhsam, put it: 'My Germanness and my Jewishness are like two brothers equally loved by the same mother.'

To be sure, such enthusiastically assimilationist sentiments were fairly novel ones at the time Riesser and Muhsam articulated them. Compared with other western European countries – France, for example, where Jews had enjoyed full emancipation under Napoleon and cultural assimilation had been assumed since the early nineteenth century – the process was a gradual one in Germany, and was resisted, sometimes violently. Pogroms were still a fact of life for German Jews in the early 1800s: witness the barbaric 'Hep! Hep!' riots that swept through Germany in 1819, a reprise of the great pogrom of 1617. So was poverty. Banned from farming, the professions, including the military, and virtually all of the crafts, half of the mid-nineteenth-century German-Jewish population were beggars or close to it, according to Amos Elon, author of *The Pity of It All*, his seminal history of German Jewry.

Until that time, one of the worst places for a German Jew had been the free imperial city of Frankfurt, where Flory's family, the Marburgers, originated. Governed by a hidebound, anti-Semitic oligarchy of patrician merchant families, the city on the river Main that Charlemagne founded in 794 had, since the fourteenth century, more or less continuously confined its Jewish population to a single ghetto street, Judengasse, which they were forbidden to leave after dark or on Sunday; they were also forbidden to walk more than two abreast. Only the Papal States treated its Jews as harshly. It was not until 1864 that all restrictions on the civil rights of Jews were removed.

The great emancipator of Germany's Jews was Otto von Bismarck, the 'Iron Chancellor' of the First Reich who presided over the unification of the disparate states and guided Germany to victory over her French neighbour in the Franco-Prussian War of 1871. It was Bismarck whose 1871 edict granted Jews full civil rights in the constitution of the new united Germany, ratifying Jewish emancipation, and expediting their assimilation into German society. 'The Jew brings to the mixture of different German breeds a certain champagne sparkle that must not be under-estimated,' the hero of the just-concluded conflict with France said. Three generations after the Jewish philosopher Moses Mendelssohn had arrived at the gates of Berlin only to be treated as an outcast, the German Jew had finally arrived.

No fewer than seven thousand Jews had displayed their fealty to the fatherland by enlisting to fight for Germany in the Franco-Prussian War. When Kaiser Wilhelm I rode through the Brandenburg Gate after the triumph of the German army, it was a Jewish maid, Molly Ring, who draped the victory wreath around his neck.

A considerable number of Jews, however, particularly those who lived in the soon-to-be-annexed provinces of Alsace and Lorraine and were of divided loyalties, chose not to wear the German uniform and fled westward: the growing ties between Jews and their fatherland were strong, but they did not yet completely bind. One of the refusants, an uncle of Flory's who would play an influential role in her life, resettled in Paris.

Still, he was an exceptional case. By the time the Second Reich entered its second decade in the 1880s, it is fair to say that most Jews saw no contradiction in being Jewish and being German. At the same time, most Germans, led by Bismarck – whose most prominent confidants included a Jew, Gerson Bleichroder – tried to suppress their inbred anti-Jewish suspicions and treat their Jewish compatriots as equals and neighbours. Most, but not all. As Paul Johnson writes in *The History of the Jews*, 'the truth is that [by the late nineteenth century], despite Germany's long tradition of vicious anti-Jewish feeling – Jews felt at home in Germany'.

Meanwhile, as the Industrial Revolution took hold, the nature of the Jewish population was changing from rural to urban, as was that of the German population. In 1870, a mere 20 per cent of the entire German-Jewish population of 100,000 lived in cities. Forty years later, the proportion of Jews living in the cities had jumped to 60 per cent.

Myrtil Frank, son of Max Frank of Breitenheim and future husband of Flory, was a member of this transitional generation of German Jews.

If there was a region of modern Germany where Jews felt freer than else-where, and less vulnerable to the anti-Semitic virus apparently embedded in the German character, it was the *Rheinland-Pfalz* (Palatinate) – the rolling, agriculturally bountiful region bounded by the Rhine on the east and the Saar on the south.* For one thing, Jews had a long history of habi-tation in this section of Germany, establishing something of a precedent for those who came later; the first Jewish settlement on the Rhine was recorded in the second century AD. Although the relative handful of Jews who were able to establish themselves in the small towns and half-timbered hamlets of the Rhineland were never free from prejudice or persecution – a Jew was persecuted for ritual murder in the village of Xanten-on-the-Rhine as late as 1911 – most came to love their land as much as their Gentile neighbours, even if they didn't necessarily subscribe to the *Nibelungenlied*, the epic poem about the river, and the corresponding myth about the lovelorn maiden who had supposedly thrown herself into its waters at the rock at Lorelei.

Of course, one of the main reasons why the Jews of the Rhineland loved their country, or at least the part they lived in, the Palatinate, was because, unlike the rest of Germany, where Jews were generally forbidden from owning land, they were able to purchase some of it to become vintners, a form of agriculture open to Jews, and which German Jews made their own. By the middle of the nineteenth century, most of the Rhenish vineyards, known for the exquisite white wine they produced, were owned by Jews.

Hence Max Frank of Breitenheim. According to Max's granddaughter Lotte, who lives in Israel, the first Frank ambled into Breitenheim, a small village whose population of several hundred has remained virtually static for the past three centuries (a 1990 census indicated 484 inhabitants), nestled amongst the peaks and valleys of the central Palatinate, in a fertile, sparsely populated, and myth-enshrouded region known as the Hünsruck. With Bad Kreuznach, the nearest town of any size, over twenty miles to the north-east – a full day on horseback, the most common form of trans-portation, if you were sufficiently well-to-do to be able to afford a horse – and the closest city of any consequence, Mainz, thirty-five miles off to

---

* Not that the neighbouring French were immune to the anti-Semitic virus, as the Dreyfus scandal would soon show.

the north, this was – and still is – about as close as you come in Germany to what Americans call the sticks. Frankfurt, the nearest major city, is even further away, nearly sixty miles to the north-east: David's great-grandson, Julius Frank, brother of Myrtil and the author's great-uncle, used to joke that Frankfurt was located half an hour away from Breitenheim by telephone.

All this was fine for the rustic-minded David Frank and his immediate heirs.

Evidently, the conservative burghers of Breitenheim also took a shine to David, who was allowed to move into house number 61, and his son, Gottlieb, born in 1815, who is listed in the town records as being a salesman of goods, including presumably wine, which was to become the family business.

The original village ordinance, drawn up in 1750, shows just how hermetic Breitenheimers were. Amongst its dozens of provisions, in which village life was regimented and organised in the most detailed – and Germanic – way, were puritanical ones declaring that any Breitenheimer who made undue noise overnight had to forfeit a bottle of wine – most of the penalties involved had something to do with wine, not surprising in this viticultural stronghold – another forbidding smoking in barns or stables, as well as several dealing with *verbotenen* strangers and beggars, including one forbidding any villager from taking in a beggar overnight. Presumably the latter proviso was basically directed at Jews, since many beggars in those days *were* Jews.

However, the Franks were allowed to stay. They became Breitenheim's one and only Jewish family and would remain so for the rest of the century, although a second family settled in 1908. They earned the respect and allegiance of the small village by dint of their industry and hard work, as well as permission, sometime around 1860 – about the time of Bismarck's reforms – to purchase and convert a vineyard outside of town and make their contribution to the area's leading industry.

'No country in the world can compare with the Rhenish Provinces in the vast variety and excellence of the wines they produce,' enthused the Baedeker for Germany published in 1878. Among the many Jewish vintners who put Rhenish wines on the map – not to mention the little country town where they were based – were Gottlieb Frank and his son, Max.

Born in 1866, the year Bismarck defeated Austria and excluded it from the rising German Reich (a move that his twentieth-century successor, Adolf Hitler, would later reverse with the aid of his Austrian handyman, and later *Reichskommissar* for the Netherlands, Arthur Seyss-Inquart), Max, who took over the winery from Gottlieb in the 1890s, was duly proud of the family business and committed to expanding and modernising it. In 1890, Max married Johanna Pump, a Jewess from the nearby village of Muhlheim, and the foundation was set for the next generation of Frank vintners. Johanna obliged Max by producing four children, two sons – Myrtil, born in 1893, and Julius, born in 1895 – and two daughters, Irma, born in 1892, and Lisbeth, born in 1897. The family lived in a large, if not opulent, three-storey house next to the winery.

Max's pride in his trade – and his life – is evident from an early 1900s letterhead from the firm. *M. FRANK WEINBAU WEINHANDLUNG*, the ornate stationery announces in large embroidered letters, and in smaller ones below, *Lager in Rhein-Nahe-Mosel-Pfalzweinen / Alle Sorten Cognac, Likör und Südwein*. The body of the letterhead is taken up by an extremely detailed, lovingly wrought etching of the winery, featuring a dozen staff contentedly and assiduously going about their appointed viticultural tasks. There in the *Kellerei* – the main wine cellar – one group of workers is hard at work tending to the great fermenting vats, while in the *Lager Keller* – the storage cellar – another squad of Frank wine workers is busy lining up the barrels of fresh-made beverage. On the top of the order slip is listed Max's telephone number, Amt Meisenheim 22 – he had yet to enter the automobile age, but was sufficiently advanced to have a telephone. In front of the family compound, which appears to take up at least five acres or so, a wagon drawn by two horses bearing barrels of the freshly made wine is ready to pull out. Presiding over this rustic Rhenish scene is the large, no-nonsense Frank family house. Atop the austere-looking manse, the highest point in the picture, a large German flag is proudly snapping in the wind. This was the world of Max Frank, and this, too, was the world his sons Myrtil and Julius inherited.

If Max was a devout vintner and a devout German, he was first and foremost a devout Jew. Every Friday he would drive his horse to Meisenheim, where the nearest synagogue was located, to attend *shul* with the other village Jews of the area, after which he would return to Breitenheim on foot, as custom stipulated. Both sons were bar mitzvahed. This, too, was the world of Max Frank, and the world he expected to pass on to his sons, and they to their sons, just as past generations of Franks had done. The only problem was that neither Myrtil nor his brother Julius was particularly interested in it.

18

Evidently Myrtil was rumbustious from a young age: the earliest story about him has him getting into a brawl with the hapless country tailor whom Max had hired to make the suit for his bar mitzvah in 1906. Something of a dandy, Myrtil – or 'Til, as he was known to his friends and family – would continue to be particular about his clothing for the rest of his life, although this was the only time his fashion sense is known to have driven him to fisticuffs.

The aforementioned qualities – as well as perhaps Myrtil's most striking personal trait, a confidence bordering on hubris – are evident in the earliest known photo of him. Taken in 1910 or 1911, when Myrtil would have been sixteen or seventeen, it shows him and three of his boarding-school classmates, evidently members of the school's crew, sitting in their scull on the river Main in Frankfurt. In the background rises one of Germany's great architectural landmarks, the soaring 300-foot red sandstone tower of St Bartholomew's Cathedral, the august ninth-century church where Roman emperors and kings were once elected and crowned, carefully restored after the 1867 fire that nearly destroyed it.

In the photo there are other oarsmen in the distance, enjoying the fine early summer or early autumn day. And in the foreground, in the middle of the boat, sits Myrtil, clearly dominant, hair neatly parted in the middle, wearing a charismatic smile, arms coyly clasped around his oar so as to better display his ample biceps for the photographer. Here, clearly, was a young man not to be trifled with.

In 1913, when Myrtil was twenty, Max sent his eldest son, who had already shown a head for business, to Frankfurt to apprentice at a commercial firm, no doubt in the expectation that Myrtil would subsequently bring the skills and acumen that he acquired in the big commercial city back to Breitenheim and the family winery. An understandable wish, but a delusory one. From his pomaded hair down to his polished boots, Myrtil Frank was, to the despair of his father, a city boy at heart, and Frankfurt, then still enjoying an economic boom that had seen its population quadruple since 1866, was an exciting city for a savvy young man. There was just no way Max was going to be able to keep Myrtil down on the vineyard after his son had seen the bright lights of Frankfurt.

It was the same for Myrtil's younger brother, Julius, who, moved by his beautiful surroundings, decided to try his hand at painting and design, to the bemusement of his parents. He would later become a professional artist.

Another revealing photograph of Myrtil Frank from this period of his life shows the young businessman, decked out in a finely tailored hat and suit (presumably he didn't beat this tailor up), again sitting by the Main, but this time with two gaily coiffed damsels seated on either side of the young Lothario and making a fuss of him. Doubtless there were other such distaff admirers. But one memorable evening in early 1914, at a performance of the Frankfurt Opera, Myrtil's roving eye fell upon the comely visage of Flory Marburger and his heart went *giocoso*.

If any German city embodied the dramatically enhanced opportunities for the emancipated German Jews of the late nineteenth-century Germany it was Frankfurt. Breaking out of the humiliating ghetto to which they had been so long confined, members of the energised Jewish community quickly moved to the forefront of the city's powerful banking, publishing and textile industries, avidly joining Frankfurt's 'money-making frenzy', as Goethe, a native son, once termed it. By the 1880s, the indigenous Rothschild, Oppenheim and Warburg families – once of the Judengasse, now happily relocated to the leafy vicinity of the *Palmengarten*, a park in the north-west quarter of the city, and other fashionable areas – had risen to become three of the biggest names in German banking. Another Jewish clan, the Sonnemans, controlled the *Frankfurter Allgemeine Zeitung*, one of the city's and the country's most widely read newspapers. By the end of the century, Frankfurt's Jewish population numbered over 25,000 out of a total population of 370,000, making it the second largest German-Jewish community after that of Berlin, and, arguably, the most influential.

'The whole appearance of the city betokens the generally diffused well-being of its inhabitants,' the 1911 edition of *Baedeker's Rhine* informed visitors. Flory's family, the Marburgers, were certainly amongst the numerous Jewish families who shared in this city-wide sense of well-being. Although not quite on the same level as the Oppenheims and Rothschilds, the Marburgers had certainly done all right. The owner of a textile manufacturing company that specialised in making linen, Herman Marburger was successful enough in the 1880s to purchase a large flat near the Palmengarten.

A somewhat dour man who devoted himself to his business, in 1890 Herman married a warm – if controlling – good-humoured girl, Leontine Ullman. From this union issued three children: two sons, the eldest, Ferdi, born in 1893, and Fred, in 1899; and one daughter, Flory, who arrived in 1897 and upon whom Herman and Leontine doted.

Like many upwardly mobile urban Jews of their watershed generation, Herman and Leontine were firm subscribers to the Jewish cult of *Bildung*, or cultivation, which maintained that the most expeditious way for a Jew to become a full, assimilated German was by absorbing German culture. Thus, while Ferdi and Fred were being groomed to be businessmen, Flory was sent to a kind of finishing school for Jewish women, where she imbibed the German classics. At the weekends, Leontine would accompany her daughter to the Städel, the renowned art museum founded by the local banker Johann Friedrich Städel, to which he had bequeathed his magnificent collection of Old Masters. Here, strolling in the halls amongst such masterpieces as Rembrandt's *Blinding of Samson* and Rubens's *Aged Salesman*, Leontine's own love of art – if not her exact tastes – rubbed off on the aesthetically impressionable girl.

Flory's passion for art was further nourished in 1913, when her *Bildung*-minded parents sent her to Paris to spend a year with the relations of a Francophile Alsatian uncle who had fled to Paris in order to escape having to fight for the Kaiser in 1871. The experience left the young Jewess with a pronounced passion for the Impressionists and other modern art, as well as an enhanced awareness of her own swan-like beauty and hourglass figure. She also learned how to play the piano. The young Flory Marburger must have turned many a male head as she promenaded down the Champs Elysées en route to the Louvre.

Not that that really mattered to her. Prim and puritanical like her father, Flory considered physical contact with men something to be avoided for as long as possible (a sentiment, it must be said, that was shared by many if not most of her pre-liberated generation); although one would hardly suspect it from the beguiling teenager with the come-hither look who peers out of the extant photos from this period.

One, a portrait of all five Marburgers on what appears to be a weekend afternoon at their Frankfurt apartment sometime around 1912, shows the immediate family seated around a large table on which a chess game is in progress. Flory, who would have been roughly fifteen at this time, and clearly the apple of her parents' eye, is seated in the middle of the photo, smiling benevolently at the photographer, head gently resting on her hand, looking slightly prim in blouse and bow tie, a sort of *ur*-Jewish princess.

On either side of her are her mother, Leontine, comfortably ensconced in a leather-upholstered chair, complete with antimacassar to avoid soiling, with a regal expression on her face; and her father, Herman – who would die suddenly the next year of appendicitis – looking rather severe, in tie and jacket and thick shaving-brush moustache. Flory's older brother Ferdi – by all accounts the most emotionally constipated of the Marburger children – is standing behind his parents and sister, wearing a well-tailored three-piece suit and extremely neat necktie. In the background, looking in from what appears to be a large garden, is Flory's younger brother Fred, the clown of the family, who evidently has just stumbled on to the scene. Pleased to bring some comic relief to the somewhat starchy picture, he wears a wide grin.

In another photo, apparently taken after her return from Paris, around 1913, the slightly older Flory is seated in profile, her sinuous figure at right angles to the viewer, wearing a lively flowered dress and an expectant look. This was the Flory Marburger whom Myrtil Frank saw when he happened to meet the fetching teenager during an interval at the Frankfurt Opera early in 1914. According to family legend, Flory, who was waiting for her mother, asked Myrtil for the time. She had no hidden agenda.

But Myrtil did. Smitten, the young businessman followed the new apple of his eye back to Flory's home, a short walk away. Carefully writing down the address, he then bombarded her with passionate letters. Flory responded.

So, in the manner of the day, the perfervid epistolary romance continued (with Leontine's permission, of course). There was talk of marriage.

There was only one problem: as Edward Grey, the Foreign Minister of Great Britain, said in August as the Continent mobilised for the monstrous conflagration of the Great War, 'The lamps are going out all over Europe: we shall not see them lit again during our lifetime.'

Not that the millions of Britons who rushed off to fight for King and Country, or the Germans who marched off to fight for Kaiser and Country – or the millions of other young men from their respective allies who threw themselves into the mêlée – would have agreed. For the British, this was to be the War To End All Wars. For the Germans, once that country's no less effective propagandists got around to rationalising the war, this clash of civilisations was about the defence of German honour and *Kultur*. A few clear-thinking anti-jingoists attempted to point out that this was all chauvinist nonsense, but they might as well have been whistling in the wind. The generation of 1914 wanted war, and war it would get.

German Jews swarmed to the colours to fight for the country they loved with no less fervour than their Gentile countrymen.

Despite – and to a certain degree, because of – their improved social and economic fortunes, the four decades since Bismarck's de facto emancipation proclamation had not been without problems for Germany's 300,000 Jews. The 1880s saw renewed outbreaks of anti-Semitic rioting. Some of the new anti-Semites were inspired by the widely disseminated remarks of Heinrich von Treitschke, a professor at the University of Berlin, who called anti-Semitism 'a natural re-action of the German national feeling against a foreign element which had usurped too large a place in our life'. '*Die Juden sind unser Unglück*,' he declared, twisting some lines from Heine: the Jews are our mis-fortune. Half a century later, Nazi propaganda chief Joseph Goebbels would resuscitate the phrase.

Nonetheless von Treitschke and his ilk were still in the minority as the nineteenth century ushered in the twentieth. Particularly heartening to German Jews were the steps that prominent German Gentiles them-selves took to contain the virus. Thus, when Kaiser Wilhelm I's court chaplain, Adolf Stöcker, established a Christian Socialist Party and insisted that Jews be forced to convert, a group of liberal Christians coun-tered by founding a Union to Combat Anti-Semitism. Its leader, Heinrich Rickert, famously told Stöcker in the Reichstag: 'I am convinced that three quarters of the German nation are on my side.' Doubtless Max Frank and Herman Marburger read with satisfaction of Rickert's riposte to Stöcker. If three quarters of the German population were on *their* side, then they had no worries.

The German-Jewish population was swayed by the jingoism of those first heady weeks of the war as the nation giddily mobilised and the War Ministry looked forward to finally putting to use General Schlieffen's plan for the speedy defeat of France. Many Jews saw the war as the apotheosis of their long struggle to be German, and to be accepted as such. As the leading German-Jewish newspaper, the *Israelit*, put it in its 1914 call to arms: 'We Jews are Germans and nothing else.' Over 100,000 Jews, one sixth of the total population, rushed to join the Big Parade. Ninety-three leading Jews from all walks of German life, including such worthies as Max Reinhardt, the great theatrical director, signed a petition supporting the war against perfidious Britain and her allies, France, Russia and Italy, as 'necessary for the defence of German culture'.

Of course, this was nonsense, but it would take five years of mindless butchery – and 1.8 million German lives (not to mention even more French and British ones) – for most of 'The Ninety-Three', like their gung-ho compatriots, to realise that.

Amongst the signatories who enthusiastically placed their talents at the service of the government was Fritz Haber, the famous chemist who directed the Kaiser Wilhelm Institute for Physical Chemistry. An intense patriot, Haber had achieved renown for inventing a process for directly synthesising ammonia from hydrogen and nitrogen. He would later win the 1918 Nobel Prize for Chemistry. During the war he directed the development of poison gas as a weapon, something about which the fanatically nationalist Jewish chemist evidently had few qualms.

Another prominent German Jew who would make an equal if not more significant contribution to the German war effort was Walther Rathenau, the famed intellectual-cum-industrialist. Born in 1867 – a year after Max Frank – Rathenau was the son of Emil Rathenau, who had been far-sighted enough to purchase the European rights for Thomas Edison's invention of the light bulb, and was the founder of the immense Allgemeine-Elektrizitäts-Gesellschaft (AEG), Germany's largest electricity combine – an august pedigree indeed.

Something of a *beau idéal* for his generation, particularly for his generation of German Jews, and a *bête noire* to his fellow industrialists, who suspected him of Bolshevist tendencies, Rathenau's first love was literature, and in 1899 he retired from industry to devote himself to his philosophical writings, in which he mused about the future of the profit motive. By the outbreak of the war, this German-Jewish prodigy and self-styled Great Man, who spoke four languages and also played the piano, had, somewhat reluctantly, returned to the family business, assuming his father's mantle as head of AEG.

Like most assimilated German Jews – like Max, certainly like Myrtil and Flory – Rathenau considered himself a German first and a Jew second. 'I am a German of the Jewish faith,' he said, by way of explaining his conspicuous loyalty. One of the few German industrialists who realised that governmental direction of the nation's economic resources would be necessary for victory, an impassioned Rathenau succeeded in convincing the government of the need for a War Raw Materials Department situated in the War Ministry to organise the logistical side of things – before agreeing to head it. More than one historian has asserted that Rathenau's brilliant contribution to the war effort allowed

Germany to continue at least a year, perhaps two years, longer than otherwise would have been possible (which he may well have regretted by then).

One German-Jewish intellectual who refused to join the bandwagon was Albert Einstein, the physicist, who had already achieved international renown for his experiments in search of a theory of relativity. Virtually alone amongst the German-Jewish intelligentsia, Einstein did not believe that the war was compulsory for the continuance of civilisation.

But then, what did Einstein know?

Max Frank of Breitenheim was certainly willing to do his part for the cause, sending all four of his children off to the war: Myrtil and Julius as infantrymen, their sisters Irma and Lisbeth as nurses. Many other equally patriotic German-Jewish families did the same, eagerly consuming the news in those first weeks of the Great War, while the situation in the West was yet fluid and anything was possible.

From the German public's point of view, the headlines looked promising, as the eighty-odd divisions assigned to the conquest of France wheeled into place, as called for by the Schlieffen Plan. Formulated in 1905, when Germany had begun planning for war, the somewhat dusty, much-tinkered-with strategic plan called for the bulk of the Kaiser's army to execute a sweeping, scythe-like attack through the Low Countries, avoiding the formidable French fortifications on the German–French border.

According to the original Schlieffen scenario, the army's initial *Schwerpunkt*, or main thrust, would fall on all three Low Countries – the Netherlands, Belgium and Luxembourg. The plan was altered by Helmuth von Moltke, the German chief of staff, who proposed that the German army bypass the Netherlands, and that Dutch neutrality, in effect since the Napoleonic Wars, again be respected, if only for the sake of convenience. Von Moltke was confident that Belgium's small army would be unable to stop German forces from quickly gaining their objectives. It was agreed: the *Schwerpunkt* would go through Flanders.

This purported revision in German plans, of course, suited the Dutch, who had no interest in being swept into the impending conflict. However, there was no guarantee that when hostilities actually broke out, the bellicose Germans would not be tempted to plough through the Netherlands anyway. When the dread guns of August finally came, the Netherlands prepared for the worst, mobilising its army of half a million, as well as constructing an electric fence around its borders, as if that would do much good.

To Holland's relief, the German army stuck to the revised Schlieffen Plan and the bristling Paris-bound German military machine pulled up short of Germany's 125-mile frontier with the Dutch at the last minute, instead bearing down on their unfortunate neighbours, Belgium and Luxembourg.

The Great War would turn out to be a time of extreme privation for metropolitan Holland, whose export trade, on which it was nearly entirely dependent, was halted by the Allied blockade of the English Channel, paralysing economic life. The Dutch army was forced to remain on alert for the rest of the war, another considerable burden. Nevertheless, compared with Belgium and Luxembourg, which were devastated by the initial German offensive, the Dutch got off lightly. Dutch neutrality was reconfirmed, endowing it with the same international status as Swiss or Swedish neutrality, and reinforcing the peaceable kingdom's belief that it somehow existed in a place apart.

Unfortunately, as the Dutch would learn on 10 May 1940, it didn't.

In the event, the war in the West did not follow the path the German General Staff had planned. The Belgians, outraged at German atrocities, of both the real and imaginary kind, put up a better fight than General Erich von Ludendorff, the German commander, and his fellow generals expected, delaying the German 'scythe'. The British Expeditionary Force also arrived more quickly than anticipated.

The inconclusive battle that finally took place in France in September 1914, in which the Germans came close to breaking through the hastily combined French and British lines, but were ultimately fended off by the Allies, would become known as the First Battle of the Marne; it also was influential in determining the remaining character of the war in the West.

Rebuffed, the Germans retreated. However, they were by no means defeated. Morale was sky-high. There was no shortage of war materiel, nor would there be for some time (thanks in no small part to Rathenau's astute logistics). The only thing which changed now was tactics. What had briefly been a war of movement now became one of position, as both the Allies and the Central Powers hunkered down in their parallel trench worlds, fastened their gas masks, fixed bayonets and proceeded to fight the most stupendous – and arguably the stupidest – battles in military history: the First Battle of the Somme, Verdun, Passchendaele; huge, heaving, ant-like battles in which infantrymen fought and died for several hundred yards of meaningless mud, before going at it again the next day.

All this might have been different; the Germans just might have won the First Battle of the Marne and broken through to Paris had they not turned left at the Dutch border. But they did – a fact that the Kaiser would ultimately be at least somewhat grateful for when, four years later, after the injection of US troops on the Allied side finally broke the stalemate in the West, causing the exhausted Germans to capitulate, Wilhelm and the abdicating Crown Prince fled across the Dutch border and were granted permanent asylum by the Dutch (which asylum the Dutch refused to revoke when, in 1919, the Allies demanded that they give him back).

One day infantryman Myrtil Frank, still the Kaiser's loyal subject, would be grateful for Dutch neutrality, too.

Like the many other German Jews who rallied to the Hohenzollerns' standard in 1914, Myrtil and Julius, the fighting Franks, did their duty for the Fatherland. Myrtil was shipped off to the Eastern Front, to do battle with the Russians, a fortunate thing in his case and doubtless a factor in why he did not become one of the disproportionate number of Jews to die; ultimately 12,000 German-Jewish soldiers died during the war – nearly one out of every eight who enlisted – most of them in the West.

Like many, if not most, war veterans of both sides, Myrtil didn't talk very much about his war service, preferring to forget what he had seen. Later, Dorrit and Sybil would only recall that he served in Russia and Poland, and that he was on the front lines, or close to them. Later, following the 1917 Revolution and the newly empowered Bolshevik government's withdrawal from the war, Myrtil, still a private, was reassigned to army headquarters in Berlin, probably dealing with supplies, which would make sense in view of his merchandising background.

The few extant photos of Myrtil in uniform and the meagre snapshots he took while he was in the service shed somewhat more light on his war years. There is a formal photo of him in his private's uniform, taken just before he was shipped out, looking resolute, if not exactly thrilled to be there, and another of him wearing the same standard issue expression on the boat. Like other soldiers eager to record their Great Adventure, Myrtil did bring a small camera with him and a series of tiny crinkled inch-square photos survives, but it is difficult to tell much from them. There are a lot of shots of smiling Russian peasants, some with long beards;

perhaps they were amongst the still-enslaved Russian Jews who were said to treat the more emancipated Germans as liberators, which would account for their beaming countenances. It is hard to say.

The destruction of German military archives by Allied bombers during World War II makes further reconstruction of Myrtil's war career difficult. If he was decorated, he kept it a secret. He was not wounded (at least insofar as is known). Like four million other Germans who answered the Kaiser's summons, Myrtil Frank did his duty. The rest is something of a mystery.

Julius also did his duty. He was sent to the West, but his regimental commander happened to notice the aspiring artist doodling away and promptly asked him to work as an artist for the regimental newspaper, for which he recorded the mayhem of Passchendaele and other battles, a task which Julius would later say saved his life.

And so Johanna and Max got their sons back. They were lucky, and for this they rejoiced. Their jubilation, however, was muted. Germany had lost the war. The monarchy had fallen. The Kaiser had abdicated. There was a revolution in Berlin. And, in a more personal blow, both sons had made it emphatically clear that they were not interested in going into the grape business.

Myrtil was never interested in politics to begin with, but the Great War (as it would be known until the next even greater one) made him a liberal, if not a radical, and shook his faith in the right of the state to make war. Half a century later, when the US was enmeshed in the quagmire of Vietnam, Myrtil vowed that he would rather send his draft-age grandson to Europe than see him fight in what he regarded as another senseless conflict. His war service seems to have given him a certain sense of invincibility, which would help explain some of the mind-boggling risks he later took when the Franks went underground in Holland. Last, but not least, it also reinforced his desire to marry the alluring Flory Marburger, who had dutifully waited for him for four long years.

On 27 November 1919, Flory and Myrtil were wed in Frankfurt. By all accounts the affair was a happy one. The wedding picture still exists: the two look absolutely radiant.

Disillusioning though it was, the war did not shake Myrtil Frank's essential faith in his fatherland or his pride in being a 'German of the Jewish faith', as his contemporary Walther Rathenau memorably put it. Indeed, if anything, the war probably reinforced it. There was nothing intrinsically wrong about Germany, he and the other surviving German Jews who had loyally served it felt; it had simply been misled. More enlightened leadership was needed.

It was no more possible in 1919 than in 1914 for either Flory or Myrtil to imagine themselves as anything *but* loyal Germans.

This, of course, would change.

CHAPTER 2

Ultra-Dada Days

A terrorist revolution under the leadership of Dr Liebknecht, the Radical Socialist, will break out Friday evening, according to reports. Liebknecht, the reports say, has 15,000 men well-armed. The population of Berlin is at the mercy of gangs of marauders, and there appears to be no authority there.

The New York Times, 5 December 1918

There comes a moment in the life of every man, be he good or bad, when appalled by the monotony and drabness of his daily life, his soul yearns for something different – he longs for the unknown, for the glamour and excitement he imagines to be the lot of the other man; the man in the street.

The opening text from the German
melodramatic film, *The Street* (1923)

Jedermann sein eigner Fussball

Title of a German dadaist publication from
the early 1920s, meaning 'Everyman his own
football'

The 1905 edition of *Baedeker's Berlin*, written when the ancient settlement on the river Spree was coming into its own as one of Europe's great cities, if not yet Germany's capital, draws an inviting portrait of a dynamic, light-dappled city, a young city, a city on the move.

Berlin's transformation from a minor crossroads into the great metropolis of central Europe, with a population – then – of just over three million, had been a quick one. As late as 1860, when the city contained fewer than 800,000 people, Henry Adams, the well-known American writer and diplomat, described Berlin, still labouring in the shadows of its more successful sister city, the port of Hamburg, as a 'poor provincial town – simple, dirty, uncivilised, and in most respects disgusting'.

Not any more. 'Almost every part of Berlin offers a pleasing picture,' declared the German guidebook writer.

> Its streets enjoy model cleanliness. There are few dark lanes or alleys even in the oldest parts of the city. Nearly all the newer houses have balconies, gay in summer with flowers and foliage. The public squares are embellished with gardens, monuments, and fountains. The centres of traffic, with their network of railway lines, and the navigation on the river, offer scenes of remarkable animation.

'It is a new city, the newest I have ever seen,' rhapsodised Mark Twain, the American writer, who visited booming post-Bismarck Berlin several times. To Twain, the Midwesterner, the bustling, new-fangled Berlin of the 1890s and early 1900s reminded him most of America's then metropolis-on-the-move, Chicago, although he liked Berlin even more.

Like many foreigners, Twain was most taken with the city's enormous boulevards. Unter den Linden and the Kurfürstendamm had been built wide by Frederick the Great in order to accommodate military manoeuvres, but now, like the Champs Elysées or Fifth Avenue, had taken on a life of their own. 'Only parts of Chicago are stately and beautiful,' enthused Twain, 'whereas all of Berlin is stately and substantial, and it is not merely in parts but uniformly beautiful.'

Above all, alongside the 'new Berlin's' contagious energy and 'animation', there was peace and order and a respect for old values – *Eine christliche Weltanschauung*, as Germans say.

This was the beguiling, even if somewhat staid, pre-1914 Berlin, the Berlin of the *Kaiserzeit*, before the Kaiser and his armies, including several hundred thousand patriotic Berliners – and thousands of equally patriotic German-Jewish Berliners – marched off to war and the abyss.

But in March 1919 that Berlin was quite dead. George Renwick, correspondent for *The New York Times*, found the *Großstadt* – the Great City – still dazed from the recent upheaval, as well as suffering from the extended Allied food blockade. 'The civil strife in Lichtenberg' – an eastern district of Berlin, where thousands of left-wing 'Spartacist' fighters had died fighting the right-wing Freikorps army units who (somewhat incongruously) had come to the aid of the shaky five-month-old Social Democratic-led republic – was, the American hopefully noted, 'almost at an end. There [is] evidence of increasing order. The trains [are] working and the underground trains [are] running.'

Still, taking a taxi through the city, Renwick was taken aback by the contrast between the gloomy city he found and the upbeat one he once knew:

> . . . Then began a ride through a phantom city for that describes Berlin today. The streets and long avenues were dimly lighted, and boys were dashing on roller skates. Shadowy people moved slowly about aimlessly, it would appear. Now and then I heard the hoarse call of some street vendor.

The benign, light-dappled Wilhelmian Berlin was now a dark, menacing place where many buildings still bore bullet holes from the recent street battles between the well-trained, well-armed Freikorps and the reds, whose leaders, Karl Liebknecht and Rosa Luxemburg, had been shot and bludgeoned in the Hotel Eden and dumped in the *Tiergarten* (not far from where the Franks would shortly set up house) just a few weeks before. Luxemburg's bloated, unrecognisable body turned up floating in the Landwehr Canal. It was a hungry, disease-ridden city: the cruelly extended Allied blockade had only just been lifted after the victors had extorted massive payments from the prostrate Germans in return for resuming emergency food shipments, a precursor of the vindictiveness shortly to emanate from the Versailles Peace Conference; the frightening, macabre city that was the inspiration for the soon-to-be-released silent film, *The Cabinet of Dr Caligari*, in which Cesare, cinema's first zombie, blindly follows his murderous master's voice and kidnaps an innocent young woman – presumably a Berliner – and carries her over the city rooftops like King Kong until, somewhat inscrutably, he drops dead from exhaustion. But there is no logic to these things.

Neither was there much logic to postwar Berlin, where the self-proclaimed 'dada' artist George Grosz celebrated the void with his scabrous, unforgettable etchings of the city, with power-hungry right-wing generals and monocled capitalists milling contentedly about while veterans begged for change. The new, nihilistic art/anti-art movement had taken the nonsense word 'dada' for its unlikely name. Grosz himself carried a mocking but accurate banner: DADA ÜBER ALLES.

'Not now brightly lighted cafés and restaurants, brilliant streets and the crush of traffic,' bemoaned the stricken Renwick. 'Overall was an underworld gloom. How different all this was when compared with the bright and busy lights of Berlin before the war!'

Just beneath Renwick's depressing report was an equally apocalyptic dispatch from the Associated Press noting that Germany's food stocks would be exhausted by the end of May.

This was the Berlin that greeted Myrtil Frank in December of that tumultuous first postwar year when he moved into his new flat in Brückenallee, a leafy street just off the *Tiergarten*, and prepared to take up his duties as one of the newly hired managers of the all-important municipal food rationing office.

To be sure, the very fact of the storm-tossed republic's continued existence itself was no small miracle. In June, just as the echoes of the last shots of the Spartacist revolt had died away, the government and the country were shocked by the promulgation of the terms agreed upon at Versailles as the final price of peace. Amongst the many onerous provisions of the treaty – or *Diktat*, as the document was quickly dubbed – were requirements that Germany cede Alsace-Lorraine back to France – no great surprise there – but also the Saar, Upper Silesia, and other parts of her territory, as well as all the former German colonies.

Additionally, under the terms of Versailles, the German army would be reduced to a rump force of 100,000. On and on the humiliating terms went, as Germans read with dismay. The German air force would be abolished. The Rhineland, including the Palatinate, was to be demilitarised and occupied by French troops: the Hunsrück, the Franks and their Breitenheim neighbours learned, would soon be swarming with *zouaves*.

Only in the creation of a League of Nations to arbitrate future conflicts was the influence of Woodrow Wilson's idealistic Fourteen Points seen. However, in the terms specifically regarding Germany, the vengeful British and the even more vengeful French had already won the day.

All this was bad enough. But the provisos that stuck the most in Germany's collective craw were Articles 227 to 232, the so-called honour clauses, particularly 231, the 'war guilt clause', which declared Germany responsible 'for causing all the loss and damage' suffered by the Allies, strongly implying that she was solely responsible for the war. Article 231 was used to justify the next clause, 232, which created a commission to determine reparations – eventually set at the ludicrous figure of 132 billion goldmarks, about 32 billion gold dollars. Germans were outraged. Certainly, few believed that Germany was solely responsible for the war. Here, ready made, was Hitler's soapbox.

As Herbert Hoover, the head of the American relief mission (and future US president) noted: 'Hate crawled in [to the Versailles negotiations] with demands for punishment, revenge, indemnities and reparations . . . We and our world must live with these seventy million Germans.' Hoover, who, ironically, would be cast out of office by American voters in 1932 for his own perceived callousness, went on to caution, 'No matter how deeply we may feel at the present moment, our vision must stretch over the next hundred years.'

But Hoover's idealistic vision, as well as Wilson's original one, failed at Versailles. Hatred triumphed. The hatred would be returned.

The provisional government in Weimar was thrown into turmoil by the publication of the proposed terms. 'What hand would not wither that binds itself and us in these fetters?' cried Philipp Scheidemann, its first president, who had declared the 'accidental' republic six months before; he resigned rather than sign the offending document. Only an ultimatum from Paris that made it plain that the Allies were prepared to invade Germany brought a reluctant German delegation – including a brave German Jew, Matthias Erzburger, who was vilified and then assassinated for his efforts – to sign the *Diktat* on 28 June 1919.

In August the still-concussed government's prestige was bolstered by the formal promulgation of the new ultra-democratic (if perhaps not entirely thought through) Weimar constitution. Combining elements drawn from both the American presidential system and the British and French parliamentary ones, the highly idealistic document, drafted by Hugo Preuss – a professor of law at the University of Berlin, a liberal and another Jew – included provisions for popular initiative and referendum, as well as a strong president elected by the whole people, and a chancellor responsible to the legislature.

Unfortunately, the Weimar constitution also contained the means of its own demise, including provisions for the autonomy of local state governments – which would soon allow Bavarian state authorities to allow the Nazis to flourish under their lenient rule – and, more fatally, Article 48, which empowered the president to rule by decree, the same provision which would eventually lead to the installation in the Chancellery of a one-time Austrian corporal named Adolf Hitler, then recovering from his wounds in hospital, and the end of the democratic Second Reich.

At the time, however, the new constitution seemed to offer Germany the basis for a new start. In September, the new republican advisers, deeming it safe to come back to the capital, if not quite safe enough to hold national elections, returned to Berlin from Weimar to – gently – take up the reins.

But Berlin wasn't really safe yet, either for governments or for ordinary people. The food distribution system that Myrtil had been hired to help straighten out was still hopelessly fouled-up. In August, to cite but one example of the ambient chaos, 75,000 food retailers closed their shops to protest the imminent commercialisation of food supplies. There were dozens of other strikes, some serious, some frivolous. Street crime was rampant. Karl Baedeker's gay, animated Berlin was gone. This, now, was Dr Caligari's Berlin, and it would remain so for some time.

Brückenallee, the once elegant street near the *Tiergarten* where Myrtil had found an apartment for Flory and himself, was somewhat grim. If one looked around, one could still find bullet holes from the recent rebellion. There were plenty of ghosts.

Not long before, during the war, the leafy street had reverberated with the sound of hearses ferrying the coffins of the war dead from the nearby Bellevue tram station. At night, this morbid spectacle had been followed by the spine-chilling cries of the animals at the once great, now abandoned Berlin zoo, being killed and devoured by starving Germans. If one listened closely enough, the Franks' neighbours swore, you could still hear the bellowing beasts.

All in all, it was not the most auspicious place to begin a new life. But the Franks refused to be disheartened. Myrtil's new, responsible position with the Berlin food administration was his chance, their chance too, and with Flory's backing, he resolved to give it everything he had, chaos be damned.

The first few years of the Weimar Republic – 1920, 1921, 1922 – coincided with the first few years of the Franks' married lives, as well as their lives as independent adults and as bona fide Berliners. It was a happy and exciting time, a flourishing in the void. In the outside world, the world of everyday Berlin, dada – chaos – still ruled all, but inside their world, at Brückenallee 4, things were fairly *gemütlich*.

Myrtil's work with the city food administration continued to be arduous, as he and his fellow logistical workers did their best to distribute the poorly coordinated supplies they received, while coping with the chaos. Despite his and his staff's energetic efforts to keep Berlin fed, the general social and economic situation continued to be extremely volatile and the prospect of a complete breakdown in the system was never far away.

In January 1920, a month after Myrtil began his logistical duties, *The*

New York Times reported that, as a result of late-arriving rural food stocks, the food situation in the capital remained 'critical'. Another Spartacist revolt was imminent, the paper reported.

Somehow, however, the desperately needed supplies were found, transported and distributed. Although Berliners – including both the general citizenry and the food merchants who had to comply with the new rationing rules – continued to grumble, there was no recurrence of the food riots that had ravaged the city the previous autumn. Catastrophe was averted. The Spartacists, or what was left of them, stayed at home.

Nevertheless, the threat of mass famine continued to hang over Berlin, and over the work of Myrtil and other senior food officials, for some time. The sight of Berlin families rummaging through the rubbish in order to supplement their meagre rations was common throughout the early 1920s. In January 1921, a then noted Swiss-based observer of world affairs by the name of F. Foerster publicly declared that because of the continued shortages Germany was on the verge of anarchy. 'Should Germany continue to suffer so acutely from underfeeding,' the professor warned, 'she will develop into a terrible powder magazine, threatening all Europe.' The near-famine conditions of the early 1920s, which were to a great degree the direct result of Allied spite (a factor in explaining why that shameful episode is all but forgotten in the West today) – the same dreadful conditions that Myrtil and his fellow workers laboured to ameliorate – were amongst the underlying resentments that eventually led to the Nazi explosion.

In the meantime, according to the same article that carried Dr Foerster's doomsday prediction, at least one eminent Berlin physician was advising young Berliners that it was their duty *not* 'to bring children into such a world'. Such a world, indeed.

The writer Ilya Ehrenburg, one of the many Russian artists and intellectuals who travelled to Berlin during the immediate postwar period – a distinguished group that included such luminaries as painter Wassily Kandinsky, who joined the inaugural faculty of the avant-garde Bauhaus school in Weimar, as well as others – was shocked by the violence and misery he found when he arrived in Berlin in 1921. 'The Germans were living as though they were at a railway station,' the amazed Russian wrote. 'No one knew what would happen from one day to the next. Shopkeepers changed their price tickets every day: the mark was falling. Herds of foreigners wandered along the Kurfürstendamm: they were buying up the remnants of former luxury for a song.'

However, factory chimneys continued to smoke, book-keepers neatly wrote out astronomical figures, prostitutes painstakingly made up their faces. At every turn there were small *Diele*, dance halls, where lean couples conscientiously jiggled up and down. Jazz blared. Popular songs proclaimed: 'Yes, we have no bananas', and 'Tomorrow's the end of the world'. However, the end of the world was postponed from one day to the next.

And Myrtil and Flory were never happier, or more in love.

Frustrating though Myrtil's job at the rationing office might be at times, it also empowered him. It was distressing, of course, to pass the line of crippled veterans selling matches or begging for change on Friedrichstrasse every day, as he went to work. Still, as Myrtil calculated the logistics of feeding Berlin – *his* Berlin – he felt he was making a contribution. Moreover, the pay wasn't bad. And every day he was making new connections, connections that would stand him in good stead in the career he wanted as a stockbroker on the Berlin exchange.

All in all, it was not bad for a young whippersnapper, particularly a Jew out of Breitenheim. When Myrtil arrived home, after walking the short distance from the Bellevue tram station, he was, more often than not, in an upbeat mood, and so was his beautiful young wife.

These were also the years when Myrtil and Flory got to know each other for the first time. There were some surprises, most of them nice. For one thing, as Flory found, her leonine husband was still in touch with his silly side, a rarity in such a serious man. In years to come, Myrtil would entertain his grandchildren by placing a silver tray on his head for no particular reason and walking around; now he performed similar stunts for Flory. He also had a huge, yelping laugh that seemed to come out of nowhere. When 'Til was business, he was all business, but when he wasn't, he was game for anything and his eyes shone with a slightly manic glee.

Flory had her own quirks, as Myrtil similarly discovered. Already a born optimist, she was a fan of autosuggestion – or self-conscious auto-suggestion, as it was technically called – the popular system of self-help that was all the rage then in Europe and America, particularly amongst suggestible young middle-class women. Devised by the French pharma-cist Emile Coué, this easy-to-use, if somewhat fatuous system of self-help – a precursor of today's positive thinking – revolved around the repeated use of the lullaby-like phrase: *Day by day, in every way, I am getting better and better.*

Flory's extreme aestheticism, the legacy of her teenage Parisian sortie, was also an aid of sorts. When she wasn't playing the piano, the musically inclined young Frankfurt native liked to hum. Flory was a great hummer. She also loved to decorate. This was welcome, except when her husband's more garish and her somewhat more sedate tastes clashed. On the rare occasion when this occurred, Myrtil, in awe of his wife in many ways, was happy to defer to her more educated judgement. After all she had spent a year in Paris!

It was not a perfect match – Myrtil's easy-going personality jarred somewhat with Flory's more conservative, controlling one – but it was a good one, and would remain so for some time. If the high-spirited Myrtil was *schnapps*, to put it in bibulous terms, Flory was *Dubonnet*. And together they made quite a party.

If all else failed, the Franks could also join the growing number of Berliners who chose to escape reality by going to the cinema. If postwar Berlin was jazz-mad, it was also movie-mad, taking to the new-fangled medium with gold-rush-like enthusiasm: in 1919, while the social fabric of revolutionary Berlin came close to disintegrating, dozens of movie palaces were erected around the city, lavish sanctuaries in which the anxiety-ridden masses could lose themselves for an hour or two as the silent images flickered before them, more often than not to live musical accompaniment.

Premièring in 1920, the aforementioned *Cabinet of Dr Caligari* was a hit with the young cinema-going audience. Even more popular, however – and more to Flory's classical tastes, when they attended the opulent Palast am Zoo located nearby – were the great historical epics, like *Madame du Barry* and *The Loves of Pharaoh*, which the renowned director Ernst Lubitsch had created for UFA, the pioneering Berlin film studio. Otto Friedrich writes in his bestselling 1972 book *Before the Deluge*:

> Almost every day in the streets of Berlin . . . there were crowds of demonstrators marching to and fro for one cause or another, but inside the shelter of the UFA Palast am Zoo, where a symphony orchestra of seventy musicians provided the accompaniment, Berliners could escape into an imaginary world in which Lubitsch's crowds were storming an artificial Berlin, or besieging an artificial Tower of London.

The Franks had each other. This was important, particularly on those occasions when the once reliable city lights really *did* go out, as they briefly did during the five-day-long Kapp Putsch.

In 1919 it had been the revolutionary left's turn to try to seize the government. It was only a matter of time before the revolutionary right attempted to do the same thing. On 13 March 1920, Berlin and the world were startled to learn that a group of right-wing soldiers, led by an obscure politician named Wolfgang Kapp, had seized the Chancellery and set up machine-gun posts around the governmental district. Backing Kapp was the veteran Ehrhardt Brigade, a battle-hardened unit which had fought in the Baltic during the Great War, and had also seen service as a Freikorps unit during the suppression of the Spartacist rebellion. The rebels also reportedly had the support of General Ludendorff, the German commander during the Great War, still acting very much his old imperious self.

On the day that the attempted *coup d'état* took place, the displaced republican government called a general strike. To its surprise and delight, the strike was heeded, as the unions, left-wing militants, the government and Berliners themselves combined to put the coup down. Berlin was already used to strikes, but this was the first time absolutely nothing worked. Not even the movies. For five days Berliners stayed at home, read by daylight and dined by candlelight.

In the end the Kapp Putsch proved more *opéra bouffe* than *coup d'état*. The hapless Kapp, who had no experience of government (as manifested by his decision to dissolve and un-dissolve the Prussian State Legislature on the same day), spent most of his time walking around the darkened, abandoned government offices in a semi-daze, before being persuaded to give it up and fly to Sweden.

'If only we had shot more people everything would have been all right,' one soldier who supported the short-lived coup said later.

On 20 May 1920, the day after Kapp flew into Swedish exile with his sobbing wife, the men of the Ehrhardt Brigade (whose battle flag was adorned with the diminutive pre-Nazi swastika) dutifully filed out of the government compound, lustily singing their barracks songs, just as they had done when they had entered five days before.

The failure of the Kapp Putsch gave Ebert, the Socialist chancellor, a last chance to carry out basic, desperately needed reforms in the civil service and armed services. Nonetheless, these changes were only partly popular with the German public, which was still divided between left and right. The government coalition failed to win a majority in the June 1920 elections, resulting in a divided Reichstag, the first of the divided Reichstags that would burden the doomed republic for the remainder of its thirteen-year existence.

But the republic survived; the end of the world was postponed. And the thin, love-possessed couples at the *Diele* continued to dance away to the tune of 'Yes, we have no bananas'.

On 27 December 1920, Myrtil's twenty-seventh birthday, Flory presented him with their first child, a daughter. An Anglophile and a Francophile, the internationally minded (but still deeply patriotic) Flory decided to name her brown-haired, hazel-eyed daughter Dorrit, after *Little Dorrit* by Charles Dickens, one of her favourite books: a gesture of true Anglo-German *rapprochement*.

True to her Dickensian roots, the Franks' beautiful daughter, who was soon gleefully waddling around the big apartment at Brückenallee 4, would turn out to be the great romantic of the family. Outspoken, strong-willed, temperamental, adorable: Dorrit was an admixture of her high-spirited father and her *grande dame*-like mother. Cassandra-like physicians be damned: Flory and Myrtil were very glad that they had decided to bring such a sparkling child into their world.

Still, certain worrying developments in the world beyond the *Hansa Viertel* or Hansa Quarter, as their smart neighbourhood was called, could not be wished away, notably the return of anti-Semitism to German public life.

This pernicious development coincided with a rise in anti-Semitism both in Europe and worldwide. This was the same period when Henry Ford, the brilliant industrialist and rabid Jew-hater, was frequently proclaiming his belief in *The Protocols of Zion* – the counterfeit nineteenth-century document supposedly 'proving' that Jews were linked with an ancient conspiracy to take over the world – in the pages of his friendly home-town newspaper, *The Dearborn Independent*. Many Americans believed him.

Meanwhile, Eastern Europe was consumed by a new wave of anti-Semitic fervour. In Hungary, so-called 'white terror' gangs attacked Jews on the streets of Budapest, while the avowedly anti-Semitic government ordered the expulsion of all Jews who had entered since 1914. Poland, historically the country most receptive to anti-Semitism, was racked by such pogroms, as was Czechoslovakia.

In heady, 'anything goes', democratic Weimar, Jews were no longer held back, but they were no longer protected by the power of the Crown as they had been under Bismarck and the Kaiser. There was more opportunity than ever before – witness Myrtil's fairly prominent position, for example – but there was also more exposure.

Attacks on Jews in public – when the attackers were sure they had a bona fide Jew in their clutches – were commonplace during this turbulent time, as a German Jew by the name of Conrad Rosenstein relates in his memoir:

> I was on a train one night on my way home from Frankfurt. The train was pitch dark. The lights were out, nothing uncommon after the war when German railroads were in utter disrepair and few things functioned orderly. It was either in 1919 or 1920, during one of the early periods of violent anti-Semitic acts which might occur anywhere, and when a Jew who had the guts to fight could become embroiled in a vicious brawl. It happened often enough on a train and it was difficult not to react to the slander and the smears poured over you. That night, we were seven or eight people in the dark, fourth-class compartment, sitting in utter silence till one of the men started the usual refrain: 'Those God-damned Jews, they are the root of all our troubles.'

Enraged, Rosenstein challenged the bullies in the dark with the fact that *he* was a Jew.

> That was the signal they needed. Now they really went after me, threatening me physically. I didn't hold my tongue as the argument went back and forth. They began jostling me till one of them next to me and near the door, probably more encouraged by the darkness than by his own valour, suggested: 'Let's throw the Jew out of the train.'

At which point Rosenstein wisely decided not to provoke them further.

Attacks on Jewish public officials – and not merely verbal ones – also escalated during this incendiary period. Were three quarters of the German nation *still* on the side of the Jews and against the anti-Semites, as Rickert had so loudly asserted in the Reichstag forty years before? It was getting hard for Jews to tell.

One anti-Semitic attack that threatened the fragility of the Weimar Republic was the cold-blooded murder in June 1922 of Walther Rathenau, then the German Foreign Minister.

The noted industrialist and Renaissance man had not initally rallied to the republic nor vice versa. At the 1919 constitutional assembly, a move to nominate Rathenau as president produced jeers from the right. Stricken, the great man withdrew his name. 'The Parliament of any other civilised state would have shown sufficient respect for a man of recognised intellectual standing,' he protested, somewhat preciously. 'But the Parliament of the German republic greeted [me] with roars and shrieks of laughter.'

Nevertheless, Rathenau, who helped the German Democratic Party, was a convinced democrat, and the new government found that it could not spare his gifts for long. In May 1921 he became Minister of Reconstruction, and in January 1922 was appointed Foreign Minister. He became a symbol for the republic, and, as its most eminent Jew, the perfect scapegoat for German nationalists who were disgruntled with it, as well as those who wished to avenge the alleged Jewish-perpetrated 'stab-in-the-back' that had led to the humiliation of Versailles.

Rathenau's policies only increased resentment against him from the right. In his controversial first speech to the Reichstag as Minister of Reconstruction, he advocated fulfilment of Germany's obligations under Versailles, however distasteful, as the best means of 'linking up with the world again'. He continued his programme of linking up with the outer world, including Germany's former enemies, by signing the Treaty of Rapallo with the Soviet Union, thus re-establishing economic and political relations with its ex-foe. A deft move, the treaty signified Germany's re-emergence as an independent agent in the arena of foreign affairs.

Unfortunately, by linking arms with the same Bolshevik government that had sponsored the Spartacists, he also opened himself up to criticism from the right that he was some sort of Communist agent – in addition to being a Jew. As it turned out, the far-sighted *rapprochement* with the Soviets – which, ironically, in the light of conservative opposition, wound up playing a catalytic role in German rearmament, as the Soviets secretly began to help the Reich rebuild its military – turned out to be the German-Jewish diplomat's death warrant.

By the spring of 1922, Rathenau had become the target of numerous death threats. In May, Karl Wirth, then the German Chancellor, was distressed to receive confirmed intelligence of a murder plot against his idealistic Foreign Minister. Worried, Wirth shared the news with Rathenau, insisting that the latter accept police protection. After a long pause to take in the news, Rathenau refused. 'Dear friend,' he reassured Wirth, putting both of his hands on the worried Chancellor's shoulders, 'it is nothing. Who would do me harm?'

On the morning of 24 June 1922, as Rathenau was being driven to work in his open car from his villa in *Grunewald*, a group of three Freikorps veterans, led by a rabid former naval lieutenant by the name of Erwin Kern, shot him as they passed in another vehicle, and tossed a grenade at the mortally wounded politician for good measure.

Rathenau's murder, Weimar's equivalent of the Kennedy assassination, stunned Germany. 'This atrocious crime has struck not only Rathenau,' declaimed President Ebert in his oration to the fallen cabinet minister, 'but the German people!' An estimated two million Berliners – more than half the city's population – lined Rathenau's funeral route or marched in simultaneous protest. As historian David Lange writes, 'Jews and Gentiles alike understood that the fragile new republic couldn't afford to lose true patriots like him.'

Amongst the Berliners who lined Rathenau's funeral route were Flory and Myrtil Frank. For cultured and assimilated Jews like the Franks, the murder of Rathenau – the ultimate child of German *Bildung* – was earth-shaking. For the first time in their adult lives, the Franks felt unsafe as Jews in Germany.

That same year, ruinous hyperinflation had destroyed the German currency. In July, the mark, already battered by Germany's economic and political unrest, stood at 670 to the dollar, compared with 331 a mere few weeks before.

The republican government, in an understandable if not particularly well-thought-out desire to act against the French government, which was still occupying the Ruhr Valley, decided to subsidise 'passive resistance' to the occupation by paying the salaries of striking workers there. However, the Weimar treasury, already near-bankrupt from the strain of reparations, had nothing to back up the specie it continued to print.

The mark now went into freefall. In February it hit 12,000 to the dollar and that was only the start. By August, it hit a million – and kept going. A tram ride that had cost 3,000 marks in July soon cost 10,000; then 50,000; then 100,000. Restaurant prices changed while diners were in the middle of their meals. If anyone needed the proof that dada truly ruled in Germany, this was it.

Middle-class citizens who lived on a fixed income and had dutifully put their money into savings accounts simply couldn't keep up. A few didn't even try. In a typical horror story, a disconsolate Berlin writer was said to have spent his entire life savings on a last subway ride through the city. Then he went home and starved himself to death.

Amongst those patriotic, hard-working Germans who were wiped out by the galloping inflation was Max Frank, who was now forced to sell the family vineyard, a move that doubtless hastened his death several years later at the relatively young age of sixty-three.

Taking in the chaos around him – including his father's bankruptcy – Myrtil in October 1923 carefully packed his wife and two-year-old daughter into a waiting taxi, accompanied them to the train station and placed them on an express train for Lugano, the Swiss resort, where he had arranged for them to stay in a chalet for the duration. Remaining behind – after all, he still needed to try to make a living – he promised to telegraph once things calmed down.

But the madness continued. At the beginning of November, the mark stood at a billion to the dollar.

Some tried to lay the blame for the tragic economic state of affairs at the doorstep of Berlin's growing Jewish community, particularly the large number of conspicuously unassimilated Jews from Eastern Europe who had recently settled in Berlin. Retaining their distinctive dress, speech and customs, the so-called *Ostjuden* settled in Berlin's *Scheunenviertel* during the early 1920s, turning it into a kind of ghetto, and making themselves an anti-Semitic lightning rod.

'In addition to finding the *Ostjuden* distasteful,' Lange writes, 'Berlin's assimilated Jews worried that this highly noticeable community might fan the fires of anti-Semitism, perhaps provoking the kind of pogrom-like violence that Germany had hitherto avoided.' And so they did. On 5 November 1923, a pogrom-like riot broke out in the old Jewish quarter, as scores of enraged unemployed men fell upon the bearded residents, who they believed – falsely – had bought up the funds guaranteeing their jobless benefits at usurious rates.

Up and up the mark soared, while down below chaos reigned. 'Now,' writes historian Sebastian Haffner in his poignant memoir, *Defying Hitler*, 'we expected the downfall of the state, even the dissolution of the Reich . . . There had never been so many rumours: the Rhineland had seceded; the Kaiser [then in exile in Holland] had come back; the French had marched in. It was difficult to distinguish the possible from the impossible. People disappeared [by] the dozens . . . Saviours appeared everywhere, people with long hair and hair shirts declaring that they had been sent by God to save the world.'

By now the mark had virtually disappeared. Sojourning in Hamburg that month, the American painter Marsden Hartley, fascinated and appalled at Germany's collective nervous breakdown, wrote a letter to his friend Alfred Stieglitz on the back of three ten-million-mark notes; he told Stieglitz that it was cheaper to do that than to use regular stationery.

Faster and faster the couples at the *Diele* danced. Perhaps, they shrugged, tomorrow indeed would be the end of the world.

On 15 November the mark stood at 4.2 billion to the dollar. Three days later, in what seemed to many a poor replay of the Kapp Putsch, Adolf Hitler, the corporal-turned-politician, made his first appearance on the German political stage, issuing a call for a national right-wing revolution in a beer hall in Munich. The self-proclaimed revolutionary and avenger of Versailles managed to get a few of his fledgling National Socialist Party comrades killed before he was hauled away by the Bavarian police. He wore short hair rather than long, but he didn't seem all that different from the other wild-eyed saviours who had preceded him.

CHAPTER 3

'Once You Had Berlin, You Had the World'

Once you had Berlin, you had the world.

Carl Zuckmayer, German-Jewish playwright
and Berliner, 1925

*So long as your panties are still hanging on the chandelier, I'll know that
you still love me . . .*

Popular Berlin ditty from the 1920s

Over the next few months, a kind of normality was restored. The
ballooning billion-dollar mark came back down to earth and was replaced
by a new, more stable currency, the Rentenmark. Buoyed by US loans,
the economy recovered. The storm passed. What Sebastian Haffner calls
the country's 'mad decade' – Germany's 1914–23 period – was over:

> The dollar stopped climbing, so did shares. And when one converted them
> into Rentenmarks, they were reduced to nothing, like everything else. So no
> one was left with anything. But wages and salaries were paid out in
> Rentenmarks, and some time later, wonder upon wonder, small change also
> appeared, solid bright coins. You could jingle them in your pockets and they
> even kept their value. On Thursday, you could still buy something for the
> money received on the previous Friday. The world was, after all, full of
> surprises.

In April 1924, Myrtil wired Flory to come home. At long last, the
lights in Germany were working again.

Technical credit for halting the ruinous inflation went to Hjalmar
Schacht, the brilliant banker with the ugly but somehow reassuring

bulbous nose, who actually developed the Rentenmark, backed by a rigorous restorative monetary programme. Certainly, Germans were agreed, as they giddily inspected the magical new currency, Schacht was a wizard. Long live Hjalmar Schacht!

However, the man who best personified the German economic recovery of the mid-to-late-1920s was another hitherto somewhat obscure German technocrat and politician, Gustav Stresemann. It was the soothing Stresemann – the administrative assistant to the head of the German Chocolate Makers' Association, before he joined the government during the war and threw his lot in with the republic – who, as German Chancellor during the topsy-turvy autumn of 1923, set the necessary conditions for currency stabilisation and made possible the return of something approaching economic and political normality.

And so Stresemann, in the manner of the blank-faced US president Calvin Coolidge, who presided over America's contemporaneous 'Era of Good Feeling', became normalcy incarnate, Germany's amulet against the void. As long as Stresemann was around, Germans felt, things would be all right.

For the next six years, Stresemann, who now became Foreign Minister, continued his martyred predecessor Walther Rathenau's policy of *rapprochement* with the West, guiding Germany back to something approaching its prior international prestige, and allowing the modest recovery to continue.

'During the Stresemann era,' Haffner says, 'people lost their interest in politics . . . money came into the country, the currency maintained its value and business was good.' All comers were welcome during Germany's own era of good feeling. 'The public sector required only competent officials and the private sector only hard-working professionals.'

Myrtil Frank, having completed his mission as city food administrator, in 1924 transferred his skills and energy from the public sector to the private one, becoming a hard-working and successful grain futures dealer.

German anti-Semitism, one of the factors in Myrtil's decision to send his family out of the country the year before, had, it appeared, been successfully contained. The void in the nation's soul left by the war and the destruction of the old established order had been banished; or so it seemed. The continuing tonic presence of Stresemann – who in 1926 won the Nobel Peace Prize for his success in reconnecting Germany with the world – Stresemann with his bowler hat and his self-effacing smile;

Stresemann 'the miracle worker', seemed proof positive of this welcome healing of the German spirit.

Of course, Hitler – then dictating his 'political testament' in the comfortable confines of Landsberg Castle where he was serving out his sentence for his role in the Munich beer hall putsch – and his ilk were still around. Confirmed democrats like Sebastian Haffner and his friends were under no illusions about that, 'but as long as Stresemann was there,' the liberal historian writes, 'we felt more or less sure that they would be held in check.'

At last Germany was on the move again. Leading the way, rising from the abyss, was Berlin. These, the *Goldene Zwanziger Jahre* – the Golden Twenties – were the years when Berlin reached its zenith as a city of youth and imagination. The bustle and 'remarkable animation' – as Baedeker had put it in 1905 – of the Berlin of the *Kaiserzeit* was back, and so, mercifully, was its civic harmony. Gone was the stodginess, the respect for the 'established order' that had held the city back from becoming the cultural furnace it now became. These were the years when Berlin became the modern *Großstadt* – the metropolis – the triumphant subject of *Berlin: die Symphonie einer Großstadt*, Walter Ruttman's noted 1926 futuristic documentary about the new Berlin.

This was the Weimar moment, and Berlin's moment too.

In this period, Berlin became the capital of renascent German Jewry. Drawn by its energy and opportunity, as Myrtil had been in 1919, the city's Jewish population, 92,000 in 1900, now jumped to 173,000, or about 4 per cent of the population – still a minority, but, increasingly, a minority whose contribution in talent, energy and capital was disproportionate to its numbers.

This, indeed, was Berlin Jewry's moment, as Conrad Rosenstein recalls:

In Berlin one had it better. The Jewish community was large and influential, thanks to Jewish capital. Taken with a grain of salt, one could say that the Jews were Germany's best taxpayers. Their exceptional intelligence had the effect of 'cranking up' business life. They stimulated artistic endeavour and the press. The Jews contributed decisively to the remarkable development of Berlin in the twenties. In those days – to be sure, for eight or nine years only – Berlin became the centre of Europe. So it seemed enticing to live in Berlin, above all, if one was a Jew.

This was how many of Berlin's privileged and prolific Jewish population felt. Everywhere one looked – in business, as well as the arts – in the great recrudescent metropolis, Jews were in the forefront. The huge new department stores, perhaps the most prominent symbols of the new prosperity – Tietz, noted for its annual 'white sale' (a favourite of Flory's), Wertheim, N. Israel, others – were Jewish-owned. The leading evening newspaper, *Das Berliner Tageblatt*, which 'Til used to read when he returned home from work, was owned by a Jew, Rudolf Mosse, who also owned the city's leading advertising agency.

Owning businesses was not, however, the same thing as *controlling* these industries. The distinction was lost upon Joseph Goebbels, the fire-breathing *Gauleiter*, or district leader, personally picked by Hitler for cosmopolitan, resolutely anti-fascist Berlin, who, incensed by the disproportionate number of prominent Jews in German economic life, railed against them in his speeches to the party faithful. 'The Jews,' he declaimed, reviving the old anti-Semitic lament, 'are our misfortune.'

But, for the moment, few Germans – and even fewer Berliners – took the future Nazi Minister of Propaganda very seriously, nor would they while the economy remained relatively strong.

Meanwhile, Jews continued to be in the vanguard of Berlin's vaunted cultural renaissance. When Berliners were not attending plays written by Carl Zuckmayer or other talented Jewish playwrights; or directed by the internationally renowned Max Reinhardt; or starring acclaimed Jewish actors like Ernst Deutsch or Max Pallenberg; they were heading off to the Municipal Opera House, to hear Bruno Walter, the Jewish conductor, or Jewish opera stars like the megaphonic Richard Tauber or the incandescent Fritzi Massary. Or watching the luminous Elisabeth Bergner, also known as 'The Bergner', one of the first German movie stars.

Not all the leading lights of the so-called Weimar Renaissance were Jewish. Bertolt Brecht, the best-known as well as the most controversial playwright of the period, was not, nor were Walter Gropius, its most celebrated architect, nor Fritz Lang, its best-known filmmaker, or many other cultural luminaries. Jews did not control the arts any more than they did business.

Then there was Einstein, the theoretical physicist. Few Jews knew or cared what the great scientist was researching. The man hadn't been to temple since his bar mitzvah, not that Berlin Jews were particularly religious – the Franks, for example, only occasionally celebrated *shab-bath*. But his co-religionists were certainly proud that the tousle-haired scientist was also a Berliner, asserting the Jewish contribution in that area of intellectual endeavour.

Did the Jews 'own' or even control Weimar Berlin? No. But they can be forgiven for thinking that they did.

These were the years – 1925–28 – that Flory, like other Berlin Jews, would later wax nostalgic about; the years when the *Hansa Viertel* regained its cachet as one of Berlin's choicest neighbourhoods; the time when, with the indulgence of her doting grain-dealer husband, their ten-room apartment blossomed into a great Berlin *home*, with a flower-adorned balcony and 'scenes of remarkable animation' inside. By 1925, the year after the birth of the Franks' second daughter, Sybil, the household staff included a cook and a nanny, as well as Schwann, the chauffeur.

This was the golden time, the time when Flory was served breakfast in bed while the *Kinder* ate in the kitchen under the benevolent, watchful eye of Annie, the family's prodigious cook; and then, after Frau Frank had arisen, Herr Schwann would drive her in the family Chrysler to visit her dressmaker in Wedding – a raffish neighbourhood of Berlin on the other side of town where many tradesmen set up shop. This was the same fashionable tailor who frequently visited Paris to shop for materials for his clients.

Or perhaps Frau Frank would join her society friends at the eightieth birthday reception for Max Liebermann, the doyen of modern art and impassioned advocate for Impressionism, still Flory's favourite movement (even though she also admired the Expressionists). Or perhaps she would have a bridge afternoon with the ladies. And afterwards, they might repair by limousine for a *Kaffee und Strudel* at Dobrieu's. And perhaps, if it was a Saturday, Dorrit and Sybil would be paraded before the ladies, provided they had their patent leather Mary Janes on (Flory would insist), for which they would be rewarded with an ice cream.

Sometimes Flory would invite her friends back to the Franks' spacious and well-decorated apartment, with its Art Deco furniture and parquet floor, and they would cast their pince-nez at the Franks' impressive art collection, its centrepiece a seventeenth-century peasant dance by Rubens: exquisite! *And did you know that Flory once spent a year in Paris?*

And then perhaps the children would once again be marched out for the amusement of the guests with the aid of one of the *Kinderfräulein*. *'Mein Gott!'* they would exclaim about button-nosed Sybil (to the evident annoyance of her older sister). 'Isn't that one *so sweet?*' And then they would be bundled back and the *Klatsch* would continue.

Perhaps, as Haffner claims, by way of explaining the void that still seethed beneath Weimar's glittery surface, most Germans 'accustomed to having the entire content of their lives delivered gratis . . . had never learned to live within themselves, how to make an ordinary private life great, beautiful and worthwhile, how to enjoy it and make it interesting'.

But the Franks certainly knew how to make life great, beautiful and worthwhile. This was particularly evident on the evenings when Flory and Myrtil entertained. 'Til might invite an official of the grain exchange, or Flory might invite her society friends, such as the Countess Heinemann and her dashing husband. And perhaps, as he often did, Myrtil's talented brother Julius, now a rising artist on the Berlin scene who lived nearby, and whom Myrtil supported, would come over, or Flory's brother Fred, a banker, to whom she was close.

And, as always, Annie would serve something exquisite. And then Flory – who probably would have been called a control freak if she lived today – would press the button under the table (how she loved that!) and the maids would come, quickly clean up and then vanish, just as she had trained them.

And then, after the company had retired to the buffed leather furniture of the living room, the mistress of the house would be prevailed upon to play an easy piece or two on the grand piano, after which the men would head off to the library for cigars and brandy and *Männer* talk – most likely about sport, for all Germany was sports-mad now, and less frequently about politics. After all, what need was there to worry about politics while Stresemann was in control?

Ah yes, the Franks, the impressed and satisfied company would say to themselves as they left Brückenallee 4 (after politely doffing their hats to the semi-comatose superintendent in the glass booth downstairs), or when they glimpsed Flory and Myrtil on summer holiday at Westerland or Nordernei or one of the other smart German North Sea resorts, dressed to the nines, dancing at night; *the Franks know how to live! And aren't they so much in love?*

Alas, they weren't. Dorrit and Sybil would later be decidedly less nostalgic about these 'golden' years than their mother. 'I had a terrible childhood,' Dorrit said flatly, half a century later.

Of course, there were some nice things about the life that Flory and Myrtil provided for their children. Dorrit enjoyed her first school, the Frau Motteck, an elite private school where she studied from 1925 to 1929. And she also liked her next school, the Kleist Lyceum, to which she transferred in 1930 and where she was able to indulge her penchant for history and English, and which also came with an up-to-date swimming pool. Flory would always make sure that Dorrit, and later Sybil, when she went to school, had a nice *Zuckertüte*, the cone of candy German children were given on their first day of school.

The household staff were also all right, sometimes better than all right. Dorrit was especially fond of Eve, an English nanny the Franks hired in 1926, who nurtured her seven-year-old charge's love of literature by reading to her from *Alice's Adventures in Wonderland, Winnie the Pooh* and other classics, and otherwise did as much as she could to make her and Sybil's world a fun one. The girls adored Eve. And, of course, they both loved Annie and Herr Schwann.

There were nice things about their world, but it was separate from that of their parents. 'They lived in their part of the apartment,' said Dorrit, 'and we lived in ours.' And rarely did the two meet. The fact that this division between parents and children was common in households like the Franks' did not matter to the girls, who often felt like orphans in their own home.

There were exceptions. Sometimes Flory would take her daughters with her in the car when she went to Wedding (which also became known as 'Red Wedding' because of the large number of Communists who lived there), to have her dresses altered. And the girls would stare out of the window at the grim, flowerless buildings all around and the not especially happy-looking children playing in the street, and it would dawn on them that there was another, grittier, less privileged world out there.

That was exciting.

Then there was the Saturday afternoon in 1928 when Flory took Dorrit to see her first movie, the Warner Brothers cartoon *Felix the Cat*, known locally as *Felix der Kater*. That was special. But there were too few such afternoons.

Moreover, for reasons that are not difficult to discern in retrospect, neither Dorrit nor Sybil was particularly keen on their mother in the first place. They *admired* her, of course, perhaps they even loved her;

they didn't know. But certainly they weren't crazy about her, even if she played the piano and knew the names of all the painters at the museum.

From afar, if one passed the Franks on Sunday in the *Tiergarten*, or strolling along the Unter den Linden, with Flory and Myrtil in their Sunday best – Flory in her newest cloche, 'Til in his fedora with the feathers in it, casually holding a cigarette – and Dorrit and Sybil politely walking beside them hand in hand with one of them holding on to a balloon, or perhaps glimpsed them together in front of the lion cages at the zoo, they certainly *looked* like a great family. And perhaps they were. You might even say they had their own *Weltanschauung*.

They just weren't a particularly happy family, or despite appearances, a particularly together one.

The real problem was that, surrounded by a revolution in sexual mores, as exemplified by the ditty on the radio urging everyone to throw their panties on the chandelier, Flory was sexually inhibited. Myrtil had always been aware of this less-than-endearing tendency on the part of his wife, but he had been willing to overlook it before 1924, when the Franks conceived Sybil, their second daughter.

Perhaps another, less sexually active man would have been willing to continue to overlook his wife's frigidity. However, Myrtil had a strong sex drive. And at a certain point he decided, with Flory's either tacit or explicit permission, to take a mistress.

The Franks evidently didn't argue about this, or if they did they did it beyond the earshot of their children – significantly, the worst argument that Dorrit and Sybil would later recall the two having occurred when Myrtil (evidently still under the vestigial influence of the Berlin school of dada) decided to lacquer the living room furniture without Flory's permission, a *faux pas* that resulted in a near-brawl.

Taking a mistress was not unusual at this time. After all, the sex-starved wife in *Blind Husbands*, the 1919 Erich von Stroheim film about a similarly inclined loveless marriage, had done so, for example. So had some of Myrtil's friends.

Myrtil's mistress was called Lola. Dorrit met her once, and at that moment she realised that her parents had a bad marriage. It took a little while longer for her younger sister to catch on, but she did.

Once, Lola, a fetching blonde in her early twenties, whom Myrtil had met at the exchange, even posed for a photo with Flory. Rather than play the role of the deceived, Flory opted to be the knowing wife.

But after this, the girls only rarely saw their father.

In contrast to their haughty, controlling mother, they loved 'Til, with his killer smile, twinkly Rhenish eyes and uproarious laugh. At least to them, he seemed to be everything that Flory wasn't: unpretentious, relaxed, warm-hearted, generous, and just a little crazy. They *worshipped* their father, but either he was working late at the grain exchange, or he was off at his hunting lodge in Spandau, or he was with . . . you know who (the girls would look at each other knowingly).

Once in a while, they would see their parents together at night, when the Franks had company. Flory and 'Til would peep into the bedroom and the girls would catch a glimpse of their father smiling, Cheshire cat-like, before disappearing, while Flory looked on benevolently.

And, of course, there were always Sundays in the park.

However, the closest thing to genuine togetherness the Franks would achieve was during the summer holiday, when Myrtil would motor to one of the North Sea resorts with Nanny in tow.

In 1924, when they were still a threesome, they holidayed at Scheveningen in Holland, long a favourite with Germans, where they rented one of the big enclosed beach-chairs-cum-umbrellas peculiar to the resort, and walked along the long promenade and bought cones of *patat-mayonais* and posed for silly concession photos just like everyone else.

After Sybil was born, the Franks tended to favour resorts like Westerland-Sylt on the German Baltic coast. Not that they had anything against the Dutch. Myrtil and Flory *loved* Scheveningen. But Westerland was closer. And after all, they *were* German, weren't they?

Or the family would motor around northern Germany, visiting the many historic sites there, like Wittenberg, where Martin Luther posted his ninety-five theses on the church door.

Then there were the skiing holidays the Franks took every winter in Switzerland.

Sometimes, too, the family would take the car or the train to Frankfurt to visit Flory's mother, Leontine, who was still living near the *Palmengarten* with her son Ferdi, or Myrtil's mother, Johanna, also living nearby – or, more sadly, grandfather Max, now living in a sanatorium, still in mourning for his lost life. And afterwards they would go walking in the Taunus hills, where sometimes they would encounter groups of *Wandervögel*, the German rambler groups, determinedly walking through the fields, strumming their guitars.

This was the Franks' world – or should one say, the Franks' *worlds*: Flory's world, Myrtil's world, and Dorrit and Sybil's world. Sometimes these worlds would combine. More often, they didn't, even if from a distance the Franks did appear to be a picture-postcard family.

It could have been worse.

But late in 1929, Gustav Stresemann dropped dead (reportedly while brushing his teeth) and the Franks' world, and the whole privileged world of Berlin Jewry, began to fracture.

The Foreign Minister's death was reportedly hastened by the fight over the Young Plan – the far-sighted, American-backed scheme to strengthen the German economy by reducing reparations by two thirds and ending the Allied occupation of the Rhineland; a sound plan that Stresemann approved, as did the Reichstag, but Hjalmar Schacht did not.

Weimar began to choke on itself. The right wing, which saw the Stresemann-backed plan, however seemingly generous, as a re-endorsement of the hated Versailles *Diktat*, used the republic's constitutional processes for popular initiatives and referenda to call for a plebiscite to force the government to repudiate the plan. To promote the plebiscite, Alfred Hugenberg, the media baron who owned UFA and much of the German media, recruited Adolf Hitler, head of the apparently moribund Nazi party.

For several years, Hitler, operating from his base in Munich, and Goebbels, who had reluctantly accepted the post of *Gauleiter* of Berlin in 1926 and made little progress there, had continued to rant without much success. In the 1928 elections, the Nazis polled only 2.8 per cent of the total vote, confirming their status as a splinter party. An article published in the *National Geographic* later that year, extolling 'Renascent Germany', contained a photograph of a small troop of SA brownshirts in Nuremberg, clutching flowers, as an example of local colour; interestingly, it also carried a photo of Stresemann, symbol of German normality, striding arm in arm with a smiling Jacob Schurman, the US ambassador, along the Unter den Linden. Who would have thought that these two countries had ever been adversaries, or would ever be again?

But now in 1929, Hugenberg – the first of a long and dishonourable line of magnates on whose backs Hitler leap-frogged to power – gave the Nazis a national platform for the first time and forced Stresemann on the defensive.

The move to rescind the magnanimous US reparations plan was a failure, enlisting only 14 per cent of the national vote, but the entire episode was stressful for Stresemann, already in ill health, and probably contributed to his demise.

In October 1929, several days after Stresemann's death, the New York stock market crashed, an event with immediate and severe repercussions for the German economy, as nervous American investors withdrew their loans. Capital assets dwindled, salaries were reduced, labourers and white-collar workers were made redundant. The shock of the crash was also felt at the grain exchange where Myrtil worked. Now, when he came home late, Flory knew it was because of work and not Lola.

By the middle of 1930 six million Germans were unemployed and the match-sellers whom Myrtil used to pass on the Friedrichstrasse in the old dada days were back. And so were those bullies-in-the-dark who had threatened to throw Conrad Rosenstein from the train years before – except that now they had a credible movement and a madly articulate *Führer*. Along with their caps and uniform, the *Sturmabteilung* now had a ready-made language they could use to apply to the objects of their loathing. Revolting words and phrases like *Einsatz* (strike force), *Volksgenosse* (racial comrade), *Untermensch* (subhuman) entered the national discourse of the language of Goethe, Schiller and Heine and Schubert.

In the September 1930 elections, the Nazis polled 6,400,000 votes, which now made them the second largest party in the country, after the Social Democrats. They were no longer a splinter party; now they were an electoral force, and Adolf Hitler – the self-proclaimed saviour of Germany and arch-nemesis of 'the Jewish-Zionist-internationalist clique' – was halfway towards realising his master plan of seizing ultimate power by constitutional means and leading the Fatherland and the *Volk* back to glory.

'It's all over with Germany; all over with Europe,' the great German-Jewish cellist George Rosenman said at three in the morning, after the final results were announced.

The rest of Hitler's meteoric rise to power, what John Gunther calls 'the savage, swooping arrow', is well known. There was storm; there was fire; there was intrigue. But the course of the Hitlerite arrow plunging through the dying body of the republic remained true.

Always, everywhere, in 1931 and 1932, as the next elections approached, there was Hitler relentlessly driving towards his goal, giving interminable incantantory speeches at the giant *Sportpalast* in Berlin or at other large venues, criss-crossing Germany by plane ('Hitler Over Germany'), repeating the same platitudes, the same lies, until people – and not just the bullies now, but an increasing number of middle-class Germans who had resisted the glittering cosmopolitan culture of Weimar and the Jews who seemed to propel it – began to believe him; while behind the scenes, the monomaniacal party leader outmanoeuvred everyone in his path, industrialists, chancellors and conservatives all.

If Hitler was ubiquitous, so was his chief propagandist and acolyte, Goebbels. 'We stand at the turning point of Germany's destiny,' he declared during the 1932 presidential campaign. 'We fight today! We fight tomorrow!'

This time the German people really were listening. Hitler achieved 36.8 per cent on the second ballot for German president, forcing Hindenburg, still respected as president, but increasingly given to mental lapses, to offer Hitler, whom he despised, the vice-chancellorship.

Hitler refused. He was intent on total power, and it was now only a matter of time.

Cabaret, the 1972 film adapted from *I Am a Camera*, Christopher Isherwood's memoir of life on the edge in late Weimar Berlin, brilliantly limns the way the Nazi contagion seemingly crept out of nowhere in the late years of the doomed Republic, before consuming it entire. Perhaps the most haunting and effective scene takes place as Sally Bowles, the high-living American cabaret singer (played by Liza Minnelli) and two of her edgy Weimar friends, a writer, Brian Roberts (Michael York), and a wealthy bisexual prince, Maximilian (Helmut Griem), come across an outdoor festival while motoring around Bavaria. Everyone is in high spirits, all is in order, until a young Hitler Youth type begins singing the Nazi song 'Tomorrow Belongs to Me', and the mood suddenly turns solemn. One by one the *Lederhosen*-clad picnickers rise to their feet like so many somnambulists, as the angelic boy keeps singing:

> Now Fatherland, Fatherland, show us the sign
> Your children have waited to see
> The morning will come when the world is mine
> Tomorrow belongs to me . . .

As Sally and her friends leave the repellent scene and motor away, the young Nazi ends his song by shooting out his right arm and the rest of the once merry picnickers follow him.

Dr Caligari was back.

The first signs of trouble came from Dorrit's school, the Kleist Lyceum. One day in 1931 or 1932 she told her parents that she had been jostled by several girls who were members of the League of German Girls. She was fine, even joked about the incident. Nevertheless, this was disturbing news to Myrtil and Flory, particularly after they discovered that a few of the teachers at their daughter's school were out-and-out Nazis who could recite from *Mein Kampf* chapter and verse.

Then the household staff were infected. Ursula, the governess hired for the girls in 1930, confided in her charges that she was a Nazi, too. Next the maids spoke in favour of the Nazis. Arms were shooting up all around the Franks now. And so it went.

Then, one Sunday, while the Franks were motoring towards the *Grunewald*, just like Sally Bowles and her friends, they came across a petrifying sight: a huge group of Nazi storm troopers marching along the Heernstrasse, evidently headed towards some sort of demonstration, or perhaps to one of the street battles with the Communists which were raging across the city at that time. There were hundreds of them. These Nazis were singing 'The Horst Wessel Song', the rousing anthem named after a brownshirt who had 'fallen in battle'. As the singing storm troopers passed, sympathetic onlookers would shoot out their arms.

To be sure, not every member of the Frank household was a Nazi. It was about this time, Dorrit recalled, that Herr Schwann (the children never learned his first name) blurted out, as he was driving the Franks around: 'Just wait, when Hitler comes to power, *I* won't be a Nazi.' Their friendly chauffeur, it turned out, was a diehard Communist.

But it was no longer *if* Hitler came to power, but *when* . . .

Several weeks later, Hitler was on the radio again, after a fanfare of trumpets, at the great Grunewald Stadium, filled to bursting with a capacity crowd, with thousands listening to loudspeakers outside. An equally awestruck German radio reporter described the scene. As millions of Germans, including the Franks, listened transfixed, there he was, bathed in light, hatless, briskly saluting, returned from the wilderness, no longer the 'madman of Munich', but the saviour of Germany incarnate.

And then Hitler began to speak – which was generally the point at which Myrtil would switch his set off.

But it was too late to switch off Hitler. The genie was out of the bottle.

There was a ray of hope in the autumn of 1932, after the November elections, in which the Nazi vote declined slightly, causing a drop in the number of Nazi deputies. Perhaps, some claimed, the Nazi tide was receding. It wasn't.

Finally, as Germany learned on 30 January 1933, after a round of back-room intrigue involving Schleicher, the chancellor, Papen, his predecessor, and Oskar Hindenburg, the son of the feeble eighty-five-year-old President, the latter was persuaded to name Hitler Chancellor. Hitler's decision, several years before, to seek power through democratic means, before vitiating those means, had seemingly been vindicated.

That evening, a massive torchlight parade of several hundred thousand jubilant Nazis marched through the Brandenburg Gate and up the Unter den Linden, shouting and singing along with the joyous crowds.

Jewish community leaders, for their part, advised caution. 'In general, today more than ever,' declared the Central Association of German Citizens of the Jewish Faith, 'we must follow the directive: wait calmly.' But German Jews knew it was their turn to be cast out again into the wilderness.

The following Friday evening, as Conrad Rosenstein writes, thousands of anxious German Jews attended *shul*:

I went to the synagogue like many other Jews . . . There I saw desperate faces full of the most profound mental anguish – pale and trembling. Never before did Jews pray more ardently than on that evening on which they experience[d] their being Jews so fundamentally. My heart, too, trembled and my soul cried secretly to its God. 'My God, why have you forsaken me?'

Later, during *shabbath*, Rosenstein broke down in front of his children:

The whole weight of the day's experiences struck me, and I broke down . . . The children either did not know or did not understand why I was crying so violently, but I knew: this was my leave-taking from everything German, my inner separation from what had been my fatherland – a burial. I buried forty-three years of my life.

The head of the Frank family also anguished; all German Jews anguished that night. Nevertheless, his main concern – his only concern, really – was to protect his family. Once again, as he had during the hyper-inflation madness, Myrtil knew he had to get his wife and children out of the country.

Holland – The Hague – was where he decided they would go; safe, peaceable, neutral Holland. They would be safe there. They knew The Hague. They had family there – 'Til's cousin, Betty, and her Dutch husband Paul. It was also close to Rotterdam, where 'Til had connections on the grain board: he could do business there.

On 27 February 1933, smoke could be seen in the distance – the smoke from the Reichstag fire. Berlin was literally aflame now.

'The final straw for us was when we heard on 15 March that the Jewish passports were being seized in Breslau and Silesia,' Flory remembered.

The March parliamentary elections were technically a disappointment for the Nazis. Despite the fact that Hitler was now Chancellor and the SA had virtually free run of the streets, the Nazis were able to poll only 43.9 per cent of the vote, still short of a majority. But on 23 March, Hitler placed before the Reichstag an Enabling Act, as set out in the original constitution – the same constitution drafted by the Jew Hugo Preuss – dissolving the body entirely. It was all over for Germany now.

Six days later, on 29 March 1933, the Franks boarded a train for The Hague.

'This isn't the way to Frankfurt!' cried Sybil. No, it wasn't, Flory assured her daughter as the train sped for the Dutch border. It would be a short journey, she promised – shorter than that to Frankfurt, just a few hours – actually it was a little longer.

The Germany the Franks were leaving looked much the same as the one of previous trips, complete with groups of *Wandervögel* rambling and singing in the fields. But now many of those same cheery *Wandervögel* were singing a new tune:

> Now Fatherland, Fatherland, show us the sign
> Your children have waited to see
> The morning will come when the world is mine
> Tomorrow belongs to me!

61

The Franks passed through customs without difficulty. Afterwards, Flory was horrified to discover that Sybil, the most religious of the family, had secreted a Jewish prayer book on her person. Did she not realise what could have happened if the Nazis had found that?

Anyway, they were safe now.

PART TWO

FALSE SANCTUARY
HOLLAND, 1933–42

CHAPTER 4

The Long Mirage

'Quaint' is no more appropriate an adjective for 1933 Holland than it is for any European land whose ways and whose past is ten times longer. 'Fascinating' it certainly is; 'picturesque', also, and its life today could likewise be aptly termed 'vigorous'. But, oh, not 'quaint'! . . .

. . . The seat of the government and the residence of the Queen, The Hague is one of the handsomest, cleanest and most fashionable cities of Holland . . .

Travel, April 1933

. . . Holland's proximity to Germany does not make her position a comfortable one at present. For centuries Holland has stood for culture and justice, for freedom of religion and of conscience – ideals for which Willem of Orange gave his life. Therefore, it is not surprising that Holland has generously received many refugees . . .

Travel, March 1939

Mr Colijn [Hendrikus Colijn, Dutch Prime Minister, 1933–39], when he visited me in 1937, explained to me the marvellous efficiency of the Dutch inundations. He could, he explained, by a telephone message from the luncheon table at Chartwell, press a button which would confront an invader with impass-able water obstacles. But all this was nonsense . . .

Winston Churchill, *Their Finest Hour*

Heinrich Heine, the great German-Jewish poet (a favourite of Flory's) once wrote that if he ever thought the world was coming to an end, he would move to Holland because, he said, everything happens fifty years later there.

But at 4.30 on the morning of 10 May 1940, after a peaceful hiatus extending back to the Napoleonic wars, contemporary history caught up with Holland and the Frank family.

Like most of their neighbours in Scheveningen, the quiet, windswept beachside annexe to The Hague where the Franks had lived since leaving Germany, Myrtil, Flory, Dorrit, Sybil and Leontine, Flory's mother, who had joined the family in Dutch exile in 1938, were comfortably ensconced in bed when a fast-moving thundercloud of German Junkers, Heinkels and Stukas appeared in the clear cobalt sky, and the first staccato report of Dutch anti-aircraft fire rent the air.

'I'll never forget that morning,' Sybil, who was then sixteen, later recalled. 'It was six in the morning [actually, it was closer to five]. Dorrit and I were fast asleep, and suddenly there was this giant BA-BA-BOOM!'

At first Sybil thought that the sound came from the troops at the nearby Alexandria Dutch army base, whose martial efforts – like those of most of Holland's peacetime soldiers – had long been a source of annoyance to Scheveningen's residents, but had never been taken very seriously.

'Oh no, we thought, the Dutch soldiers are playing at war again. But we had never heard anything quite that loud – or quite that early in the morning.'

Weren't those *bombs*? And what was this – *parachutes*?

It must be borne in mind that in May 1940, the idea of using parachutists as a means of war was a fairly novel thing, as the then Dutch Foreign Minister, E.N. van Kleffens (who had actually received firm intelligence regarding the attack the evening before, the most recent of numerous warnings of German intentions), recalled in his somewhat breathless memoir, *The Rape of the Netherlands*, published in England later that year, after he and the rest of the Cabinet escaped to London via seaplane:

> The government soon began to receive reports of a particularly alarming nature. Telephone messages were coming in from many places around The Hague, of parachutists who had landed in a wide circle surrounding the seat of government. These men were dropped from especially designed aeroplanes: the pilot, when finding himself above the indicated spot, merely had to pull a lever by his side in order to cause the bottom of the plane to open up, thereby dropping the parachutists out into space. These men carried not only small firearms, but also machine guns and radio sets.

Sybil continued: 'So we ran to the window, and we saw all these *white things* coming down – and what were they? German parachutes! We couldn't believe it!'

The reaction of their mother, who had also run to the window, along with her husband, was more detached – as if she was watching some sort of giant canvas by Kandinsky or Nolde, writ large in the cerulean.

'I remember seeing the anti-aircraft artillery bursts in the sky and thinking how much they resembled flowers – red on the inside, orange on the outside,' said Flory, ever the aesthete. 'It was strange, but I didn't feel in danger at all.'

But the direness of Holland's situation became all too clear as the Franks turned on their large Philips radio, and listened, transfixed, to the reports of the mechanised terror that Hitler had unleashed on all three Low Countries, as well as France.

It was hard to take everything in: in the east of the country, German Panzer tanks had crushed the vaunted Dutch border defences and were racing towards their other objectives. German paratroopers had also landed at Moerdijk, near Rotterdam, where they had already seized the critical bridges over the Meuse and Waal rivers. Belgium had been invaded. Luxembourg was gone.

'The Low Countries were swept by a hurricane of aerial war [today],' the Associated Press reported. 'Nothing like this has ever been seen before. The Polish *blitzkrieg* pales by comparison.'

In the distance, near the Queen's palace, more shooting could be heard as a detachment of German paratroopers assigned to capture the airfield outside town, as well as Wilhelmina, the Dutch sovereign, shot it out with Dutch forces which included, it was later learned, the Queen's stalwart son-in-law, Prince Bernhard.

Sunlight was streaming into the room now.

One of the things that everyone remembers about 10 May – the Dutch Pearl Harbor – was how good the weather was.

'It was such a *beautiful* spring morning – crystal clear, no rain,' Dorrit recalled half a century later, still wistful at the recollection of the innocence she and Holland lost that day. 'And then, of course, the Germans came.'

The head of the household sat back in his chair, overcome. For seven years, ever since the Franks had debarked from their train from Berlin at the main railroad station of The Hague, Station Staatsspoor, Myrtil, proud of his record of reacting to events with vigour and celerity, had been confident that he had made the correct move in choosing Dutch exile for his family. That response had enabled him to exit with both his family and his assets intact; too many other German Jews, particularly well-to-do ones, preferred to await the course of events, as German-Jewish community leaders had suggested.

Few countries were as palpably safe from the rising Nazi menace as peaceful, tolerant, *gezellig** Holland. The family was familiar with Dutch hospitality, having holidayed there several times already. When the girls found that their new home at 6 Mechelschstraat was located but a short bicycle ride from the beach at Scheveningen, and saw the famous long pier extending into the sea and the even longer promenade stretching off into the distance, and the circling sea gulls and the barnacled old fishermen down by the old harbour who still plied their ancient trade, they were thrilled.

Of course, there was a period of adjustment. It was not easy for the Franks – particularly 'Til and Flory – to reconcile themselves to the loss of their many German family and friends, now scattered to the four winds, or to the extinction of the comfortable life they had enjoyed at Brückenallee 4, or to the idea of exile.

Perhaps not surprisingly, the change was most difficult for Flory. She missed meeting her crowd at the Café Dobrieu and the Kempinsky; she missed having staff, and the little button under the table she used to summon them – although, thankfully, the Franks were later joined by their cook, Annie. Flory missed her world; she missed being a Berliner; she missed being German.

For the first few years of Dutch exile, Flory consoled herself with the thought that the Franks might yet return to Germany, that Hitler would somehow make a misstep and topple from power, that the sensible majority of the German people who she knew, in her heart, still stood with the Jews would see the light and disavow the Nazi revolution; that the anti-Semitic tide that had since ravaged her homeland might subside, just as it had after the inflation madness was cured, and that she could go home again.

For her part, Flory was not yet ready, as her disillusioned countryman Conrad Rosenstein put it, to take leave of everything German. The presence of an expatriate German-Jewish population of nearly two thousand in Scheveningen – the latest additions to an established Jewish community that stretched back to the early nineteenth-century – helped the émigré, who was thirty-six when she fled her homeland, to remain in her mental cocoon.

The transition from German of the Jewish faith to expatriate had also

* An emblematic Dutch word that defies exact translation, *gezellig* roughly means cosy.

been a strain for her husband. Myrtil, who turned forty in December 1933, the first year of their exile, also missed his cushy and secure (if somewhat loveless) life in Berlin. He didn't miss Flory's dinner table bell (which had always annoyed him), or some of the other perquisites of the Franks' now lost life. He missed his hunting lodge in Spandau. He missed his Lola. He missed being a Big Shot.

But he adjusted, and so, in time, did Flory.

Unsurprisingly, the girls found acclimatising easier, though living in Holland was not entirely a romp, especially for Dorrit. Enrolled in the Nieuwe Meijses School, a private girls' school in The Hague, the impressionable twelve-year-old found herself looked down upon by some of her classmates. Perhaps grown-up Dutch people were tolerant and friendly, but in the cut-and-parry world of the *meijses* who attended the Nieuwe Meisjes School, refugees, particularly refugees from Germany – whether they were Jewish or not – were not especially popular.

Holland and Germany had traditionally had a love–hate relationship, even before the advent of Hitler. Every summer, hordes of loud-mouthed German tourists, obnoxious to Dutch eyes and ears, 'took over' the beach at Scheveningen. How keenly Dutch people, and not merely children, enjoyed correcting any German who tried to speak in the throaty local dialect (which Edmondo de Amicis, the nineteenth-century travel writer, accurately described as like German, but 'with a hair in your throat'). Try as they might, German tourists couldn't come close to the correct pronunciation of Scheveningen, with its long-drawn-out, gargly first syllable – *Scheee*veningen – and most didn't bother to try. Later it was said that the Dutch resistance used the pronunciation of Scheveningen as a means of ferreting out German double agents.

Then, too, there was the small matter of how the German newcomer dressed. 'All the girls were dressed to kill,' Dorrit recalled. 'They had outfits from Bonnetierie [a high-end Dutch department store in The Hague] and I didn't.'

Then a fellow-*meijse*, Gerda Buchsbaum, took Dorrit under her wing, and that, essentially, was the end of her adjustment problem. Gerda was also Jewish, which made it easier for her to empathise with Dorrit, and the two quickly became best friends. Years later, Dorrit would have fond memories of hanging out with her new Dutch friend. 'We would go to the dunes and have our first cigarettes and laugh about it all. She [Gerda] saved my life, really.' And sometimes she spent time with another young Dutch Jewish girl, Edith Velmans.

Dorrit's affinity for languages, including Dutch, also proved helpful; she even managed the correct pronunciation of her new home town. 'Yes, you see,' she would say to her sceptical classmates, '*I* can pronounce *Schkeeeveningen* too!'

Confidentially, of course, Dorrit preferred English to Dutch. By the mid-1930s, when she was in her middle teens, the ardent Anglophile lived in a virtual Anglo-American world, her recreational reading consisting mostly of back issues of *Vogue* and *Harper's Bazaar*, which she would devour in her stylishly decorated room on the top floor of the Franks' three-storey terraced house; sometimes Gerda would also bring along the latest movie magazines to flip through.

Galsworthy was Dorrit's favourite author, followed closely by Dickens, after whose work she had been named. Errol Flynn, whom she saw with Gerda in the popular 1935 swashbuckler *Captain Blood*, was a big hero. So was Brenda Frazier, the reigning It Girl – or 'celebutante', as the gossip columnist Walter Winchell called her. Like millions of other teenagers on both sides of the Atlantic, Dorrit had her 'Brenda Fraser' period, characterised by a swept-back hairdo and carefully stencilled red lips.

In time, Dorrit would learn how to dress stylishly too, just like her schoolmates (although she didn't have nearly as much money to spend on clothing). By 1937, when the young German-Jewish émigré was sixteen, she had told her parents that she wanted to be a clothing designer, and Myrtil and Flory dutifully made enquiries about a possible design school for their style-conscious daughter.

In a real sense, Dorrit blossomed in Holland, and so did her younger sister, Sybil. Only eight years old when she arrived with her secreted prayer book, Sybil had the least problem adjusting of the entire family. Enrolled in a local public school, the Harting School, she quickly learnt Dutch, and, unlike her more extroverted sister, was less likely to preen about it. Less romantic, more studious, more hard-nosed – and, as the feisty youngster was quick to point out, just as bright as her older sibling – Sybil found herself drawn to subjects like maths and chemistry.

She too loved Holland, easily adapting to the local ways. Sybil also had a flowery side, or at least a floral one, as she convincingly demonstrated in 1935 when she entered a garlanded bicycle contest, a Dutch youth rite, and to the delight of her friends and family, and with the aid of her sister, who made the requisite paper garlands, won.

The Franks' life in exile was much less extravagant than it had been in Berlin. There was no chauffeur any more, no squadron of housemaids, no nannies. But this was fine with their daughters. They certainly didn't miss having nannies (except Eve, of course), and with fewer intermediaries around, they were able to spend more time with their mother, accompanying her to the fine local art museums, especially the bejewelled Mauritshuis, Europe's most celebrated small museum, with its Vermeers and Rembrandts, where Flory would share her voluminous knowledge of Dutch art with them, as well as with a steady stream of bemused and fascinated eavesdroppers, who enjoyed hearing the exiled *grande dame* hold forth. She was always at her best then.

The girls saw their father frequently – certainly more often than they had in the old days. 'We were definitely closer in the thirties,' Sybil agreed. The snapshots of the Franks dating from the first five years of their Dutch exile are mostly happy ones, depicting the girls and their friends – as well as Flory, with just a trace of sadness in her face – laughing or clowning in the sand at Scheveningen as they waited for the photographer, often their father, to snap the shutter. When Myrtil himself appears in the frame, dapper and well groomed as ever – are those *striped* swimsuits? – his smile is always the widest.

And why not? Everything had turned out for the best, hadn't it? So the Franks weren't well-to-do any more. It didn't really matter; the happy-go-lucky former Rhinelander had never been that much of a materialist anyway. Myrtil's income on the grain bourse in Rotterdam was only a fraction of what it had been in Berlin, but that was all right. He was still able to afford to take the family on motoring holidays, but this time he did the driving himself.

Thus, in 1937, in what turned out to be perhaps the nicest holiday the family took together, the Franks drove to Paris, where they visited the Invalides and ogled the futuristic pavilions at the Paris Expo. One day, at Myrtil's suggestion, they went on a tour of Verdun, the site of the Great War's most savage battle, where so many French, British and German soldiers had fallen, marked by a giant cenotaph and a sea of graves, where they mused on the futility of war. They also spent an afternoon with Flory's brother Ferdi, who had become a stamp dealer in exile, which, all agreed, was a profession that well suited his pinched personality. Then, after buying some last snaps, they drove back to Scheveningen.

'We had a nice life in Holland,' Flory said.

Like the thousands of other German Jews who had found refuge in Holland by then, the Franks were concerned, in 1935, when the local

Nazi variant, the NSB (Nationaal-Socialistische Beweging), led by a self-styled Napoleon and former water engineer named Anton Mussert, polled 8 per cent of the vote in that year's provincial elections. Democrats around the world were also concerned. Had the Netherlands, they wondered, caught the Nazi virus?

Happily, it hadn't. The party's strident propaganda, which emphasised Holland's Germanic 'blood ties', and extolled the fascist virtues embodied by the one-man state across the border, grated on Dutch ears, and the party's support fell. In the next major poll, the 1937 election for the *Staats-General*, the Dutch parliament, the NSB's share of the vote dropped to 5 per cent, which, under Holland's system of proportional representation, was good for only four seats, far short of what many had feared and Mussert had gloatingly predicted. Coalitions dominated by the resolutely anti-fascist (but also anti-Semitic) Social Democratic party remained in power for the rest of the decade.

'Thumbs down: Hollanders Smack Fascism at Polls', read the headline in the leading American magazine *Literary Digest* that week.

Meanwhile, support for the Dutch monarchy remained strong throughout society. Few modern-day sovereigns have been as popular with their peoples as Queen Wilhelmina was with the Dutch during the two decades between the world wars, the period which turned out to be the Indian summer of the Dutch empire, then with its vast East Indies holdings the third largest in the world.

There had been a brief crisis in 1918, after the Dutch socialist leader Troelstra called for a leftist revolution similar to the one that had just taken place in Russia and might take place next door in Germany. With typical Dutch thoroughness, Troelstra announced *his* revolution a week in advance! But the Communist seed didn't take root in Holland's soil any better than the fascist. In the event, the day earmarked for the inauguration of the Dutch republic became the occasion for one of the greatest ever demonstrations of loyalty to the monarchy since Holland's sixteenth-century founding by William the Silent, as thousands of the loyal subjects of the Queen, faced with a possible revolution (however properly announced), descended on the Palace Noordeinde near the centre of The Hague, to show their support for her and her family, as well as their contempt for the stillborn republic.

Older Hagenaars could yet recall that emotional and historic scene, as Wilhelmina, moved by the extraordinary display, her only child, nine-year-old Princess Juliana, enfolded in her arms, asked that her landau be led slowly around the palace courtyard. 'I'd like to see who pays me this tribute,' she had said to her protective escorts. At which point a voice boomed out, 'All Holland, Your Majesty,' as thousands of other cheering spectators joined in. So much for the so-called Dutch republic.

Seventeen years later, The Hague was the scene of yet another such outpouring of support, following the marriage of Juliana – who, like her mother, had since impressed her future subjects with her democratic, unselfconscious character – to her German fiancé Bernhard, or Benno, as many Dutchmen, who had first looked askance at the princess's choice, called the newest adopted member of the extended royal family.

'This is the marriage of my daughter to the man she loves, whom I have found worthy of her,' declared Wilhelmina (who had also taken a German consort, Heinrich of Mecklenburg) in response to critics of the union, 'not the marriage of Holland to Germany!' Dutch critics of the betrothal were partly mollified by Bernhard's decision, the previous September, to completely relinquish all his affiliations with the Reich in preparation for Dutch citizenship. They were even more pleased when, as further proof that he had changed his colours from German brown to Dutch orange, the former storm trooper allowed authorities to substitute a rollicking song extolling Lippe-Biesterfeld, capital of his extinct principality, for the obligatory Nazi anthem.

Years later, Dorrit recalled Bernhard speaking on Dutch radio to ease opposition to the controversial match. 'I remember him talking about how he wasn't really from Germany, he was from *Lippe-Biesterfeld*, this lovely little country *within* Germany,' said Dorrit, who by then, like her sister, considered herself a loyal subject of the Queen.

If these moves to disassociate himself from Germany – along with his future mother-in-law's aforementioned rejoinder – helped to placate the Dutch, they incensed Berlin. *Essner Nationale Zeitung*, the mouthpiece of Nazi Air Minister General Hermann Goering, denounced Bernhard for his 'lack of character'. The foppish *Reichsmarshall*, then Hitler's number two, who had been looking forward to attending the event in his dress vanilla suit with all of his medals, threw a fit when his bid for a wedding invitation was refused.

Berlin grew even angrier when anti-Nazi Dutchmen staged several demonstrations against the Reich in the weeks leading up to the wedding. The bilateral tempest in a teapot finally culminated in Berlin's confiscation of the passports of three German princesses scheduled to act as Juliana's bridesmaids. The bridesmaids – along with the rest of

Bernhard's family, including his brother Aschwin, a German air force pilot – were allowed to attend only after Wilhelmina, in an extraordinary move, wrote a personal letter to Hitler requesting that the women be admitted.

Hitler, who as yet had no designs on his small neighbour and wished to avoid an international incident, tried to make amends by sending warm greetings to the couple on the day of the wedding. For his part, Joseph Goebbels, now Nazi Minister of Propaganda and Public Enlightenment, made it clear that he was definitely *not* appeased by withdrawing from The Hague all but one of the Reich's newspaper correspondents.

On 14 January 1937, the day of the wedding, when hundreds of thousands of Dutchmen descended on the capital to show their support for the royal newlyweds and for the House of Orange, the teary-eyed Frank girls were amongst those who greeted the happy couple as they exited the *Groote Kerk* with the traditional Dutch cheer: 'Hold the sea! Hold the sea!'

Not even the sight of the prince's smiling brother, in his dress *Luftwaffe* uniform – the same *Luftwaffe* which, three years hence, would incinerate the heart of Rotterdam – waving to the crowd along with Juliana and Bernhard was sufficient to dampen the enthusiasm of the spectators, or that of the Franks.

Just in case the Germans harboured any ideas about invading their neutral neighbour, Hendrikus Colijn, the no-nonsense Dutch Prime Minister, who had ably served as Dutch defence minister during the Great War, wanted the country – and the world – to know that Holland was prepared for any eventuality. Between 1935 and 1937, Colijn, the so-called 'Dutch strongman', presided over a mammoth $47 million rearmament plan, a tremendous sum for a country whose total budget was then less than $400 million. In a crisis, asserted Colijn, who was a friend and confidant of Wilhelmina's, he could mobilise at least 300,000 men, possibly more. Colijn's impressive plan also provided for 100 bombing planes (as they were then called), as well as new submarines and cruisers for defending the Dutch East Indies.

The centrepiece of Colijn's plan to stave off a possible German invasion was his scheme to employ Holland's watery topography itself against the aggressor by a series of huge, linked inundations, as he explained to Winston Churchill during a visit to England in 1937. Churchill later recalled: '[he] explained to me the marvellous efficiency of the Dutch

(*Above*) Breitenheim, the tiny Rhenish town
that was home to the Franks since 1749.
(*Right*) Like most German Jews of his generation,
Max, seen here posing proudly with two
uniformed nephews during The First World War,
was a patriot.
(*Below*) The letterhead from Max's prosperous
winery.

(*Below left*) Max's son, Myrtil, was a
city boy at heart. Here he is
(centre) in Frankfurt with some
of his schoolmates after a day
sculling on the Main.
(*Below*) It wasn't long before
the debonair Myrtil graduated
to other sports.

(*Above*) The apple of their eye. Flory Marburger with her family at their home in Frankfurt *c*.1910. From left: Leontine, her grande-damish mother, the mischievous Fred, dour Ferdi, and father Herbert. After Myrtil met Flory one day at the Opera she became the apple of his eye as well.

(*Below*) Whipper-snapper. Turning his back on the family business, Myrtil decided to learn the ins and outs of the grain business in Frankfurt instead. Here he is with two of his colleagues, looking his usual natty self.

(*Above*) A wan and world-weary Myrtil returns home from the war in 1918. Over one hundred thousand German Jews loyally fought for the Kaiser in World War I; 12,000 died. Myrtil saw service on the Eastern Front, and was one of the fortunate ones, emerging intact and anxious to get on with his life.

(*Right*) One of the first things Myrtil did was to marry Flory. The couple are pictured shortly after their marriage in November, 1919.

(*Below*) The newlyweds immediately moved to Berlin, where, thanks to his new job with the rationing authority, Myrtil was able to find a large flat near the Tiergarten. They found a city in tumult, as right-wing Freikorps battled insurgent Spartacists.

(*Below*) A crippled veteran begging for change, a commonplace scene in postwar Berlin.
(*Right*) The jarring contrast between luxury and famine and the general nihilism of the times was captured in the savage drawings of self-proclaimed 'dadaist' George Grosz.

(*Above*) Walter Rathenau, first foreign minister of the Weimar Republic, was a *beau ideal* for his generation of German Jews. His murder in 1922 was one factor, along with rampant hyperinflation, that moved Myrtil to send his wife and daughter, Dorrit, out of the country.
(*Right*) Dorrit, the young exile, with her grandmother, Leontine, in Switzerland.

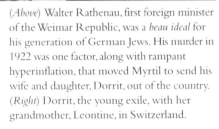

Happy Days. The mid-1920s were good years for renascent Berlin, and as its perilously prominent Jewish community. Flory and Myrtil smoking cigars by the Spree; Myrtil at his hunting lodge in Spandau; Dorrit and Sybil clown in the back of the Franks' chauffered Chrysler; Flory trips the light fantastic.

(*Right*) The calm before the storm. As late as 1928, the Nazis, who drew only 3% of the vote in that year's Reichstag elections, were considered a fringe party. Here a smart group of charter stormtroopers, bearing flowers, rally in Nuremberg. Soon they would exchange the bouquets for blackjacks.

From afar the Franks seemed an ideal couple as well as an ideal family. The reality was somewhat different. (*Above*) The Franks exchange meaningful looks on a North Sea holiday. (*Left*) Sunday in the Tiergarten.

(*Right*) In the world beyond the Franks' comfortable household, everything seemed under control. Gustav Stresemann, the republic's able foreign minister, was the era's emblem of normalcy: as long as Stresemann was around, people felt, all would be fine. Then in 1928 he died and things went rapidly downhill. Here the benign diplomat strolls arm in arm with U.S. Ambassador Jacob Schurman.

Sturm breaks loose. The Nazis made a strong showing in the 1930 national election, thanks in great part to the fiery Joseph Goebbels (*above left*). In January 1933 (*left*) a weary President Hindenburg asked Hitler to become Chancellor. A month later, the Reichstag burned down (*above right*). Three weeks later the Franks fled to Holland.

Sanctuary.
(*Above*) Dorrit and Sybil in Scheveningen, shortly after the move, 1934.
(*Above right*) Flory and the girls tour the Dutch interior, 1935.
(*Right*) Sybil wins a garlanded bicycle contest, 1936.

(*Right*) In 1934 Myrtil returned to Germany to bring Johanna back to Holland, whence she emigrated to Palestine, where Myrtil's sister, Lisbeth, had already settled. Both, understandably, fearful.

(*Below*) In Breitenheim in 1938 a group of young men celebrated in front of the Franks' former house. All but one of the seven men pictured would soon die serving *Fuehrer* and Fatherland.

Evening Standard

NAZIS INVADE HOLLAND, BELGIUM, LUXEMBURG: MANY AIRPORTS BOMBED

Allies Answer Call for Aid:
R.A.F. Planes are in Action

HITLER HAS INVADED HOLLAND, BELGIUM AND LUXEMBURG. HIS PARACHUTE TROOPS ARE LANDING AT SCORES OF POINTS AND MANY AIRPORTS ARE BEING BOMBED.

THE DUTCH HAVE OPENED THEIR FLOOD-GATES AND CLAIM TO HAVE BROUGHT DOWN A DOZEN BOMBERS.

You Must Carry Your Gas Mask

(*Left*) Escaping Buchenwald. Flory's brother Fred stayed with the Franks before fleeing to the U.S. in 1937.

(*Right*) *Blitzkreig.* Once again the 25,000 German Jews in exile in Holland found themselves under the shadow of the Reich. Several hundred killed themselves.

(*Below right*) Sybil with Jeanne Houtepen, who would later help the Franks.

inundations. He could, he explained, by a telephone message from the luncheon table at Chartwell, press a button which would confront an invader with impassable water obstacles. But all this was nonsense.'

Amongst the first wave of German Jews who chose the seemingly prudent Dutch path, along with Myrtil, was Otto Frank, his namesake and fellow Great War veteran – and former neighbour of Flory's from Frankfurt. In December 1933, after Otto and his wife Edith had made several preliminary trips, the Frankfurt businessman put Edith and his two daughters, Anne and Margot, on a Holland-bound train. Otto Frank chose to resettle his family in Amsterdam. His reasons for choosing Holland were virtually the same as the approximately 25,000 German Jews who took up Dutch exile during the early to mid-thirties, before the Dutch began shutting the gate: he already had family and business connections there; and of course, because Holland was safe, especially for Jews. Religious freedom and tolerance, after all, were one of the pillars of the Dutch state. There had been Jews in Holland for centuries. Rembrandt had painted them. Where, indeed, could they be safer?

It was only the following year, 1938, the year of the *Anschluss* and the Munich crisis, and other aggressive moves by the Reich, coupled with the frightening escalation in anti-Semitic violence on the other side of the border, culminating in that year's government-organised *Kristallnacht* pogrom, that Myrtil and Flory began to have second thoughts about their choice of exile.

In February and March, the Franks listened, fascinated and appalled, as the juggernaut engineered by Hitler and Goebbels (with help from their Trojan horse, Arthur Seyss-Inquart, the lawyer who was leader of Austria's Nazi Party) inexorably rolled over Austria: the summons from the *Führer* to Kurt Von Schuschnigg, the hard-pressed Austrian Chancellor, to parley with him at Berchtesgaden, Hitler's mountaintop retreat; Hitler's browbeating of the latter into appointing Seyss-Inquart Minister of the Interior and otherwise giving the local Nazis a free hand; the recalcitrant Von Schuschnigg's brave repudiation of the agreement and decision to call for a plebiscite.

The Western powers watched from the sidelines, just as they had during the remilitarisation of the Rhineland: they saw the browbeating of Von Schuschnigg into cancelling the plebiscite; his resignation and imprisonment after the *Anschluss*; the 'peaceful' invasion by the German army; Hitler's triumphal return to Linz, his home town, in company with his beaming fifth-columnist, Seyss-Inquart (about whom the world, and especially the Dutch, would soon hear more); and, finally, Hitler's speech to a crowd of over a million Austrians cheering themselves hoarse in Vienna's Heldenplatz.

Then, after the summer of 1938, a reasonably happy one and the last time the Franks would travel *en famille* out of the country, came the equally electrifying Czech crisis, as Hitler decided to also add the Sudetenland, the German-speaking section of Czechoslovakia, to his growing empire. The Franks, along with the vast majority of their Dutch neighbours, were again appalled when the British and French caved in at Munich and agreed to dismember formerly sovereign Czechoslovakia in order to further appease 'That Man' as the German dictator was increasingly referred to by his small but growing number of detractors in the West, led by Winston Churchill, the outspoken British MP. They listened as Chamberlain proclaimed upon returning to London from his meeting with Herr Hitler, that the deal meant 'peace in our time', while at the time of signature, the Czech president, Benes, waited abjectly in an adjoining room.

Meanwhile, the Franks followed with alarm the telephoned reports they received from their Jewish friends and family still in Germany of the fast-rising and increasingly violent campaign against the remaining German-Jewish population.

After years of boycotts and other restrictions aimed at ostracising the rump German-Jewish community of 300,000 (down from its pre-Nazi high water mark of over half a million), the Nazis now moved to crush what was left of the Jewish professions and economic life. One of the targets of the new measures was Flory's brother, Fred, who had stayed behind partly in order to take care of their mother, Leontine. One day in 1937 the police showed up at his door. Vague, obviously trumped-up charges were read to him (a formality soon to be dispensed with). Several days later, Fred found himself incarcerated at Buchenwald, the Nazis' newly opened concentration camp (the first, Dachau, had been set up in 1933).

That might have been the end of the end of the line for him. But Fred Marburger was a very clever man. He still had some funds that the Nazis didn't know about. Several weeks later, he was mysteriously released. Next Fred applied, successfully, for a visa to the United States, where he – reluctantly – moved the following year, 1938, leaving Leontine.

Then, on 9–10 November 1938, this new wave of anti-Semitic measures culminated in the horrifying *Kristallnacht* pogrom, so called because of the large numbers of windows of Jewish businesses and synagogues that were 'spontaneously' destroyed. The specific trigger for the horror was the assassination of Ernst von Rath, the third secretary of the German embassy in Paris, by one Herschel Grynszpan, a Polish-Jewish student. But that was only a pretext. For months Hitler's henchmen had been looking for an excuse to ratchet up the anti-Jewish campaign, preparatory to expelling them completely from the life of the Reich. There was no talk of extermination; Hitler was undecided at that point about what to do with the Jews, or where to send them; nor did the Nazis care, particularly, where they ultimately went. If other countries like Holland and England wanted to accept their *Juden*, that was still all right, at least at that point, as long as they left their valuables behind; there was even some discussion about the possibility of setting up a Jewish exile community in Madagascar. The only point upon which Himmler and Goebbels and Goering were evidently agreed, at that juncture of their prolonged skirmishing campaign with the Jews, was that it had to be escalated: it was time to truly make war with 'the Jew'. However, for the sake of appearances an excuse of some kind was needed. There was still the matter of form.

And then, as a result of a tragic serendipity, while Hitler was in Munich celebrating the anniversary of the beer hall putsch, came word of the von Rath assassination. That evening and the next the skies over many German cities blazed red as over one hundred synagogues were put to the torch. It was the beginning of the end for what remained of German Jewry.

One of those who was caught up in the backdraught of *Kristallnacht* was Leontine, who, along with thousands of other wealthy Jews, found herself expropriated and ordered to leave the country. Myrtil – now technically a 'stateless' Jew as a result of the cancellation of his and the family's passports in 1937 – risked arrest by returning to Frankfurt to escort his shaken mother-in-law back to Scheveningen and safe harbour.

As his train chugged towards the German–Dutch border Myrtil, accompanied by the pallid Leontine, must have wondered whether he had, in fact, made the right choice five years ago; whether he might not have been better off putting his family on a boat train for England, as his brother Julius and his wife Else did in 1936; or to Palestine, where his sister Lisbeth, who also fled that year, settled in the then-wilderness northern Palestinian town of Nahariyah, shortly to be joined by her mother Johanna, after her two sons put her on a boat in Marseilles; or to America, where Fred, lucky to be alive after his brush with the Nazis, had resettled in Canton, Ohio, in the safe heartland of America.

Myrtil was able to finesse his way through German customs, even though he didn't have a valid passport, but then Myrtil was always very good at finessing things. In any event, there weren't any problems; and now the Franks were five.

At one point on the way back to Holland, Myrtil's train passed within sixty miles of Breitenheim, his once beloved birthplace and home town. What had become of Breitenheim, or of his father's business and house, he feared to think.

In the event, a book about Breitenheim published in 1992 on the occasion of its 700th anniversary lends some light on the matter. On one page there is a photo of the Franks' former house which is listed as number 61. According to the photo, dated that same year, 1938, the house had been converted into something called the Gasthaus Heinrich, an inn. Standing in front of the *Gasthaus* is a jovial group of seven young local males, healthy specimens all – and happy ones too, to judge from their smiles and the huge stein of beer that one of the celebrants, Alfred Miller, is showing off.

Happy days for Germany, and happy days, evidently, for Breitenheim as well.

That would change, however, as another section of the book indicates. This contains a list of the several dozen men from the village who would give their lives during the Second World War. A quick comparison of the names of the young men gathered in front of house number 61 on that happy day in Breitenheim in 1938 with the war casualty list shows that no less than six of the seven, including Alfred Miller, were to be killed in the war.

For their part, none of Max's children ever saw Breitenheim again.

Myrtil liked the sound of America. In December 1938, shortly after he returned to The Hague with Leontine, he went to Rotterdam to apply for visas for the family from the US consulate. The American consul politely accepted Myrtil's application. However, the official was also duty-bound to inform the disappointed asylum-seeker that there was little chance of its being approved within the foreseeable future. There was this matter of quotas, you see. Perhaps in a few years things might open up, he told his crestfallen visitor.

A few years, Myrtil thought. He might just as well have said an eternity. The US proved just how unenthusiastic it was about accepting

German-Jewish refugees the next year, when the *St Louis*, a passenger ship bearing several thousand, was not allowed to dock in New York – or anywhere else – and ultimately had to return to Germany (an episode immortalised in Katherine Porter's book *Ship of Fools*).

The Dutch were also growing wary of accepting large numbers of German-Jewish refugees. Over 7,000 German Jews applied for Dutch asylum in the wake of *Kristallnacht*. However, only a fortunate few, like Leontine, who already had family in the Netherlands, were allowed in. Most of the rest were turned back, while several thousand of the new 'limbo Jews' were housed in a special squatters' camp the Dutch government built for them in the northern province of Drenthe, near a place the Franks had never heard of before, a village called Westerbork.

So that was that. Upon learning of the indefinite wait for American asylum, Myrtil postponed planning to reach any other destination. Perhaps, he and Flory began to persuade themselves, Holland had not been such a bad choice after all. Perhaps the international situation *would* improve.

Then again, as their fearless prime minister kept reminding them, there were always the dykes.

Hitler's appetite was not quelled by the offering of the Sudetenland; it only grew. Hardly had the cheering for Chamberlain ceased when, that winter, it became clear that the German dictator wanted the non-German-speaking rump of Czechoslovakia as well without any pretence of self-determination. The following March he greedily seized it. Now Prague was his as well. Meanwhile his intentions for the Jewish population continued to crystallise.

Chagrined but determined, Britain and France belatedly joined ranks, refusing to cede any more of Europe without a fight. The *Wehrmacht*, now the world's second largest army after Russia's and by far the most modern, was ready. The *Luftwaffe*, whose aerial terror tactics had been honed during the recent Spanish Civil War – the same offensive air force that the Germans had supposedly been forbidden to build by the Versailles Treaty – was ready. Germany, united behind its *Führer*, all doubts quelled, virtually all remaining resistance quashed, was ready.

The only question was where and when the Reich would strike. Soon it became clear: Poland. This was where the line would be drawn. The necessary defensive alliance was prepared. The Poles signed. Europe mobilised. The world waited.

Confident of *his* rearmament plan, confident in his dykes, Hendrikus Colijn cautioned his countrymen not to despair. 'I advise all not to be unduly anxious,' the stout-hearted Dutch leader declared at the end of April, after he ordered the Dutch armed forces to mobilise.

Over the rest of the Continent, war clouds billowed, but from where the venerable Dutch statesman stood, it still looked like peace in our time. 'Humanity's destiny is not in the hands of one man,' Colijn declared. 'We shall not be blown like reeds in the wind.'

Holland wanted to believe Colijn. The Franks, too, wanted to believe him. Not that they had much choice at that point. And so they did, or they convinced themselves that they did.

Meanwhile the life the Franks had built amidst the sheltering dunes of Scheveningen had begun to fall apart. Myrtil's income on the Rotterdam grain bourse dropped, as the uncertain economic situation affected the European food business; he decided to supplement his earnings through work as a dental equipment salesman. He had also become romantically involved with a new woman, Tine van der Sluijs, an attractive Hagenaar fifteen years his junior and the sister of Dorrit's former Dutch tutor, who now became his mistress. At a certain point in 1938 or 1939 he moved out to live with her, casting a pall over the Frank household. Sometimes he was home, sometimes he was not. All in all, it was not a good situation, particularly for the girls. Their friends guessed that something was wrong.

Dorrit recollected: 'Gerda would say, "Where is your father? He's never home." I didn't know what to tell her.'

It was for this reason, as well as the clearly worsening international situation, that the Franks didn't take their usual family holiday abroad during the summer of 1939. They weren't really a cohesive family unit any more.

Then Julius, who had managed to establish himself as a successful wallpaper designer with a studio and house in the London suburb of Hendon, called with an idea: perhaps Dorrit would like to take a holiday in London? He was, of course, aware of the family's troubles. Perhaps, he suggested, she could help out around the studio as well.

Naturally, his Anglophile eighteen-year-old niece, who had just completed her apprenticeship at an Amsterdam design studio, was elated. England! She was going to England! Her parents were all for it. It was a good idea, they agreed, that she should get away for a bit. Hitler could wait.

So in mid-July off Dorrit went by boat to spend what she expected to be a fulfilling two-month sojourn in England.

But what to wear? She hadn't any clothes! The Franks couldn't afford them. 'I remember when I went to England I had almost nothing to wear,' Dorrit said. This was one of those times when she missed her former luxuries like having a dressmaker at the ready, as they had in Berlin. But she would be fine. Anyway, she still had her Brenda Fraser hairdo.

As expected, Dorrit had a lovely time with her uncle. She saw the sights. She helped Julius around the studio. She used her English; no one corrected her. It was glorious; even the weather was grand.

But Hitler would not wait. As August approached, Berlin began to make trouble over the Free City of Danzig. It became clear that the start of the Second World War was only weeks away.

'I remember they were building trenches in Hyde Park,' Dorrit said.

Worried, Myrtil and Flory called Julius and asked him to send his niece home, back to Holland, where – they assumed – she would be safe when hostilities broke out. After all, everyone knew Holland was neutral. This was what the Queen and the Dutch cabinet – now led by a new, equally tough-talking Premier, D.J. de Geer, after the defeat of Colijn's Catholic party in the midsummer elections – thought. This what most Dutchmen thought. After all, Hitler had guaranteed it!

And so, on 30 August, as Germany made overt preparations to invade Poland, an upbeat Julius escorted his niece to Euston Station to take the boat train to Harwich and then cross the still quiet, still safe English Channel back to Hoek van Holland.

Before she departed, Julius, impressed with Dorrit's grasp of design and sales skills, asked her if she would like to try selling some of his wallpaper designs for him in Holland. She told him that she'd love to.

Not to worry, uncle and niece assured each other, in words that echoed dozens of other emotional conversations taking place on the same platform. Everything would be all right. They would see each other soon.

Flory, Myrtil and Sybil were all waiting on the dock when Dorrit's ferry arrived. For a brief, delirious moment, as her parents and sister excitedly debriefed her, and Dorrit, pointedly speaking in English, chatted away about her uncle's *brilliant* studio and the *brilliant* this and that, the fractured Franks were a family again. Most important, Dorrit was safe.

The next day, 1 September, Hitler invaded Poland, and the Polish people got their own taste of *blitzkrieg*.

Later, Dorrit remembered that she was on the tennis court of the Jewish tennis club with her first boyfriend, a handsome fellow by the name of Ed Weinreb, when another friend came over and hollered out the news. There was a brief pause, as the tennis players took it in.

Then they resumed their rally.

Two days later, a weary and chagrined Neville Chamberlain, his last warnings to Hitler ignored, went on the BBC to make it official.

And so it had begun, again.

Aside from the admittedly horrific Polish campaign, highlighted by the terror bombing and flattening of Warsaw and the successful pursuit by the British Navy of the German pocket battleship *Graf Spee*, which ultimately scuttled herself outside Montevideo Harbour as millions avidly followed the dramatic naval shootout – the Second World War hardly seemed worthy of the name, during these first relatively bloodless months. Particularly comical was the *Sitzkrieg*, or sitting war, on the Western Front, as the French and British troops waited on their side of the Maginot Line for something to happen while the Germans, evidently content to do nothing as well, sat on their side of the no less formidable and static Siegfried Line.

'*We're going to hang out the washing on the Siegfried Line*,' went that autumn's most popular London ditty. '*Have you any dirty washing, mother dear?*' In the Netherlands, the Dutch, as pleased as anyone by the absence of combat, merrily sang along as well. Decades later, the Frank girls could repeat every line.

However, the Germans were decidedly not doing nothing. In October, the *Führer* instructed his *Wehrmacht* staff to begin planning in earnest for an invasion of France and the Low Countries the following spring.

Despite reports from their own agents and other sources asserting that, the *Führer*'s protestations to the contrary, Herr Hitler did have plans for Holland, the Dutch government and nation remained palpably unworried.

A 'Letter from Amsterdam' in the 9 March 1940 issue of *The New Yorker* captures the mood of complacency and denial that pervaded the country at that late date, a mere eight weeks before Hitler's spring offensive. 'The Dutch give the impression of indifference to the progress of the war around them,' observed the magazine's correspondent. Meanwhile Amsterdam had become a centre of intrigue as Gestapo and British agents mingled freely in Dutch cafés and bars. Occasionally, in the febrile atmosphere, the two sides stepped on each other's toes, though this being neutral Holland, the matter could still be settled musically.

In one incident that may have been the inspiration for the famous scene in the 1942 film *Casablanca*, a group of visiting Nazis tried to bully the orchestra of a hotel in The Hague into playing their fighting song, 'Deutschland Über Alles'. The British in the audience strongly objected to this, as did their French comrades, who asked that the orchestra play their anthem, *La Marseillaise*, which the now frazzled orchestra leader, trying his best to keep to Dutch neutrality, likewise refused. However, he *was* amenable to playing another, more innocuous suggestion from the British side, 'Whistle While You Work'. What the poor Dutchman didn't know was that the Brits had revised the lyrics:

> Whistle while you work!
> Ribbentrop's a twerp!
> Hitler's barmy
> Like his army
> Whistle while you work!

The delighted British sang at the top of their voices, as the red-faced Germans walked out.

The correspondent from America – still avowedly neutral itself – was less than impressed with the state of Dutch preparedness, painting a surreal scene:

> Rotund Dutchmen solemnly thump their tables in the Astoria Restaurant while waiting for the waiter to clean up the shells of a dozen Zeeland oysters, or the remains of a brace of brown roasted pullets, and declare with conviction that Holland will soon do to Germany what Finland is doing to Russia.

It was a bad comparison. On 19 March, ten days after the article's publication, Finland, after holding off the Russian bear for four months, finally capitulated. Also, Holland was not Finland. The Grebbe Line – the outer line of dykes that would allegedly stop any German invasion – was not, as the world would soon learn, the Mannerheim Line.

The New Yorker's correspondent was not taken in, concluding: 'There are British military experts who think the Dutch Army would hold up a German advance for just about five minutes.'

Even after the Germans invaded Denmark and Norway in April, ending the *Sitzkrieg*, the Dutch continued to play ostrich.

Dorrit was attending a play in The Hague with Gerda on the day Hitler made his surprise Scandinavian move. The shocking event was extraordinary enough for the master of ceremonies to note it in his opening remarks. *'Doe gewoon dan blyft het ook gewoon,'* he advised anxious playgoers: 'Act as if nothing happened, and nothing will happen.'

The next day Queen Wilhelmina said much the same thing in her speech to her worried subjects. And Her Majesty's worried subjects, including the Franks, wanted to believe her.

At that point Myrtil could probably still have removed his family from Holland to England, where Julius possibly could have attested for him; to Palestine, to join his sister and mother, Lisbeth and Johanna; to Portugal, where Flory's brother, Ferdi, had just settled; or perhaps elsewhere, like South Africa, where a sizeable number of the German-Jewish diaspora had fled, or even Morocco, where Ferdi ultimately settled after he left France following the German invasion. It would have been difficult, but it could have been managed.

Instead, Myrtil and Flory, trusting in the wisdom of their original decision, and in the soundness of Dutch neutrality, as well as the sturdiness of Dutch dykes, elected to remain where they were, in The Hague, much like the estimated total of 20,000 other German and Austrian Jews.

Thus it was with utter bafflement and incomprehension that the residents of The Hague and Rotterdam awoke on the morning of 10 May 1940 to find the sunny skies above them speckled with thousands of German parachutists, while hundreds of German fighters and dive-bombers, guns and cannons ablaze, swarmed down upon them, shooting up predesignated military targets – and anything else that struck their fancy: boats, bridges, civilians, as well as quite a few bewildered Dutch cows.

The supposedly fail-safe dyke inundation system was not of much aid – not against *blitzkrieg*. Churchill later wrote:

The power of a great State against a small one under modern conditions is overwhelming. The Germans broke through at every point, bridging the canals or seizing the locks and water-controls. In a single day all the outer line of the Dutch defences was mastered. At the same time the German Air Force began to use its might upon a defenceless country. The Dutch hope that they would be bypassed by the German right-handed swing as in the former war was vain.

Dutch sanctuary, Dutch exile, Dutch neutrality – it had all been a mirage, Myrtil and Flory realised, a long mirage. And now, as the sound of the gunfire outside reminded them, it was time to wake up.

Myrtil did not stay baffled for long. Twice before, in 1923 and 1933, he had moved quickly to remove his family out of harm's way, and so he did again that day. He would do something, he promised his worried family. Didn't he always? And so he did.

The following day, the second day of the invasion, 11 May, while the lopsided battle between the Dutch army and the *Wehrmacht* continued to be fought out in the streets of The Hague, Myrtil raced down to the Old Harbour and tried to hire a boat to ferry the Franks to England.

There were no takers. Most of the fishermen foolhardy enough to undertake such a risky voyage had already left. A number had already been strafed and sunk by the *Luftwaffe*. The fishermen must have been quite scared: Myrtil Frank could be a very persuasive man, and he had brought money with him. It was no use. That exit was closed.

Across the Channel, in London, Julius read the banner headlines in the *Evening Standard* and wondered if he would ever see his brother and his family again.

CHAPTER 5

Shadowland

*Although 5,000 Wehrmacht and Dutch soldiers are dead, there is no animosity
in our hearts . . . We will not persecute, nor will we force our convictions upon
the population . . .*

> Arthur Seyss-Inquart, German *Reichskommissar*
> for the Netherlands, June 1940

*Many Dutchmen have been persuaded that Germany is bound to dominate Europe
and that the best policy for Dutchmen is to cooperate with Germany . . .*

> From an article about occupied Holland in the
> *Saturday Evening Post*, February 1941

They spent many beautiful hours . . .

> The inscription below a panel from the
> sketchbook of Edgar Reich, an artist interned
> at Kamp Westerbork, a Dutch-based German
> work camp, in which he depicts his romance,
> during the winter of 1942, with his fiancée,
> Dorrit Frank; the panel shows them dancing

The war in Holland was over as soon as it had started. The British military experts quoted two months before in *The New Yorker* were very
nearly right. The Dutch were able to hold off the Germans for five days.
Not five minutes, but close enough.

Not that they didn't fight. They did. The Dutch air force, including
the squadron of 'bombing planes' that Prime Minister Colijn had thought-
fully purchased several years before, fought spectacularly. Doomed from
the moment they took off, every available pilot from the ready pool flew

into combat. Every Dutch pilot was downed, though not before an equal number of German planes were also shot down.

The Dutch army, under its commander General Henri Winkelman, gave a sufficiently good account of itself, capturing or dispersing the German forces that had landed near The Hague, as well as holding Rotterdam, as to move Hitler, who was following the unequal battle from his western command post and wished to use some of the troops bogged down in Holland to exploit a new opportunity that had just opened up in France, into issuing one of his rare special directives.

'The power of resistance of the Dutch army has proved to be stronger than anticipated,' stated Hitler's Directive No. 11, issued on the morning of 14 May, the fifth day of invasion. 'Political as well as military considerations require that this resistance be broken *speedily*.'

And so it was. Later that same morning, while Winkelman (whose men, despite having lost 3,000 of their number, still had a good bit of fight in them) was considering German terms, a covey of *Luftwaffe* bombers appeared over the centre of Rotterdam, Holland's second largest city and busiest port, and without warning dropped their high-explosive loads. Instantly a square-mile area was levelled. Over 800 civilians were killed, several thousand more were wounded, 78,000 were made homeless. Rotterdam, like Guernica before it, became a byword for aerial terror.

And it remained so for several years, together with Coventry, the English Midlands city which the *Luftwaffe* also bombed to smithereens later that year during the Battle of Britain – until the far more devastating strategic bombing raids, often comprising as many as 1,000 bombers or more, which the RAF and the US Eighth Air Force directed at Germany later in the war.

But in May 1940, all that was far in the future. One Rotterdam was sufficient to take the wind out of the Dutch. That afternoon, Winkelman surrendered. Within hours German tanks had moved into Amsterdam and The Hague, taking control of central points, as the benumbed local populace looked on. For the first time since the Spanish Wars of Independence, metropolitan Holland was under foreign occupation.

Although every Jew living in Holland that week was terrified by this turn of events, none were more distraught than the estimated 20,000 German and Austrian-Jewish refugees who suddenly found themselves under German rule again. No doubt Myrtil was not the only German Jew who tried – and failed – to hire a boat out of Scheveningen that day. Escape by land was equally pointless: the closest neutral country –

Switzerland – lay across three well-guarded frontiers. 'Nowhere,' as Gerald Ratlinger writes in *The Final Solution*, 'was the Jewish population more trapped than in Holland.'

For some, suicide represented the only way out. During the first week of the German occupation, an estimated 250 German Jews took their lives rather than have to face their Nazi tormentors again. The Franks knew one Scheveningen couple who died by their own hand. 'They just walked into the dunes,' Flory remembered, 'and they never came back.'

However, the whirlwind that most Jews, especially German ones, feared in the wake of the German *blitzkrieg* did not come to pass, and the shock of those first traumatic post-invasion days gradually subsided.

In June 1940, Arthur Seyss-Inquart, the newly appointed *Reichskommissar* of the Netherlands, gave his inaugural speech at the Binnenhof, site of the soon-to-be-disbanded Dutch legislature in The Hague. Seyss-Inquart's name was already familiar to most Dutchmen from the 1938 *Anschluss*, and his subsequent position as deputy to Hans Frank, the fanatical governor of occupied Poland.

Understandably they were apprehensive about what to expect from their newly imposed regent. At least they did not need to feel slighted by the appointment: Hitler had clearly sent one of his top men to Holland to run things there. At the same time, by dint of Seyss-Inquart's appointment and the installation of a civilian administration in the Netherlands, it was also apparent that Hitler's plans for the Dutch were different from those for most of the other newly acquired territories of the Reich including Belgium and France, which had military governments imposed on them. Amongst the occupied territories of western Europe, only Norway, where Seyss-Inquart's civilian counterpart, Josef Terboven, had just been installed, were given this dubious privilege.

What did this mean? What, in fact, *were* the Reich's plans for Holland? The music-loving Nazi proconsul did his best to allay Dutch suspicions in his placatory speech, which was accompanied by violins. 'We will not persecute nor will we force our convictions upon the population,' he declared. Most heartening to those who wished to believe him – and at that point many if not most Dutchmen did – Seyss-Inquart vowed to uphold Dutch law, including (although he did not explicitly say so) the venerable laws and traditions dating from the seventeenth century regarding religious freedom and the rights of religious asylum. Seyss-Inquart did not even specifically mention the Jews.

And so the pogroms that the Jews had feared would occur in Holland, as they already had in Poland and elsewhere in the occupied eastern European countries, did not take place. As Seyss-Inquart's emollient speech demonstrated, the Germans, at least at that early juncture of the war, were still trying to win over the Dutch. As far as the bombing of Rotterdam was concerned, the *Luftwaffe* said, there had been a communications error.

Over the next few years, as Seyss-Inquart and his cohorts realised how deeply most Dutch resented them, Germans would see the futility of his wish, but at that point, while the Germans were still hoping eventually to incorporate Holland into the Greater Reich itself (a hope that Seyss-Inquart would eventually make explicit in early 1942, before abandoning it soon thereafter), the general policy was to be nice to the Dutch, which also meant being nice to 'their Jews'.

Holland's 'Jewish problem' could be dealt with later. But for now, the tune was softly, softly. A German military band even came to Scheveningen in June to serenade the crowds.

Only one restriction was placed on the Jewish population: Jewish members of the civil anti-aircraft service had to resign. And that was it. That wasn't so bad, was it?

'It was very strange,' said Flory. 'Suddenly there were Germans around.' A large number of *Wehrmacht* were billeted in Scheveningen. And yet they didn't seem to be shooting anyone. Quite the opposite, in fact; many Dutchmen were impressed by the 'correct' behaviour of the occupying soldiers, just as many Frenchmen were at first impressed by the discipline and tact of the German troops who now came into their midst.

On 29 June, Prince Bernhard's birthday, Seyss-Inquart realised that the job of winning Dutch hearts and minds might be a little more difficult than anticipated when, in a spontaneous show of support for the exiled prince and the House of Orange, Dutchmen sported white carnations on their lapels, as Bernhard was famous for doing. Some even went so far as to hang the Dutch tricolour out of their windows. The *Reichskommissar* was annoyed, but not deterred. The Dutch, he was confident, would see the light in the end. Meanwhile, as a precautionary measure, Dutch mothers were forbidden to name their children Wilhelmina, Juliana or Bernhard. But that was just a slap on the hand.

The pre-existing civil bureaucracy was essentially allowed to remain in place. Only a thin layer of Germans and local (more often than not incompetent) NSB members were imposed from above; the vast majority of Dutch civil servants had no official contact with the Germans, which suited them fine, and kept on working at their jobs without protest, continuing to do so for most of the five-year-long occupation. Some, especially those involved with essential services like rationing, would claim that such cooperation was necessary for the nation's well-being and that if they had protested or resigned they would have been replaced by less competent NSB types (as later, those who did resign were) and the country would have suffered even more than it ultimately did.

In any event, the byword of the day for the civil service in 1940 (and for roughly four years afterwards) was cooperation. Thus, when, as a so-called 'precautionary measure', the Germans asked mid- and top-level civil servants to sign the 'Aryan attestation', in which the 12,000-odd respondents were asked to state their religious affiliation, only one solitary conscientious objector refused. He was fired. As Christopher Browning observes in his recent, definitive work, *The Origins of the Final Solution*, the harnessing of a compliant, dutiful, and impeccably efficient Dutch officialdom to implement Nazi racial policy was to be one of the keys to explain the record fatality rate of Dutch Jews in comparison to other west European countries.

The Franks were not quite as taken in. And yet, and yet . . . everything seemed nearly OK. Trying to be practical, Flory sent Dorrit and Sybil out to buy shoes. That would be the first thing the Germans would want, she figured. And so the girls went out shopping, while the Franks all tried to get used to the perturbing Nazi sights and sounds that now confronted them everywhere, on the street, on the beach, on the radio.

Still, maybe things would be OK. Of course, they didn't have very much choice: they were trapped.

Then, in September 1940, a new German edict ordered foreign Jews, including German Jews, to move away from the coast on the grounds that they might abet a future English invasion. This was the first move in a protracted campaign to isolate and concentrate the entire Jewish population, an insidious cat-and-mouse game that the Germans would play for the next two years – and one that would end in the destruction of Dutch Jewry. As Seyss-Inquart said at his 1946 trial in Nuremberg, 'It happened step by step.' This was one of the first steps, the first swipe of the cat's paw.

At this point there were concentration camps for Jews and other 'criminal elements' – but no extermination camps, at least not yet. Perhaps a few hundred Jews – out of a total population of 140,000 – went underground at this time, no more. There was no need.

The impact of the unpleasant new edict on the Franks and the 2,000-odd German Jews affected by the relocation order was mitigated by the fact that those affected were granted a sizeable area in which to relocate. Instead of being herded into a small ghetto-like neighbourhood, as many feared – and as had occurred in Poland – the Franks and their fellow deracinated Jews were merely enjoined to move to a new locale at least forty kilometres (twenty-five miles) from the coast. An inconvenience, yes, but not so bad.

The relocation order gave the Franks only three days to move. Nonetheless, after a short, frenetic search, Myrtil was able to find a large house in Hilversum, the medium-sized 'garden city' twenty miles east of Amsterdam, for his wife, daughters and elderly and increasingly frail mother-in-law. And so, after a short intervening stay in the town of Bussum, just outside Hilversum, where they rented an apartment for a few weeks, they moved late in 1940, the first year of the German occupation. They were even allowed to take their furniture with them, although Myrtil and Flory chose not to, a decision they didn't take with much thought. As they later discovered, it was very well that they didn't.*

Although the Franks missed the sea and their friends in Scheveningen, the family soon became attached to their new home in Hilversum, which was actually larger than the one they had had in Scheveningen, and came with a pleasant garden, something that Hilversum was famous for. It was located on a leafy, well-tended street – Frans Halslaan, named after the famous Dutch painter – round the corner from the neighbourhood school. Myrtil continued to struggle to make ends meet, but, as Flory later said, 'We tried to get as much out of life as we could. We did a little entertaining,' she recollected. 'We even went mushroom hunting. Of course, things were getting more difficult, I could see that. Basically, we were happy to be alive.'

Dorrit would later recall the seventeen months the Franks spent in Hilversum as 'surreal'. 'It was like living in the twilight zone,' she said. Still allowed to work, she resumed her apprenticeship at yet another design studio in Amsterdam. She also fell in with a new high-spirited circle of friends, young Jews from the Hilversum–Utrecht area, mostly

---

*When the Germans first began their internal deportations to Westerbork a year later, most of the first families to be selected were those who had brought their furniture and effects with them. Those who did not have furniture to confiscate, like the Franks, were less attractive. Later, of course, when the Germans were seizing *all* Jews, this distinction became pointless, but at that point it helped save the Franks.

in their late teens and early twenties. Every Saturday, ten or twelve of them would get together in the Franks' living room on Frans Halslaan to talk and gossip and dance to Big Band music or java jive.

The sensation of being in limbo, of not knowing what the seemingly omnipotent Germans – who were currently marching on Russia – would do next, lent such occasions a manic intensity.

Already, by the spring of 1941, there had been some violent incidents in the Jewish quarter of Amsterdam, one of which, in February, had resulted in the death of a Dutch militiaman, to which the Germans reacted by staging a raid on Jonas Daniël Meyerplein in Amsterdam in which over 400 Jewish men were swept up off the street, never to be heard of again.

Meanwhile, an angry Dr H. Böhmcker, Seyss-Inquart's special commissioner for the city of Amsterdam, summoned the leaders of the two Jewish communities (Ashkenazi and Sephardic) and insisted that they form a twenty-member *Judenrat*, or Jewish Council, similar to ones the Germans formed in other occupied countries, as a means of transmitting their orders to, and better controlling, the general population.

Amsterdammers reacted to the raids, and what was perceived as the increasing persecution of the Jewish population, by participating in an extraordinary strike. Led by Communist activists, the *Februaristaking*, as it was called, quickly spread across the city, affecting transport, department stores, shipyards and factories. For nearly two days the entire industrial centre of Amsterdam was shut down. The 15,000 workers at the Philips plant in Hilversum also joined in, as did some in nearby Haarlem and Zaandam.

'A seething indignation filled the city,' noted the underground newspaper, *Het Parool*, later. 'Were we going to look on passively while our Jewish brothers were beaten?' The strike, the resistance paper noted, 'was primarily a strong protest against the scandalous anti-Semitic terror which the German barbarians started in our country'.

The Jews of Amsterdam and environs were, of course, heartened by the action, which Louis de Jong would later describe as 'the only anti-pogrom strike in history'. As Geert Mak put it, 'The Jew knew, if only for a moment, that [he] was not alone.'

But it was only a moment. Initially taken by surprise by the action, Rauter, Böhmcker and their German colleagues soon suppressed it with the aid of a German police battalion and two SS *Totenkopf* police battalions, as *Het Parool* describes:

The German police [were] sent into the streets in innumerable trucks and they began to shoot everyone who did not get out of the way. Machine guns were brought into position on streetcorners and swept the corners clean. On many occasions hand grenades were used . . . And through this din one heard German curses and the hoarse cannibal battle screams of the uniformed Nazis charging into the unarmed masses.

The strong Nazi response effectively brought the strike to an end within forty-eight hours. By that time nine Amsterdammers had been shot dead.

And then the extraordinary moment, one of the most stirring examples of popular resistance to the Nazi persecution of the Jews to take place anywhere in Europe during the war, as well as the last one to take place in Holland, was over, never to be repeated, at least in Holland.*

One of those who disappeared during the raids that precipitated the *Februaristaking* was Dorrit's friend Ed Weinreb. One day in February, she had had an appointment to meet her old tennis partner in Amsterdam. But Ed didn't turn up. Several weeks later, his parents received a letter from the authorities stating that he had been sent to the German concentration camp at Mauthausen, but that he was all right.

By May 1941, every one of the 400 Jews picked up in the February raids, including Ed Weinreb, was dead.

But no one knew this immediately: the Germans would stagger the death notices so that they seemed accidental. Despite everything, it was still possible to believe that things would turn out for the best, if one wished, and most Jews fervently so wished.

And what was that knock on the door?

This is what this strange interlude was like, if you were a Jew trapped in occupied Holland. It was, of course, distressing to see the signs in the parks that declared 'BEPERKTE BEWEGINGSVRIJHEID VOOR JODEN' – limited liberty of movement for Jews – but at least Jews still had *some* liberty. All they had to do was to follow the clearly worded instructions of the *Joodsche Raad*, the Jewish Council, as transmitted from German headquarters, promulgated each week in *Het Joodsche Weekblad*, the Jewish weekly, undersigned by the two co-chairmen of the Council,

---

* Two years later, in September 1943, in an equally stirring, mass form of resistance, the Danish people, spearheaded by their king, Christian X, and the Danish churches, as well as the Swedish government, succeeded in rescuing virtually the entire (albeit considerably smaller) Jewish population of 7,200 of that occupied country, along with 700 non-Jewish relatives, and trasporting them to neutral Sweden and safety.

Abraham Asscher and Dr David Cohen, and everything would work out. That was the prevailing feeling amongst most Dutch Jews. Even Myrtil subscribed to this compliant attitude.

In November 1941, the German authorities ordered the Dutch to make a detailed census of the Jewish population, and the heads of all Jewish households were ordered to report to their local police station to fill out the census forms. Virtually all complied. The Dutch civil authorities, unaware of, or oblivious to the possible uses to which such a census might be put, agreed to carry it out; across the border in Belgium, by contrast, the less cowed and/or compliant authorities refused a similar request. But the obedient Dutch officials agreed to execute the census, which would soon become a key instrument in the continuing Jewish persecution. The spirit of the *Februaristaking* of nine months before (to which the great majority of serving public officials were immune anyway) had evidently vanished. There was really nothing to worry about, the friendly Dutch policemen assured the tens of thousands of weary-looking Jewish men around the country, including Myrtil who dutifully reported for the census. Not to worry, just a formality.

That month, November 1941, thanks to the unceasing efforts of Joseph Goebbels, now in his ninth year as Nazi Minister of Propaganda and Public Enlightenment, and still as Jew-obsessed as ever, the first transport made up from the sixty thousand or so Jews still living in Berlin left for Poland. In an essay in *Das Reich*, the 'prestige' Nazi publication, Goebbels justified the 'evacuations' (as the transports were euphemistically called) and made a chilling prophecy which echoed a similar one Hitler made in 1939: 'If the Jews involved in international high finance were to succeed in dragging the peoples of the world into another war,' the Reich's official hate-monger declared, 'the result would be the extermination of the Jewish race in Europe.' Two months later that prophecy, which was already being translated into reality in Poland, would be turned into systematic, planned reality at the Wannsee Conference.

But few Dutchmen, including Jews, read *Das Reich* and, even if they did, they would doubtless have called Goebbels' prophecy propoganda.

The Germans continued to issue new and incrementally more humiliating regulations through the autumn of 1941 and the spring of 1942, including ones forbidding Jews from travelling or moving to another house without a permit (7/11/41), from entering non-Jewish hotels, theatres, and swimming pools (21/11/41), from driving cars (1/1/42), from marrying non-Jews (23/1/42), and so on and on and on: the list was getting to be quite long now. If Myrtil had plans for taking the family 'under' at that point, he kept them to himself. Everything would be OK, he would say when he returned to Frans Halslaan from his onerous salesman rounds. Meanwhile, Dorrit still continued to go to Amsterdam to work as an apprentice designer.

And then Dorrit fell in love with one of the Jewish boys who came to her house on Saturdays. His name was Edgar Reich and he was nineteen. But Edgar and his family were almost immediately sent to Westerbork, the German internment camp in the north-east . . .

Six months later, on Friday 15 May 1942, Dorrit – a six-pointed yellow Jewish star conspicuously affixed to her left breast – is sitting aboard the 1.15 p.m. train out of Amsterdam, bound for Assen, in north-eastern Holland, a trip of approximately three hours. Some of the other, un-starred passengers in Dorrit's second-class carriage glance at her, doubt-less wondering who this 'special' passenger is.

Dorrit looks away and stares out of the window, oblivious to the atten-tion, engrossed in thought – benign thoughts, mostly, for Dorrit is in love and she is going to visit her fiancé, Edgar Reich, in a place called Kamp Westerbork. Edgar is interned there, has been since February. It's not so bad, he told her the last time they met, in Amsterdam in late March, when he was allowed to leave Westerbork and return to Amsterdam in order to register for the new Jewish census.

Now – after receiving special permission for the long trip from the helpful, if stressed, staff at the *Joodsche Raad* – Dorrit is about to see what Westerbork is like for herself.

As the steam-powered train gets under way, Dorrit looks up to check her bicycle, parked at the end of the carriage; she has brought it along in order to cover the last leg of her trip, from Assen to the farmhouse where, again with the aid of the Jewish Council, she has arranged to lodge for two evenings.

As the gabled roofline of Amsterdam gives way to the blur of semi-detached houses of the suburbs, Dorrit returns to the security of her private internal cinema, replaying scenes from the short reel entitled *Dorrit and Edgar*, in between occasional bored looks at the vista whizzing by; Dorrit is particularly familiar with this stretch, having traversed it many times on her way from her job in Amsterdam to the Franks' just-evacuated home on Frans Halslaan. The interior panorama is much more interesting . . .

Engrossed in her own thoughts the young Jewess replays the Saturday evening in the Franks' living room in Hilversum the previous September, when she first met Edgar, an Austrian Jew whose family moved to Utrecht from Rotterdam at the same time that the Franks were forced to evacuate The Hague. Thinking back, she recalls how impressed she was with the suave nineteen-year-old commercial artist with the curly blond hair; impressed, but not attracted. Perhaps they stole glances at each other, amidst the slightly forced frivolity of their cosy little group. But it was not love at first sight – at least not on Dorrit's part. Edgar, though, evidently took an immediate liking to her, at least so he claimed later.

Dorrit glances out of the clean window. The train has arrived at Hilversum, and she catches sight of the city's most famous landmark, the Raadhuis, the Cubist yellow-brick city hall, its tower concealed by a hideous green camouflage net: nervous that Allied bombers would use the tower to help them locate *Wehrmacht* headquarters, located nearby, the Germans, oblivious to the architectural wonder in their midst, at first wanted to paint the tower green, a plan from which they were dissuaded with some difficulty by local officials. Hence the net welcoming Dorrit home.

Home, she muses, as the train takes on a typical midday, midweek complement of mostly students and elderly passengers. *Home*. A curious concept. What does home mean *now*? When – and where – will we ever be *home* again?

Too depressing to think about. Dissolve to another, happier scene from *Dorrit and Edgar*, one that took place at this very station, the first week of January, several months after the star-crossed lovers met, when Edgar volunteered to walk Dorrit to the station – their crush was mutual then – so she could catch the train to her job in Amsterdam and he could get the train back to Utrecht. Instead of the chaste kiss on the cheek that Dorrit expected, Edgar suddenly kissed her full on the lips and confessed that he was in love with her, as the stony-faced Dutchmen standing on the platform looked on with varying degrees of interest.

Now *that* is a scene worth dwelling on, Dorrit remarks to herself with a smile, as the train finally pulls out of the station.

At the next few stops Dorrit barely looks up, for she has seen them all before. Now, however, an hour out of Amsterdam, the exterior scenery begins to change noticeably. As the train swings to the north upon leaving Amersfoort, it occurs to Dorrit that in the nine years she has lived in Holland she has never been to the north of the country before. The novel aspect of the trip is underlined as the locomotive nears Hardwijk and the vast, blue, tranquil expanse of the IJsselmeer – site of the great south-east polder which the Dutch land reclamation authorities had hoped to build before the war dynamited their plans – appears in the carriage window.

Dorrit takes in the pleasing diorama before her as the train curves to the east and plunges into forestland, then hungrily returns to the feature for today. In her mind's eye appears a montage of pleasing scenes from the weeks that followed the kiss: Edgar and Dorrit dancing alone in her living room as 'Ole Guappa', their favourite song, wafts from her scratchy but reliable record player; Sybil, who already knew the dashing *artiste* from their Saturday group, also approved.

Then, of course, how could she not? Anyone could see that Edgar is a dreamboat. And, as the engraved ring that Dorrit now happily twirls around her finger proves – the same ring they hastily purchased in Utrecht, the night before Edgar and his parents were dispatched to Westerbork, to confirm their love (they hesitated to call it an engagement ring) – he belongs to her!

The train reaches the halfway point: Zwolle, ancient capital of Overijssel, former member of the Hanseatic League. Slowly they cross the railway bridge over the tiny *Zwarte Water* – one of numerous bridges the Dutch army destroyed in May 1940 in a futile attempt to staunch the Nazi tide, now rebuilt and in business again, serving Holland's German masters, just like new.

'*V = VICTORIE, WANT DUITSCHLAND WINT VOOR EUROPA OP ALLE FRONTEN*' ('V = Victory for Germany on all fronts') – shouts a propaganda banner stretched over the awning of the station, part of the Germans' strained effort to subvert the meaning of the angrily scrawled 'V's that have sprouted on Dutch walls to mean victory for the Allies. In May 1942, Berlin is still trying to convert the hearts and minds of its subject Dutch 'friends'.

'Victory on all fronts – God forbid,' Dorrit mutters to herself – even though the Germans do seem to be winning on all fronts of late – before the train heads off again in the direction of Drenthe, the dreary, wind-swept north-east province sometimes known as 'the Siberia of Holland'.

The next station is Meppel, current population 5,000; current Jewish population 260; home of the representative of the Jewish Council for Drenthe, the esteemed Meyer Lobstein. Recently, Lobstein had appealed to Dutch Jews, worried by the German authorities' effort to isolate them from the rest of the population, to obey the authorities and not resist, a message that was also consonant with Dutch legalistic impulses. Obedience, not resistance – *that* was the right way, the Jewish way, the widely respected Lobstein asserted.

Dorrit herself, like most Dutch Jews, is undecided about the best course of action, content to take each day of the German occupation as it comes, preferring not to think about where all this – the yellow star, the Franks' enforced move to Amsterdam, Edgar's deportation to Westerbork – is leading. Denial, or partial denial, contemporary psychologists would call this state of mind, which the soothing pronouncements of Lobstein and other deluded members of the Jewish Council only serve to reinforce.

Still, it is hard for Dorrit to put out of her mind some of the traumatic scenes she had witnessed in recent months, as the Germans have played out their horrid game with the hapless Jewish population; particularly the unforgettable one that took place on the platform of the Utrecht train station three months ago, when the Reichs and 150 other 'stateless' Jewish families finally, reluctantly, reported for embarkation to Westerbork, under the watchful eyes of the security police.

Now, despite Dorrit's best efforts to suppress it, that dreadful image swamps her mind: the clusters of weeping tearful deportees and worried, despairing, disconsolate friends and loved ones who have come to see them off, reluctantly letting go of each other as they board the dread train; others, already on board, shouting or reaching out through the open carriage windows to clutch the hands of their friends . . . the knots of uniformed German police in place to ensure that this, the second mass shipment of human cargo for Westerbork – the first, comprised of an unfortunate group of other relocated Jews from the Hilversum area, who had reportedly brought their furniture with them (which the Germans were intent on seizing) – goes off without a hitch; all wreathed in the swirling, Dante-esque smoke of the impatient locomotive . . .

And there is Dorrit herself, a pathetic, wretched mess, the yolks of the eggs Edgar's mother has given her running down the front of her coat – she has inadvertently crushed them against herself in the press of the crowd – waving goodbye.

Enough. Dorrit looks out. The landscape outside is all barren moors. Assen, her final destination, is approaching.

Dorrit fast-forwards her internal reel to the somewhat happier scene of her last meeting with Edgar, six weeks ago, in Amsterdam. Somewhat to his surprise, Edgar was released from Westerbork for forty-eight hours in order to register for the new census. Hastily Dorrit arranged for the two to spend the night at the home of her cousin, Liesl. The understanding Liesl gave the couple a room of their own.

Edgar didn't talk much about his life at Westerbork; obviously, it wasn't very pleasant. The Dutch camp commandant, Schol, had instituted some changes in the camp regime in recent weeks that gave the place more of a prison-like feel, he told her quietly as they lay side by side in Liesl's house in the old Jewish quarter. For example, daily roll-call, never exactly a joy to begin with, Edgar drolly noted, had been moved up to early dawn. There was also an abominable new unit of camp police – *Jewish* police, *Jüdischer Ordungdienst*, so-called OD – to augment the Dutch police at the camp, Schol having been impressed with the argument of one of the so-called Long-Term Residents, a German Jew by the name of Kurt Schlesinger, who had been at Westerbork since 1940, to allow the internees to administer and police themselves rather than have the Germans do it. Jews policing Jews: it sounded horrible. But he had no complaints, Edgar said, lighting a cigarette.

Dorrit's reverie is interrupted by the Dutch conductor's flat voice informing her that she has arrived at her final destination. Looking out at the unfamiliar train station, festooned with the by now all-too-familiar German propaganda posters, she moves to retrieve her bicycle, and strides off into the night to find the farm where she will stay. She is smiling, for tomorrow she will see her lover again.

When she eventually arrives at the farmhouse, she finds it is a primitive place – no running water, no hot water, no heat. There is a basin of cold water waiting for her in her room, a Delft basin she will later recall, Delft blue. The long trip has exhausted her; she falls asleep immediately.

In the morning, the farmer points her in the direction of the camp. It isn't hard to find, he says, gesturing in the direction of the refugee camp that the Dutch government built in 1939 – before the occupation – for the internment of Jews who had illegally entered the country. After all, there isn't much else out there. In six weeks, a motorised flotilla from the *Befehlshaber der Sicherheitspolizei des SD* (SD), complete with a company of SS troops, will arrive to take formal charge of Westerbork, and this hitherto minimum-security internment camp will be transformed into something quite different and more sinister: a 'police transit camp', surrounded by barbed wire and guard towers; a hellish place whence each week for approximately the next one hundred weeks a thousand – sometimes more, sometimes less – of its angry, weeping, resigned inhabitants will be herded by the OD on to trains bound for 'labour deployment camps' in the East, 'camps' with names like Auschwitz, Sobibor and Bergen-Belsen.

However, at this particular juncture in Westerbork's tortured history, while this God-forsaken place in the wilds of Drenthe is still administered by the Dutch Ministry of the Interior – and before anyone in Holland outside Adolf Eichmann's satellite offices in Amsterdam has any notion of what the designation 'labour deployment' really means – there is no reason why Dorrit's farmer host should hesitate to give a Jewish girl directions to Westerbork, nor any reason why she ought to fear going there.

And so Dorrit eagerly pedals off, down a sandy, windswept path. The ride is a long one, the birds circling overhead her only companions. Later she estimates the journey back and forth takes an hour.

And then the outline of one of the larger camp barracks appears on the horizon, followed by the two hundred smaller 'cottages', row upon immaculate row, each with its tiny furze-fringed garden, the yellow flowers just beginning to bloom. And at the entrance – just as he promised in his last missive – there is Edgar, standing outside the cottage assigned to the Reich family, looking as debonair as possible for the occasion, waiting for her, cigarette dangling from his lips.

They embrace. Edgar leads Dorrit inside, where she is warmly greeted by his parents, who are nearly as thrilled to see this emissary from the 'free' world and their former normal lives as their lovelorn son is. You must be hungry, her hosts say to the wayfarer. She is indeed. Good, Frau Reich replies, struggling to maintain her composure, she has cooked something special for her on her electric plate! Dorrit will forget what she ate; she is not concentrating on the food. But it is good.

And so the happily reunited lovers sit down to their specially cooked lunch under the proud eyes of the Reichs, in their little cottage in the moors, almost as if they were all on holiday.

Later, Edgar takes Dorrit for a walk, making wry comments as they go – there is the field where he lines up for roll-call, lovely place, isn't it, he says drolly . . . there is the camp hospital, actually it's quite good, he says – until they reach the Big Barracks, the long wooden building in the centre of the vast encampment. The Big Barracks doubles as Westerbork's main administration building, and, on weekend evenings like this, as camp entertainment centre. This, he explains, leading Dorrit inside, is where the camp orchestra plays. He plays accordion. The orchestra is quite good, Edgar says seriously; recently it gave a performance of *A Midsummer Night's Dream* by the composer Felix Mendelssohn (descendant of Moses). He is not sure what is on tonight. Dorrit wishes she could stay. But she can't, it is getting dark. She must leave soon, or risk getting lost out there on the unforgiving moors.

Anticipating this, Edgar has already summoned the members of the orchestra to the Big Barracks to meet his attractive fiancée. One by one he proudly introduces Dorrit to his musical colleagues and fellow internees. Obviously, he has given her a big build-up.

And then it is time to go.

But Dorrit's visit to Kamp Westerbork – which sixty years later she will recall in minute detail, including her exact train of thought – is not over. The Jewish Council has given her permission to come back the next day, Saturday.

So the following morning she pedals back to the camp for a few more precious hours with her beloved. This time Dorrit and Edgar want to be alone, and they walk off into the heather for as much privacy as the circumstances allow. Six weeks hence such a walk will not be possible. Yet later, after Westerbork's true function as a transit station to hell has become clear, Dorrit will marvel that she ever visited it at all.

But she is glad that she did. For this will be the last time she and Edgar will ever see each other.

As they embrace in the heather and talk fitfully about 'the future', it is Edgar's turn to be worried, and Dorrit's to calm him. 'I'll come back soon,' she promises. Later, she will recall distinctly that there was a dog barking in the distance.

And then, with a hug and a wave, Dorrit is off to catch the train back to the shadows of Amsterdam.

CHAPTER 6

The Decision

To the decree of 30 June 1942 D III 516 g with references to my teletype
messages – No. 250 of 17 July 1942 . . .

Subject: Deportation of Jews

. . . The deportation of the Dutch Jews has proceeded undisturbed. Today's
train brings the total of Dutch Jews deported up to 6,000. The deportation
[has] proceeded without any disturbances. Of course, the Dutch popu-
lation became aware of this measure and some temporary excitement was
noticeable . . .

From a secret message from Otto Bene, the
representative of the German Foreign Office in
The Hague, to Reich Commissioner Seyss-Inquart
confirming the start of the deportation of the
Dutch Jews to the East, dated 31 July 1942

Despite his studied casualness, Myrtil Frank was by spring 1942 doubtless aware of German intentions towards the Jewish population. Although
he had reluctantly obeyed each of the incrementally humiliating Nazi
edicts since the invasion two years before, from the family's enforced
move from the Dutch coast, through the compulsory census of January
1941, and all the other restrictions the Germans had imposed since then,
he was able to keep his wits about him.

Not that it had been easy. By the end of 1941, the stress of the occupation, coupled with his growing money worries, in addition to the
increasingly difficult task of finding food for the family, had turned the

103

now forty-eight-year-old Jewish water pic salesman into a very nervous and anxious man.

The difference between Dorrit's state of mind and that of her father is readily evident in a snapshot taken of the two in the garden of the Hilversum house. Dorrit, her hair neatly coiffed, looks as if she hasn't a care in the world. By contrast, Myrtil, hair visibly greying, fingers clenched around a half-smoked cigarette, looks tense and forlorn; the smile he wears is forced; the old killer grin is gone. Clearly, daughter and father were living in different worlds. Dorrit is smiling broadly, while her father is trying to figure out how to keep his family alive. We can see this from his expression; we know it from the courageous decision he will shortly make, to take the family into hiding. Perhaps the thought of going into hiding had already occurred to Myrtil by the time the photo was taken. In any event, it is very possible if not likely that the idea of resisting had already occurred to him.

This, the ability and willingness to resist mentally in the first place – and to resist the herd instinct amongst Jews *not* to resist – was the first prerequisite for becoming a successful *onderduiker*. As he had already proved on numerous occasions, Myrtil Frank possessed this prerequisite, along with the necessary courage to effect that resistance. So did his namesake, Otto Frank. As such, both men – along with the thousands of others who doubtless were entertaining similarly subversive thoughts at this time – were part of a minority.

However, it is important to recall that there were other preconditions for 'diving under'. For even those Jews who were willing to countenance the thought of going into hiding needed other essential things before they could consider taking such a serious step, namely: money for renting and provisioning a hiding place for an indeterminate amount of time; a place where it was safe to hide, whether in the city or the countryside; and Gentile helpers or protectors who could be counted on to bring additional supplies for the duration of the 'dive', and who would not betray them or blackmail them, as a few mercenary-minded Dutchmen did.

One year hence, by which time the resistance had created a sophisticated nationwide support system to aid both Jewish and non-Jewish *onderduikers*, these additional preconditions – money, food, addresses and helpers – would not be as difficult to come by. But, of course, no one could see that far into the future, then, in spring 1942. In any case, a year later, in 1943 it was too late for many Jews, for the great majority of them had already been deported and killed.

However, in the spring and summer of 1942, before the trains out of Westerbork bound for the East began rolling, when the conditions were 'good' for diving under, before the great *razzias* that would soon sweep across Amsterdam *Zuid*, these preconditions made all the difference. As Bob Moore, an historian of the Dutch Holocaust, writes, 'the real tragedy remained that the vast majority of Jews . . . had neither the money nor [an] "address" to go to [in 1942]'. 'The logistics [of going into hiding] were daunting,' said Leo Ullman, who survived the war after his parents hid him with a sympathetic Dutch policeman in Amsterdam.

This helps explain one of the great unanswered questions surrounding the near-extirpation of Dutch Jewry: why, according to historians, did only one out of seven Jews in the occupied Netherlands decide to dive under at all?

One must consider further. Something more was generally required to dive under, or to contemplate doing so: the willingness to think the unthinkable – to contemplate where the tracks to Westerbork really led. And who, in the spring of 1942, could possibly know that the tracks to Westerbork ultimately led to Auschwitz and Sobibor? No one knew about the gas chambers yet. No one had gassed an entire race, or tried to. 'People were not aware until much, much later that there was risk of death,' said Leo Ullman. 'Rather, the risk [in 1942] was transport to a work camp in Germany, and people thought that this might be tolerable and that life would go on.'

Myrtil didn't think so. Neither did Otto Frank, and neither did a relatively small proportion of Dutch Jews. They had a hunch, in their case informed by previous experience with the Germans, that something life-threatening awaited them and their families at Westerbork, or after Westerbork – and they preferred not to find out exactly what.

Fortunately for Myrtil, the various things he needed to go into hiding fell into place – or perhaps more accurately, he caused them to fall into place – just in time. When the moment came for him to act, after his family were warned, he would be able to do so.

The requisite monies came at this time from the payment he received for the sale of the Rubens painting which he and Flory owned, the one with the whirling, dancing peasants which used to dazzle visitors to their Berlin home. Fortunately Myrtil had been able to take the painting, the family's most valuable asset, with him when the Franks left Berlin, one of the advantages of the family's early exit. Now the seventeenth-century masterpiece would prove its true worth.

Exactly, or even roughly, how much the unknown buyer paid in the illicit transaction, which took place sometime during the winter of 1941, is unclear. No doubt Myrtil preferred it that way, as presumably did the buyer. Myrtil was almost certainly only able to realise a small fraction of the painting's value, which even in 1942 would have been in the tens, if not hundreds, of thousands of guilders. Nevertheless the forbidden sale of the unregistered painting – also a crime at that point – was a major coup.

Who purchased the painting, which Myrtil left behind in The Hague with friends, is anyone's guess. Outside of a few extremely wealthy private collectors and the German officers and Nazi officials stationed in Holland who might have been interested in bringing a Rubens home to put on the mantel next to the *de rigueur* portrait of the *Führer*, it is hard to think of many people in occupied Holland who would be interested in such an expensive, unique and easily identifiable work.

Most likely the sale was effected through an intermediary, possibly through L.*, an art dealer in The Hague whom Myrtil knew from before the war and whose gallery would later become an occasional hang-out of his after the family dived under.

But he did tell them about the sale. He couldn't help it. 'I remember that he came into the studio in Amsterdam after he sold the painting,' Dorrit recalled. 'He was so happy.' Myrtil also confided the sale to Jeanne Houtepen, a pre-war schoolmate of Sybil's who had lately also become a good friend of Dorrit's, and who now was working as a bank teller in The Hague.

'With this money,' she recalled him saying, 'I can get through the war.' He was nearly right.

Now that he had these life-saving monies in hand, that still left the matter of finding the other things Myrtil needed to take the family under. To wit: a physical hiding place, and one or more people to help support the Franks after they had hidden themselves, both of which were also difficult to come by in the densely populated, closely watched, thoroughly cowed Holland of 1942. These components coalesced after Myrtil had a conversation with Annie van der Sluijs, Dorrit's former Dutch teacher and the sister of Tine, his secretary – and his former girlfriend – sometime during this tense and murky 'twilight zone' period (as Dorrit described it), before the deportations began.

---

* The family prefers not to name.

Perhaps Annie approached Myrtil. Or perhaps Tine broached the subject with her sister. Without Myrtil's testimony, it is hard to say; years later, both his wife and daughters were unsure about the exact sequence of events. Clearly, Myrtil was playing his cards very close to his chest.

In any case, sometime during this period the conversation took place and the idea of going into hiding was formulated, fleshed out and put into motion.

While novel, the idea was certainly not original. By this point, two years after the invasion, a small number of Jews, perhaps a few hundred, perhaps a few more, had already dived under, along with known Communists and other political fugitives. Eventually, by the end of the war, the total number of *onderduikers* of all kinds – including the estimated 25,000 Jews who ultimately dived under – would reach the hundreds of thousands. However, at that point of the occupation it certainly required some imagination, as well as daring, not to mention the other aforementioned qualities, to do so.

In any event, sometime during this fraught period Annie offered to let Myrtil use a pied-à-terre she maintained in The Hague for teaching her Dutch students, should the time come for making the decision to take the family into hiding. The flat, located on a short street – Pieter van den Zandestraat – was small, tiny really, merely three rooms. Perhaps it would do.

It would, Myrtil decided. Of course, neither Myrtil nor Annie had any notion of how long the war would last. If he had known that the Franks would have to dive under for as long as they did – nearly three years – he might have baulked at the notion of subjecting the family to confinement in such a small space.

As the time for making the decision to dive under approached, Annie's sisters Tine and Ans also volunteered to help the Franks. Dorrit's friend, Jeanne, said she would help too.

Myrtil probably made the decision to commence the physical preparations for diving under sometime between February and April 1942. In February, as we have seen, Edgar and his parents were forcibly sent to Westerbork, the first enforced shipment of Jews within Holland proper, an event that upset and concerned Myrtil, for its import both for Dorrit and for the whole family.

'Dad was very disturbed when the Reichs were sent to Westerbork,' said Sybil. 'He didn't trust the Germans. He said we're not *going there.*'

Then in April, the Franks received the order to move to Amsterdam, and it was at this point that it became a matter of not *if* they should dive under, but *when*. Unlike the September 1940 edict ordering them to move from the coast, there was no leeway in interpreting this directive: not only were the Franks specifically told to move to Amsterdam, they, along with several hundred other Jews living in Hilversum, were ordered to move to one of three areas of the city designated as Jewish districts.

In a sense, the Franks were lucky. By mid-April, when the order came down, Kamp Westerbork was filled to capacity; otherwise, the harrowing scene that Dorrit had witnessed at the Utrecht station would have been repeated at Hilversum, and their fate, like that of the Reichs, would most likely have been decided then and there. Not that they felt particularly lucky as they stood on the platform of the Hilversum train station, sniffling and miserable in the cold. They were even less reassured when they arrived in Amsterdam and saw what the Nazis were doing.

'This, clearly, was different,' Flory said, after she saw the barbed wire and signs with which the Germans were isolating Jews from their Gentile neighbours. 'The Germans were dividing the city into ghettos.'

After another feverish round of flat-hunting, which was becoming something of a family ritual by now, Myrtil decided to move to the nicest of those 'ghettos', the *Rivierenbuurt*, or River Quarter. Ever since the traffic of Jewish émigrés from Germany had begun in 1933, this district of Amsterdam *Zuid* had been the preferred destination for German Jews.

As the Franks later learned – and in one of the numerous coincidences between the two oddly parallel family sagas – one of those who had already settled in this district was Otto Frank. By the time Myrtil and his wife and daughters arrived, Otto Frank, his wife Edith and daughters Anne and Margot had been living in an apartment on Merwedeplein, in the centre of the comfortable, if not especially attractive quarter, since December 1933.

There, Otto's family had been able to begin life anew. In 1933, the River Quarter *was* a good place for German-Jewish émigrés to start, linked as it was to the city centre by the fast and convenient Amsterdam trams – on which the conductors often spoke German – as well as being with one's own people; in 1937, a synagogue was built on Lekstraat to cater to the burgeoning Jewish population. The middle-class area also boasted its own Hebrew bookshop, an up-to-date playground, where the children of the restricted neighbourhood – including Anne Frank – often played, as well as its own street market, where clothing and produce, including ice cream and chocolate, could be had. It was here that the paths of the two Frank families came closest to intersecting.

However, by the time Myrtil Frank moved to the area, in April 1942, he was not looking to begin life anew, as Otto had done nine years before. He was simply looking for a temporary abode for his family, before he found a way to take them under.

It was not easy to find. When Otto's family had moved into the River Quarter, he had had a wide of choice of vacant apartments from which to choose. However, by the spring of 1942, with the Germans consciously concentrating the Jewish population in the increasingly crowded quarters, there were few apartments to be had and Myrtil was not at first able to find one large enough to house both him and his wife, their daughters and his mother-in-law.

As always, Myrtil's first concern was for the health and safety of his daughters. So the Franks did something they only did once during the entire war: they split up. After making enquiries, he was able to place Dorrit and Sybil in the large canalside house of friends of his who owned a large department store in the city. The well-to-do couple, named Cohen, could be relied upon to give the girls the best of care. Sybil's still fragile health – she had been ill with pleurisy – was also a factor in the decision.

After the shocks and privations of the previous months, the girls revelled in the luxuriously appointed house, a world which in the surviving Franks' collective retrospect resembles that of the Finzi-Continis, the wealthy Italian-Jewish family later portrayed in *The Garden of the Finzi-Continis*, the poignant memoir-cum-novel by Giorgio Bassani that captured the lost idyll of Italian Jewry.

The Cohen's magnificent house created a sense of déjà vu for the two girls. Like their former home on Brückenallee, the residence boasted a capacious, well-stocked kitchen, something not easy to achieve in those lean times, as well as a library where they could rummage through the hundreds of leather-bound volumes. Most of all they had something else that the Franks were not to experience for a while: space. 'It was so nice and reassuring to be in this big house,' Sybil remembered. Like the hermetic Finzi-Continis, their hosts also seemed to be innocent of or oblivious to the nasty goings-on just beyond their knockered door – which, of course, was fine with the girls, especially Dorrit, who was still preoccupied with thoughts of Edgar in distant Westerbork.

While Sybil and Dorrit luxuriated in the temporary sanctuary of the De B. house (where Sybil also recovered her health), Myrtil found his mother-in-law, Leontine, a place in a pension in another part of the River Quarter. He and Flory, meanwhile, stayed at the flat of other friends in the district.

Although Flory and Myrtil were pained to be separated from their daughters, the temporary split was advantageous in that it allowed Myrtil to focus on making preparations for the anticipated dive. In the meantime, he continued to look for an apartment large enough to house the whole family. After weeks of searching, he finally found one, a drab but serviceable two–bedroom apartment, set amidst a typical 'new housing' block of attached two-storey apartments at 9 Eendrachtstraat, near the southern perimeter of the district, and at the beginning of May, after collecting his daughters from the De B.s' and extending his thanks for their hospitality, the four of them moved in. Apart from Leontine, the Franks were a family unit again.

Meanwhile, they did their best to cope with the most traumatic of all of the restrictions the Germans had hurled at them: the yellow so-called 'Jewish' star (*ster*).

On 29 April 1942, the *Joodsche Weekblad* carried the thunderbolt announcement that the Germans had passed on to the *Joodsche Raad*, which was that 'as of Sunday next, a so-called "Jewish star" will have to be worn by every Jew. A maximum of four stars is available per person. The price of a star is four cents.'

Every feature of the humiliating star had been thought out by the German authorities, including – and especially – the colour, which was ordained to be a sickly, lymph-like yellow. The Jewish Council protested: couldn't the *sterren* at least be a different, healthier shade of yellow, perhaps like that of the life-giving sun, or a bright orange? No. The Germans didn't want the *sterren* – which resembled the stigmata that Jews in Poland and other parts of the Greater Reich had already been wearing for months – to be badges of pride; they wanted them to be badges of shame. The sickly shade of yellow stayed.

Visiting Berlin, the American diplomat George Kennan described in his journal the traumatic effect the enforced wearing of stars had already had on the approximately 40,000 remaining Jews of the Franks' former home town, as well as the surprising sympathy shown them by other Berliners, who, one would have thought, might have been hardened to such sights by now:

The major change has been the wearing of the stars by the Jews. That is a fantastically barbaric thing. I shall never forget the faces of the people on the subway with the great yellow star sewed on to their overcoats, standing, not daring to sit down or to brush against anybody, staring straight ahead of them with eyes like terrified beasts – nor the sight of little children running around with those badges sewn on them. As far as I could see, the mass of the public was shocked and troubled by the measure, and such demonstrations as were provoked were mostly ones of friendliness and consideration (for the victims).

Unfortunately, as Kennan noted, the surprising sympathy of their fellow Berliners (or at least some of them) doesn't seem to have done Jews much good – in fact, the opposite: 'Because of this fact,' he writes, 'the remaining Jews are now deported in large batches and very few are seen any more.'

In Holland, a number of non-Jews went further, insisting on wearing makeshift *sterren* themselves to show their solidarity with their forcibly starred neighbours and turning them into veritable badges of courage.

'I remember seeing obviously non-Jewish people wearing the yellow star,' Dorrit said. 'There weren't very many of them, but we appreciated them all the same.'

'Measure against Dutch Jews foiled,' *The Times* reported in early May, observing – rather hopefully – that 'the Dutch people have responded magnificently to the suggestion by Radio Oranje' – the London-based radio station of the government-in-exile which used the facilities of the BBC – 'that they wear a similar sign and thereby frustrate the German plan of creating a division among them'.

This, unfortunately, was propaganda: the measure was not 'foiled'. Jews continued to wear their stars on pain of arrest; a few Gentiles who were found to be wearing them were sent to prison. In fact the Jewish population was further alienated and demoralised, just as it had been in Berlin and elsewhere – just as it had been in twelfth-century Germany, when the Jewish star had first been used.

Indeed, as Dienke Hondius, the historian of the Anne Frank House in Amsterdam, observes, insofar as it further alienated the Jewish population from the non-Jewish one, thereby making it easier to detach and deport the former from the latter, the yellow star edict was a considerable success. 'The awareness that the Jews were different from non-Jews and the slightly increased feeling of distance between these groups was perhaps all that was needed at the time,' observes Hondius.

* * *

What then, it is reasonable to ask, was the mood of the Dutch as a whole at this time, as the cat-and-mouse game that the Germans had been playing with the Dutch Jewish population approached its climax?

It depends on whom you asked.

'The Dutch are defiant, not despondent,' averred A.J. Barnouw, Queen Wilhelmina Professor of the History, Languages and Literature of the Netherlands at Columbia University, in a sulphurous article published on Sunday 10 May 1942 – the second anniversary of the German invasion – in *The New York Times Magazine*. 'They are firmly convinced that Nazi tyranny cannot last. And that conviction gives them strength to endure the present hardships and trials. They are looking forward to the day of reckoning. They call it *Bijltjesdag*, Hatchet Day', referring to the dramatic day, 140 years before, when the workmen employed in the Amsterdam shipyards broke out in open revolt against the French, who were then ruling Holland.

In fact, the revolutionary flame to which Barnouw alluded had died down considerably over the year since the *Februaristaking*. Although a few brave Amsterdammers may have puckishly worn black – or *sterren* – to mark the sad occasion, most went about their daily business, just as did the populace of occupied Prague or Budapest. The remnants of Holland's once formidable navy had just been annihilated in the Battle of the Java Sea by Germany's Axis ally Japan, and while Berlin continued to tighten its control on the Continent, most Dutchmen were more or less resigned to the prospect of indefinite German rule.

Despite the brave talk out of London and Washington about creating a Second Front, it was fairly clear to Dutchmen in the spring of 1942 that the Allies were losing the war, whether they got their news from the BBC or the NSB mouthpiece *Volk en Vaderland*. Two years after Dunkirk, the British and their American allies hadn't set foot on the Continent in any significant numbers; nor would they until the British–Canadian raid on the port of Dieppe, later that year (which, of course, was a disaster). Even the Allies admitted that Berlin was winning the 'tonnage war' in the Atlantic; this was the 'happy time' for Dönitz's U-boat marauders, who sank US and British freighters with virtual impunity, threatening Britain's lifeline and making even the indomitable Churchill worry. The year-old invasion of Russia was going well, as the *Wehrmacht* inexorably advanced through the steppes towards Moscow.

These were facts. Whether one looked at the globe through Axis or Allied eyes, it seemed to be a fascist world. As Moore observes, 'There was no hope in the medium term [in early 1942], or in the long term, that the Germans might be driven out of the Netherlands.' All other things being equal, this 'hopeless' view, which certainly describes the Franks' thinking – 'It looked like the Germans were going to be in charge for ever,' as Flory put it – would have been a factor in deciding to submerge for the duration.

This pessimistic, or brutally realistic, point of view could also work the other way, deterring some prospective fugitives from going forward with their plans for diving under. After all, what was the point? some would-be Jewish *onderduikers* no doubt said to themselves as they looked at all the swastikas around them.

While the mass of Dutchmen – like the mass of Frenchmen or Belgians or Greeks or Norwegians – continued to be willing to cooperate, if not actively collaborate, with Seyss-Inquart and his underlings, a growing number of individual Dutchmen *had* taken up the hatchet in recent months. Some did so literally by joining the fighting resistance, which was responsible for a small but growing number of 'actions', including individual assassinations and attacks on railway lines, like those being carried out in occupied France by their resistant brethren, the *Maquis*; or they joined the burgeoning underground Dutch press.

It is probably an exaggeration to say that there was a bona fide resistance movement by spring 1942, especially since the dozens of ad hoc groups that comprised the insurrectionary forces continued to disagree on their war aims, or on coordinating their actions, a situation that would worsen before it improved.

But there definitely was a resistance, and Hitler and his SS chief, *Reichsführer* Heinrich Himmler, were determined to stamp it out by whatever means, including the generous use of the firing squad and noose. On 13 April, the first major Dutch resistance leader, Henk Sneevliet, was executed. Three weeks later, on 3 May, seventy-two more resistance fighters were executed after being found guilty at one of the first mass-resistance trials. The following day 460 well-known Dutchmen were taken hostage against acts of resistance. It didn't have much of a deterrent effect: that same day a confiscated arms factory in Arnhem was put to the torch. A grim pattern of resistance and reprisal had been set. On 11 May the Germans executed twenty-four more resistance workers.

This cycle of resistance and reprisal was avidly reported in both the Nazi-controlled and the underground press. Whether it had an incendiary or intimidating effect on the Dutch populace as a whole is difficult to gauge, but it must have given courage to those who were thinking about resisting, including those who, like Myrtil and Otto, were contemplating diving under. For – make no mistake about it – diving under was a form of resistance; passive resistance, but resistance nonetheless. The Germans certainly considered it as such.

In May 1942 Adolf Hitler was concerned enough about the security situation in the Netherlands to dispatch Himmler to see what his designated chief enforcer could do about it.

Thus, on 15 May, while Dorrit was en route to visit her imprisoned fiancé at Westerbork, a party of SS was headed from Berlin to Amsterdam. Amongst the visiting jackboots was Himmler's second-in-command and protégé and one of Hitler's personal favourites, forty-two-year-old Reinhard Heydrich, the up-and-coming head of the Gestapo and the SD, who the previous November had taken on the additional title and responsibility of *Reichsprotektor* of Bohemia and Moravia (what the Germans called what was left of Czechoslovakia after they annexed the Sudetenland in 1939). Widely seen as Himmler's heir-apparent, Heydrich had gained high marks in Berlin for the robust and demonstrably effective manner with which he had tamed the recalcitrant Czechs, simultaneously quashing the indigenous resistance – in the first two months of his 'protectorship' he had ordered more than 500 executions, as well as over 5,000 arrests – while coercing cooperation from Czech labour and industry with productivity-based incentives – the carrot-and-stick method.

From the Reich's point of view, Heydrich's administrative philosophy had worked marvellously. Overt Czech resistance had virtually died. Factories had sprung back to life. Bohemia and Moravia were marching forward.

This was why Heydrich had been dispatched to Amsterdam. Despite the accelerating rate of arrests and executions in Holland, evidently some in Berlin were beginning to wonder whether their man in The Hague, Seyss-Inquart, was really up to the job of keeping the Dutch in line. Perhaps, it was thought, some of Heydrich's 'magic' might rub off on Seyss-Inquart and Rauter.

For the same reason the diehard Nazi – like the manager of a show-case department store who is bussed around to other less successful branches to boost morale – was also scheduled to make similar uplifting visits to his fascist confrères in Brussels and Paris.

Busy man, that Reinhard. In addition to his duties as Himmler's No. 2

and chief German proconsul at Prague, Heydrich, one of the architects of the Final Solution, had also chaired, the past January, the top secret Wannsee Conference, at which the blueprint for the extermination of European Jewry was agreed. No doubt another one of the reasons for his inclusion in Himmler's party was to bring the staff of Referat IV B4 (IVB4), the secret department of the SS in Holland charged with carrying out the Final Solution (*Endlösung*), and the select few who were also in the know, up to date on the latest developments; particularly now that the SS 'branch offices', Auschwitz, Sobibor, et al., were ready, or nearly ready, to shift into action.

Most of Himmler's and Heydrich's work in Holland was, of necessity, behind-the-scenes. But on 17 May, the two men, together with a covey of assorted Nazis, including Seyss-Inquart and an appropriately fawning NSB delegation headed by Mussert (the latter had been led to believe that the real purpose of Himmler's mission was to make him titular head of the Netherlands, equivalent to his black-shirted Norwegian counterpart, Vidkun Quisling, a hope in which he was to be disappointed), lent their combined eminence to the swearing-in of 800 Dutchmen to the SS at the Durentsin, an auditorium in The Hague. Hands clutching their new SS hats, each topped off with a shiny skull-and-crossbones, right arms raised, throats distended (a Nazi news photo of the moving ceremony survives), the ready-and-eager fascist recruits, the vanguard of the 50,000 Dutchmen who would put on German uniforms during the war, bellowed the SS pledge in Dutch:

> *Adolf Hitler*
> *Germanisch Führer*
> *Zweer ik hou en trouw*
> *U en aan de door U gestelde gehoorzaamheid tot in den dood*
> *Zoo helpe mij God!*

> Adolf Hitler
> German *Führer*
> I pledge my life to thee
> To fight for the great cause until my death if necessary
> So help me God!

Soon most of these impassioned Nazi associates would be dispatched to Russia, where the *Wehrmacht* was just then approaching the Don, and where ultimately many would die in the snows of Stalingrad. But for the moment all was sweetness and *gezelligheid* as the new skull-and-cross-bones men celebrated their induction along with their jackbooted heroes.

The New York Times took note of the SS men's flying visit to Holland in a vitriolic editorial on 21 May. 'Heinrich Himmler has taken a modest pride as Germany's official murderer,' it began:

> He has more corpses to his credit than any man alive. Now Hitler has sent him to Holland. The Germans there have just shot ninety-six people and taken 460 hostages. But Himmler will try to do better. By gibbet, block and rifle he will attempt to restore a terror the Dutch have not known since the Duke of Alva [the cruel sixteenth-century Spanish proconsul who administered Holland for King Philip].
>
> Defiance will not die. Himmler and his pupil, Reinhard Heydrich, have done their best; but the very victims they have slain seem to rise up and oppose them. The Himmler system, which worked so well in Germany, can never subdue people who have once known freedom.

Although the newspaper's partisan estimate of the state of resistance in the German-occupied territories, including Holland, was somewhat over-optimistic, it was prescient in one respect. On 27 May, six days later, shortly after his return to Prague from his triumphant tour of the provinces, and feeling confident enough to ride in an open car (something that the more cautious, less headstrong Seyss-Inquart rarely did), the *Reichsprotektor* was set upon by a two-man Czech assassination team as he motored from his villa to Prague airport. Recruited and trained by the British and the Czech government-in-exile for the express purpose of removing the Reich's most successful proconsul, the two men botched the job somewhat, lobbing a hand grenade at Heydrich's car and spraying machine-gunfire without quite finishing him off. The wounded Heydrich was even able to chase them before collapsing.

Nevertheless, the agents, Jan Kubis and Joset Gabchik (who must have known that they were doomed when they took on their high-risk mission), did well enough. After lingering for ten days, while his devoted wife and son kept a stern bedside vigil, Heydrich, 'the perfect Nazi', was dead.

Hitler's vengeance was swift, terrible and sure. While the SS were successfully tracking down the fugitive assassins with the aid of a Czech turncoat, cornering them in the basement of a Prague church, then flooding it, moving Kubis and Gabchik to commit joint suicide, another party of Germans was assigned to carry out a reprisal raid on the tiny Czech town of Lidice, population 567, which the incensed Hitler ordered to be completely wiped out. (The town may have been selected because several of its men who had escaped to England were serving in the RAF.) And so it was. After the 173 men of Lidice were taken out and shot, the remaining women and children of the village were shipped to concentration camps, most never to return. After Lidice was depopulated, all buildings were razed. Then, as Radio Berlin proudly reported, 'The name of the town was eliminated.'

Although the Nazis had committed mass atrocities before, the erasure of Lidice was something different: a wholesale killing of innocents specifically intended to terrorise the populace of an occupied territory – and by promulgating it the way the Germans did, the rest of the Reich. And this time, unlike the terror bombing of Rotterdam, the Germans didn't pretend to have made a mistake.

The Czechs got the message. Shortly after the vanishing of Lidice and a wave of other lesser reprisals, several hundred thousand Czechs, brought together by nothing more – or less – than shared terror and a desire to prevent more such killings, gathered abjectly in Prague's main square, Wenceslas Square, to publicly reaffirm their loyalty to the Reich and the *Führer*.

Hitler was appeased, more or less. After an ornate state funeral for Heydrich, at which The Leader himself appeared (while privately excoriating the martyr for his carelessness), Heydrich was replaced by a lesser star in the Nazi firmament, Ernst Kaltenbrunner, an efficient, ruthless German functionary who could be counted on to keep the Czechs under control, as his predecessor had done, as well as to crack the whip when necessary. And so he did.

As intended, word of the Germans' instructive terror at Lidice also carried to the other corners of the Greater Reich – not to mention the rest of the world – including Holland, where the Dutch duly noted the latest Nazi atrocity.

Holland was not Czechoslovakia. Demonstrations of mass fear and fealty such as Wenceslas Square had just witnessed were neither required nor expected from the Dutch. There would be no Lidices in Holland. Seyss-Inquart and Rauter knew that that would be going too far. Besides, as Seyss-Inquart frequently professed (and would continue to profess right up until Nuremberg), he *liked* the Dutch, whereas Heydrich never pretended to like the Czechs.

In the meantime, behind the scenes at IVB4, somewhat incongruously installed in a mansion in the centre of The Hague, and throughout the Greater Reich, at the vast, newly constructed death camps at Auschwitz and Sobibor, those who were involved with the preparations for the Final Solution that had been sketched out at the Wannsee Conference were determined to step up the pace as a testament to the martyred Heydrich. The camps, the electrified fences, the crematoria, all would be ready even sooner than was planned. His will be done!

Already, by May, the first few 'experimental' trainloads of French Jews, mostly unlucky 'stateless' Jews from Germany, had been shipped to the Auschwitz station, ordered out of their trains and herded into the ovens without major difficulty.

Within weeks, it would be Dutch Jewry's turn.

June saw a hailstorm of new restrictions rain down upon the Jews of Holland. By this point, 80,000 Jews – just over half of the total – had been concentrated in the three areas of Amsterdam that had been set aside for them, while about half of the remainder continued to reside in The Hague and Rotterdam. The rest were scattered in small towns and villages around the country.

Although the Amsterdam Jews, in their ghettos, were more aware of their newly segregated status, the basic parameters of what it meant to be a Jew in Holland in 1942 – the routine of having to affix the Jewish star to one's clothing before venturing outside, of having to read *Het Joodsche Weekblad* to learn about the latest anti-Jewish edict, of not being able to do *this* and not being able to go *there*, of having to put on a brave smile for one's wife and children or grandparents or friends – were the same for Jews everywhere. In some cases, the details of a particular restriction varied from locality to locality, but the community-wide effect of the decrees issuing from Seyss-Inquart's offices at the Plein, in The Hague, was cumulative and uniform.

The only Jews who perhaps felt more immune from the palpably escalating persecution because of their artificially elevated position within the Jewish community were Asscher and Cohen, the deluded leaders of the *Joodsche Raad*, and their vast 17,500 full and part-time 'staff', about one out of eight of all Dutch Jews – the Germans were quite indulgent in this respect – who had persuaded themselves that by their ministrations they were tempering the Nazi terror and keeping the Jewish community together.

Of course, as would soon become all too clear, the *Raad* was not tempering the Nazi terror but helping to broker it. Soon enough, too – in fifteen months, to be exact – it would also be consumed by it.

Anne Frank, still unaware of the secret counter-preparations her father had been making, wrote of the numbing effect of the seemingly endless decrees in her diary on 19 June 1942.

The thirteen-year-old diarist, then living five blocks away from her namesakes on Eendrachtstraat, described the long list of edicts and concomitant humiliations in the past tense, even though several had only just been promulgated by the *Joodsche Raad* in *Het Joodsche Weekblad*, its weekly mouthpiece. 'After 1940, the good times were few and far between,' she confided in 'Kitty', the name that she had given to her new journal. 'First there was the war, then the capitulation and then the arrival of the Germans, which is when the trouble started for the Jews.'

Then, telescoping the recent, accelerated repression, the young diarist continued:

> Our freedom was severely restricted by a series of anti-Jewish decrees; Jews were required to wear a yellow star; Jews were required to turn in their bicycles; Jews were forbidden to use streetcars; Jews were forbidden to ride in cars, even their own; Jews were required to do their shopping between 3 and 5 p.m.; Jews were required to frequent only Jewish-owned barbershops and beauty parlours; Jews were forbidden to be out on the streets between 8 p.m. and 6 a.m.; Jews were forbidden to attend theatres, movies or any other forms of entertainment; Jews were forbidden to use swimming pools, tennis courts, hockey fields or any other athletic fields; Jews were forbidden to go rowing; Jews were forbidden to take part in any athletic activity in public; Jews were forbidden to sit in their gardens or those of their friends after 8 p.m.; Jews were forbidden to visit Christians in their homes; Jews were required to attend Jewish schools, etc.

'You couldn't do this and you couldn't do that,' she summed up. 'But life went on.'

It did, perhaps, at least for an upbeat thirteen-year-old. However, by June, it was getting harder for even the most hopeful adult to maintain the illusion that all was well. *Something* was clearly about to happen.

Dorrit, for her part, had been shocked out of her half-daze by an encounter with the NSB, which still had the run of the city, while she was out in the neighbourhood one evening in late June. 'You better be in by eight o'clock, you Jew!' the diminutive blackshirt snapped at her. 'Or else!'

The next day Dorrit was still shaking. Her nerves were not helped by a photo of Edgar she received in the post. Dated 23 June, the photo showed him in the camp outfit of workmen's trousers and clogs, with a shovel. He looked fit, as he leaned against the side of one of the barracks and stared at the unknown photographer, presumably another inmate of Kamp Westerbork. But he looked grim. '*To Dorrit*,' it read, '*yours for ever.*'

By this time, both Myrtil and Otto Frank had made the decision to take their respective families into hiding as soon as the opportunity to do so presented itself.

For some months, Otto had been preparing and provisioning a secret annexe – or *achterhuis* – in the rear of his canalside business offices, at 263 Prinsengracht, in the Jordaan district, a mile or so to the north-east of the River Quarter, in the heart of Amsterdam. Because he owned the building in which the annexe was located, Otto didn't have to worry about rent, as did most *onderduikers*, who often wound up being forced to pay high rents, and in a few cases were turned out when their funds ran out. However, this arrangement did entail either active or passive complicity from Frank's staff and their families. Upon them his own family would ultimately depend for their supplies, and their safety. In this respect, Otto realised, he would have to chance it. Anyway, there was no such thing as complete security for an *onderduiker*. All things considered, he calculated, his family would be safer underground.

Equipped to house himself, his wife and daughters, as well as an unde-termined number of friends once they reached the same decision that he had – ultimately there would be four others – the relatively capa-cious, six-room *onderduikadres* (hiding place) that Otto, a capable and resourceful man like his Amsterdam neighbour Myrtil, had carefully and stealthily constructed that spring was cleverly concealed behind a false bookcase.

While Otto hurried to stock up his hiding place, Myrtil pressed on with his arrangement to take his family under in Annie's flat back in *Den Haag*. Even though all plans for going into hiding were risky, several things made Myrtil's unusual, and, seemingly, riskier than most. Firstly, his projected hiding place was located not in Amsterdam but in The Hague. As a consequence of the new complete ban on travel by Jews, the process both of preparing his *onderduikadres* and of ultimately getting the family there meant having to take the now officially forbidden railway and not wearing the compulsory Jewish *sterren* for the duration of the trip, so exposing both him and his family to considerable, prolonged danger. It was an additional risk, Myrtil decided, he would have to take. It turned out to be a good risk.

Myrtil's sang-froid and fearlessness came in useful during the two trips he made to The Hague in June and early July to prepare for the dive. With the Dutch police on the alert for fugitive Allied airmen and other illegal passengers, including prospective *onderduikers*, Myrtil had to be prepared for the probability that his papers would be checked, or 'controlled' as it was called, at least once during the hour-long trip from Amsterdam to The Hague and back.

He was able to bluff his way through; or at least he never mentioned it later. Then again, like most risk-takers, he didn't discuss many of the risks he took. He just took them. Still, he must have worried what would happen when the day came when his wife and daughters would also have to take their *sterren* off and run the same risk.

Once he got to The Hague, Myrtil was pleased with what he found. He especially liked the address itself, Pieter van den Zandestraat. A small street located at the end of a maze of similar streets in the centre of the city, it was as out of the way a destination as could be found within The Hague proper. A fifteen-minute walk from the Binnenhof and German headquarters, Annie's flat was located right under the Nazis' noses. The *moffen* – the derogatory term the Dutch had come to use to describe their occupiers – would never look for the Franks there, Myrtil gauged as he surveyed the immediate area.

At the same time, he also apprehended another major potential problem – which was that Annie's apartment at number 14 did not contain any hidden compartment, cellar or attic where the Franks could further secrete themselves in case of a raid (as, for example, his namesakes did). His family, he quickly discerned, would be hiding in plain sight there, their safety dependent on the collusion or ignorance of people he didn't know, notably the several dozen families who lived on this one-block street, and who were bound to be suspicious of the comings and goings there.

So Myrtil decided to employ verbal camouflage, devising a false double identity for himself and Flory for the benefit of their nosy soon-to-be-neighbours. Walking into the only commercial establishment on the street, the corner grocery at number 2, the apparent focal point of the compact community. He struck up a conversation with the proprietor and in a loud voice – loud enough for the other customers in the store to hear – announced in German-accented Dutch that he was a German-Swiss doctor.

This ruse was quite brilliant. Famous, amongst other things, as the place where the German novelist Thomas Mann wrote *The Magic Mountain*, the eastern, German-speaking region of Switzerland was, despite Swiss neutrality, known to be sympathetic to German interests; injured German soldiers were encouraged to take the cure there, where they were treated by local doctors.

And so, in a very short space of time – hours, probably – the hundred or so residents of Pieter van den Zandestraat learned that a German-Swiss doctor would soon be moving to their street.

The mystery physician coupled that clever piece of disinformation with another disturbing bit about his unseen partner. 'My wife,' he informed the wide-eyed grocer, pointing to his own head, 'is not all that well.'

Myrtil had no idea whether it would work, but it was worth a try.

The final sequence of events which led Otto Frank and Myrtil Frank – who, though neither related nor acquainted, certainly shared similar instincts – to activate their respective plans for going into hiding began in Berlin on 23 June 1942 with a phone call from Adolf Eichmann to Franz Rademacher, his contact man at the Foreign Office in Berlin. From the middle of July, Eichmann told Rademacher, the deportation trains from the West would run every day according to the schedule he had made up, transporting in all some 90,000 Jews – 40,000 from Holland, 40,000 from France and 10,000 from Belgium.

The wheels had begun turning in March, when Willy Zopf, an official from IVB4 in The Hague, and his SS colleagues from Paris and Brussels, Theodor Dannecker and Kurt Asche, respectively, met with Adolf Eichmann at the latter's office at 116 Kurfürtenstrasse in Berlin. It was at that meeting, Asche later recalled, that 'Eichmann told us that on the basis of an order from the *Führer* the Jews were to be deported from occupied western Europe. Large petroleum and Buna rubber factories had been set up in Auschwitz and the Jews were to work there.' Dannecker was ordered to have 40,000 Jews sent from France, Zopf 15,000 from Holland and Asche 10,000 from Belgium. The new revised 'extermination manifest' with the

25,000 additional Dutch Jews was duly passed on to Willy Zopf at IVB4 in The Hague, and his co-workers at the *Zentralstelle für jüdische Auswanderung*, or 'Office of Jewish Emigration', the office that was charged with coordinating the entire operation and moving the selected Jews to Westerbork and thence to the East.

Three days later, on 26 June, the head of the *Zentralstelle*, Ferdinand Aus der Fünten, called the Jewish Council and informed them, encoding his words in the agreed-upon German doublespeak, that an indeterminate number of Jewish men and women between the ages of sixteen and forty would soon be sent to work 'under police guard' to perform 'labour service' in Germany. The Dutch-Jewish *Joodsche Raad* was once again assured by the smooth-talking German that those called up would be 'stateless', i.e., German Jews, playing on the undeniable and unfortunate divide between Dutch Jews and foreign ones. 'Jews who lived in the Riverenbuurt were far less assimilated in Dutch culture and society than the long-standing [sic] Dutch Jewish population,' notes Leo Ullman, and this division was also seen in neighbouring Belgium, where native Jews tended to look askance at their more recently-arrived brethren. The authorities in both countries worked to their advantage. No need to worry, Aus der Fünten said, in so many words, this doesn't affect you.

Still, there was concern. Even if they themselves were not affected by the new plan, the Council were not entirely oblivious to the fate of foreign Jews. More importantly, the raids and deportations that had taken place – most notably the one in 1941 in which Dorrit's friend Ed Weinreb had been caught up – however horrible, had taken place only incidentally, as punishment or reprisal for some 'act of terror' in which the hapless victim had taken absolutely no part. Now they were to take place systematically. This was new.

After twenty-six months of playing cat and mouse with the Jewish population, the Nazi cat was about to strike. A fresh surge of fear and tension rippled out into the Jewish population. To add to the general discomfort, a heat wave descended on the country.

Nine days later, on Sunday 5 July, the first groups of German Jews received their summonses by special post to report for 'labour deployment'.

Amongst the hundreds of doors that the special postmen knocked on was that of Otto Frank and his family at 31 Merwedeplein, in the River Quarter. All four Franks were at home at the time.

'At three o'clock the doorbell rang,' Anne Frank wrote, recalling the blood-freezing moment. 'I didn't hear it, since I was out on the balcony, lazily reading in the sun. A little while later Margot appeared in the kitchen doorway looking very agitated. "Father has received a call-up notice from the SS," she whispered. I was stunned. A call-up, everyone knows what that means: visions of concentration camps and lonely cells raced through my head.'

The daydreaming schoolgirl had, after all, given some thought to the unthinkable.

But Margot was mistaken, as Anne soon learned: 'The call-up was not for Father, but her. I began to cry.'

Meanwhile, at the offices of the Jewish Council at Nieuwe Keizersgracht 58, 'all hell [broke loose]'. Although most of those on the first call-up list were, as Aus der Fünten had promised, German Jews, there were also a number of Dutch Jews on the initial manifest, causing outright panic: 'Everyone hunted for rubber stamps and exemptions, everyone was found to be indispensable, everyone had been baptised or wounded or was an invalid; everyone queued up for doctor's certificates, letters from the church, *Ausweise* [identity cards]; failing all these, a week's deferments [from having to report for Westerbork] were begged for.'

Over the next few days Dutch postmen bearing the dread notices continued to knock on doors around the River Quarter and the other Jewish districts.

'Once the notices went out there was tremendous tension and fear,' recalled Leo Ullman, who was about to dive under himself.

Jacques Presser, an historian and survivor who lived to write the monumental 1966 study, *The Destruction of the Dutch Jews*, recalled a typical scene that took place at an end-of-term celebration at the Jewish Lyceum, where he was then a teacher. This began in an atmosphere of sweetness and light, as well as considerable denial, as people spoke inspiring words and ceremonial music was played. Still, one could cut the tension in the room with a knife, tension made all the more unbearable by the fact that some of the graduates, mostly fifteen- and sixteen-year-old girls, had received their summonses. Suddenly a girl from the highest class shot up and began speaking. She and her sister had each received a summons, she said, in a quiet but deliberate voice. 'What should we do?' she asked the adults present.

'There stood the girl, 17 years old,' Presser painfully recalled twenty years later, 'and with her final term report full of high marks, quite alone and unprotected, directly in front of the green board [at the Lyceum] behind which the teachers were sitting. To this historian, it is as though he can still see her standing there, a kind, intelligent child, utterly decent; he can still hear her question, a question he will never forget: "Ladies and gentlemen, *please tell us what must we do?*"'

Presser concludes: 'Nobody knew, nobody could help, and they were deported.'

Otto Frank knew what *he* had to do. The notice for Margot was his final trigger. He knew that he had to move quickly: 'Failure to report would give a short breathing space but the address of the individuals was on file and would undoubtedly be the target of a police raid within days, or sometimes [later on] within hours' (as Bob Moore writes).

And so the morning after he received the notice for Margot, 6 July 1942, Otto, Edith, Margot and Anne Frank dived under as a family. They removed the stitched-on yellow stars from their clothing as carefully as they could and walked to the *achterhuis* that Otto had prepared for them in the back of the three-storey building overlooking the Prinsengracht at number 263, now better known as the Anne Frank House. The fact that Anne and Margot had walked this route to visit their father's workplace many times before made the hellish half-hour trip somewhat easier.

Myrtil Frank also knew what to do when, on 11 or 12 July – one of the dates about which the surviving Franks differ – the grim-faced postman delivered notices for Dorrit and Sybil to report for 'labour service'.

That evening, at 9 Eendrachtstraat, in an emotional scene that mirrored the one that had taken place at Otto Frank's apartment and hundreds of others that would do so as the first major wave of Jewish *onderduikers* revealed their plans to their surprised and frightened families, Myrtil told his startled children of his plan for taking the family under. Flory had been in on the secret from nearly the beginning.

Dorrit baulked at first. She didn't want to go into hiding, she insisted. She *wanted* to go to Westerbork. Then she could be with Edgar. Sybil, for her part, said that she also wanted to go. That way, she felt, she could somehow 'save' her parents.

Both were noble sentiments, but, Myrtil said, as Flory nodded her assent, there were no two ways about it: the Franks were going into hiding. That was the only way they would save themselves, he said. Edgar would be OK, he assured the weeping Dorrit.

Reluctantly, the girls came around to his view.

There was just one problem: what about their grandmother, Leontine? the girls asked. Would she be going into hiding too?

No, she wouldn't, Myrtil said. Leontine would remain in her pension.

She would be fine. He had discussed the plan with her several days before, and she had agreed, saying she was too old for that sort of thing. Anyway, the Nazis weren't interested in bothering old people. Do what you have to do, she said to her grim-faced son-in-law and daughter at their final meeting. I will be fine.

Whether she was just saying that to make things easier for the four Franks, we shall never know. Of course, as Myrtil must have recognised, as no doubt did Leontine, bringing the frail seventy-two-year-old with them to the small apartment at number 14 Pieter van den Zandestraat would have created enormous difficulties.

Anyway, the Nazis weren't interested in bothering old people, were they?

'That's what we really felt at the time,' said Sybil. 'That she would be OK.'

'Of course, if we had known what would happen,' said Flory, years later, still stricken at the memory, 'we would have brought her with us. After all, she was my *mother*. But we didn't. We didn't know *anything*. We just knew that this was what we needed to do at that time to save ourselves.'

PART THREE

DIVING UNDER
HOLLAND, 1942–44

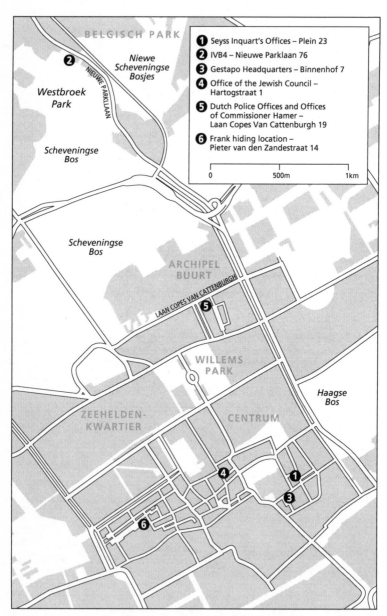

❶	Seyss Inquart's Offices – Plein 23
❷	IVB4 – Nieuwe Parklaan 76
❸	Gestapo Headquarters – Binnenhof 7
❹	Office of the Jewish Council – Hartogstraat 1
❺	Dutch Police Offices and Offices of Commissioner Hamer – Laan Copes Van Cattenburgh 19
❻	Frank hiding location – Pieter van den Zandestraat 14

BELGISCH PARK

Niewe Scheveningse Bosjes

Westbroek Park

Scheveningse Bos

Scheveningse Bos

ARCHIPEL BUURT

LAAN COPES VAN CATTENBURGH

WILLEMS PARK

Haagse Bos

ZEEHELDEN-KWARTIER

CENTRUM

0   500m   1km

The Hague during the Occupation

CHAPTER 7

Submerging

The Germans have begun to carry out their scheme of depopulating the Netherlands. As was to be expected, the Dutch Jews are the first victims. Every day, 600 Dutch Jews, aged between 18 and 40, are transported eastwards. Their property is confiscated by the Germans . . .

From a report in *The Times*, 27 July 1942

And so, on the morning of 14 July, Myrtil Frank and his wife and daughters removed the hideous yellow stars from their clothing and prepared to set out on the dangerous journey to The Hague and number 14 Pieter van den Zandestraat.

It is not clear why Myrtil decided to leave on that particular day, rather than the day before, following the arrival of the summonses for Dorrit and Sybil, but it is fortunate that he did. In the event, the Germans, unhappy with the fact that only a fraction of the 4,000 Jews who had been summoned for 'labour deployment' had reported as ordered to their local police stations, were preparing to raid the Jewish sections of the city, including the River Quarter. The raid – the first such action the Germans had undertaken against the Jewish population since the one of February 1941 that had precipitated the *Februaristaking* – was not directed against the Jews who had not answered their special summons. Rather, Rauter and his lieutenant, Wilhelm Harster, chief of the security services, decided that the best way to enforce compliance and instil the Jewish population with proper respect for 'the authorities' would be to instead pick up a large number of Jewish hostages at random and hold them until a sufficient number of the missing *Juden* showed up to 'rescue' their brethren, thus simultaneously playing on Jews' sense of fear and their sense of responsibility for the lives of their fellow Jews.

A cunning strategy, and, events would prove, an effective one.

Referring to the deportations, one of the leading underground newspapers, *Het Parool*, alluded on 14 July to the over eight hundred men who had been picked up during the original February 1941 raid, as well as several subsequent raids around the country, who had been dispatched to Mauthausen, and who the German authorities now acknowledged were dead (from 'natural causes'): 'Based on our experience with Mauthausen, it is our belief that those Jews who are deported for the East will not come back.'

Perhaps it was just as well that the Franks generally did not read the underground press. But the situation was clear. 'The penalties for non-compliance' – incarceration in Amersfoort prison, the largest of the several prisons the Germans established on Dutch soil, or, worse, being shipped to Mauthausen in Germany, and certain death – 'were severe and well-publicised' (according to Moore). Potential Jewish *onderduikers* were not 'in any doubt what this form of punishment meant'.

In short, neither the Franks nor the hundreds of others who comprised the first great wave of Jewish *onderduikers* needed to know about the killing machine awaiting them and their neighbours in the East in order to grasp that by diving under at that time, in mid-1942, they were consciously taking their lives in their own hands.

As Flory put it, 'We knew what we were getting into, even if we didn't *really* know what we were getting into.'

There was a deceptive calm that morning as Dorrit and Flory, accompanied by Sybil and Annie, departed 9 Eendrachtstraat for the last time. There was no turning back, they knew. They would either succeed in their risky mission of reaching The Hague or, well, there was no point in thinking about the alternative.

The penalty for a Gentile, like Annie, who assisted an *onderduiker* was less clear at that point; it wasn't as if the Germans had clear guidelines for this sort of thing. They certainly wouldn't have been very happy with her, particularly if she was caught in the company of three Jews who had illegally removed their stars, two of whom had failed to report for 'labour deployment'.

However, if Annie was worried, she didn't show it. As far as she was concerned, she was simply doing what she had to do.

According to Geert Mak, in *Shoah*, the scorching 1972 documentary by Claude Lanzman about the Nazi genocide, 'the attitude of the average Dutch non-Jew was little different' from that of the Poles who lived near Auschwitz: 'naïve, inert, cowardly, sometimes magnanimous, on occasion extraordinarily courageous'.

The four Dutchwomen who comprised the core of the Franks' 'external diving crew' – Annie, Jeanne and (to a lesser extent) Annie's sisters Tine and Ans – belonged to the small but not insignificant minority of Dutch whose courageous behaviour redeems the complicity of the rest in the destruction of Dutch Jewry, a tragedy which continues to haunt Holland until the present day.

As they set out on their perilous expedition, Flory, Dorrit and Sybil could take some heart from the fact that Myrtil had successfully under-taken the same dangerous journey several times before. But Myrtil, of course, was Myrtil. 'My father had the courage of a lion,' Dorrit said later. 'We were just three ordinary women – and we were scared out of our minds. Maybe that's why I remember so little about that day.'

If only, the girls had pleaded the previous night, Father would accom-pany them. But he couldn't, he said. A group of five, led by a man, would, he felt, be more likely to rouse suspicion. They would have to make the initial 'plunge' alone.

And so out they went, literally under the eyes of the Germans: up Eendrachtstraat and away from the restricted area of the River Quarter; to Ferdinand Bolstraat, where, just a few hundred yards away, in a court-yard enclosed by the Cornelis Troostplein and the Hillegaertstraat, was situated, in a former school, the headquarters of the Dutch collabora-tionist police; further north along Bolstraat where it becomes Vijzelgracht, the fugitives walked by the State Bank, where another Dutch Nazi confi-dently surveyed his domain; then north along Vijzelstraat to the Muntplein with its venerable De Munt clocktower, which had been telling the time for Amsterdammers since nearly the last occasion the city had been occupied, 380 years before, by the Spanish. Behind the Munt Tower, which struck eleven just after the Franks passed, was the elegant Hotel Carlton, once a favourite of foreigners – including spies – now the head-quarters of *Luftgaukommando Holland*, a key German air force staff unit, just then engaged in trying to foil the new bombing offensive of the Royal Air Force (soon to be joined by the US Eighth Air Force), whose lumbering messengers, their silvery forms silhouetted in the groping searchlights that played across the night skies, often flew over Amsterdam in order to reach their targets in Germany.

'LUCHT – ALARM . . . *onmiddellijk dekking zoeken!*' warned a smart, typically well-designed Dutch air-raid poster of the day; perhaps not surprisingly for the nation that produced Rembrandt and Vermeer and the avant-garde *de Stijl* group, of all the occupied countries under the Nazi aegis, the Dutch produced the most stylish posters. This one showed a well-dressed woman in high heels with her son in hand dashing for the sanctuary of a shelter, along with an equally well-turned-out man equipped with hat, briefcase and umbrella. 'WHEN YOU HEAR THE ALARM . . . *immediately take cover!*'

And so, as instructed, the Franks, like their neighbours in the *Rivierenbuurt*, had taken cover in the nearest bomb shelter during the British air raids; if anything, like many Dutchmen of Allied sympathies, they were heartened by the sight of the bomb-laden Lancasters ploughing their way through the skies to wreak vengeance on their former home-land. The Second Front might be far away, the Franks could tell them-selves as they waited for the all-clear, along with their bestarred neighbours and a smattering of non-Jews who happened to be caught in the raid, looking embarrassed, sympathetic or studiously indifferent, but at least the English were doing *something*.

Now, however, the family were taking cover from the most immediate danger to them – the Nazis themselves.

Just before the group reached Centraal Station, they passed within several blocks of the place where, nine days before, Otto Frank and his wife and daughters had gone into hiding. Up until that point, the move-ments of the two German-Jewish exile families had closely paralleled each other. Now, however, the destinies of the two Frank families diverged.

Somehow the women's luck held up during the remainder of the walk to the station; and during the tense train trip as well; and again on the walk from Station Hollandspoor to 14 Pieter van den Zandestraat. Their papers were not checked. If they aroused the suspicions of any of the people they passed in the street or who walked by their train compart-ment, they kept those suspicions to themselves. If there was a guard on their train – and there was a guard or policeman on most trains – they did not see him.

'We made it,' an exhausted and relieved Flory said as they entered the small ground-floor flat. But there was no celebration until several hours later Myrtil too arrived.

'We got out just in time,' he said, as he closed the door behind him.

'Everything is closed off,' he added, referring to the preparations for the hostage-taking *razzia* that the Germans had planned for that evening.

The *razzia* was successful. The night's yield: 700 Jews, to be held under 'protective custody' until a sufficient number of their brethren showed up to fill the first train.

A thousand Jews, responding to the Nazi strong-arm tactics, now reluctantly appeared at their local police stations, whence they were conveyed by tram to the Centraal Station and placed aboard the special Westerbork train the *Zentralstelle* had ordered from Dutch Railways for that evening. At Hooghalen, six miles away, the nearest train station to the camp, the intended deportees fitfully disembarked and were marched to Westerbork, where they were kept separate from the rest of the camp inmates so they could be speedily transferred to the next day's first scheduled train for Auschwitz.

But Erich Deppner, the new SS commander – a Heydrich man through and through – was not satisfied. The first trainload was supposed to be slightly larger: 200 more Jewish bodies were needed. And so, that evening, as the Franks were tentatively celebrating having achieved at least a temporary safe haven, the male population of the police camp was herded into the central barracks for the requisite selection to be made. It is not known what criteria Deppner used to select the additional deportees.

The next morning, the 15th, the original group of 1,000 plus the new group of 200 were marched out of the camp to the station at Hooghalen and placed aboard the first train bound for Auschwitz. Among the passengers on the train, as the carefully typed passenger manifest states, was Edgar Reich.

For the Franks, newly minted *onderduikers*, the first few weeks at number 14 had a truly bathyscopic feeling, as if they had been lowered into a remote, uncharted sea. Although they could still see out of the oblong four-by-six-foot front window, with its Mondrian-patterned coloured glass top pane, when they peered through the curtains, in every other way the environment seemed disorientating, with its own sense of time, light and space.

'The contrasts came gradually,' Flory said. Just as water magnifies, so did the process of diving under. 'The smallish things become big, because after a while you realise that you are not the same person any more.'

The sparse, almost doll's-house feeling of the three-hundred-square-foot apartment – furnished with little more than a wooden kitchen table and matching chairs, a nondescript couch bed where Myrtil and Flory slept, two cot beds for the girls, and what little else Annie's prior subtenants, two German Jews by the name of Alfred and Eva Schnell (now themselves in hiding near Zwolle) had left them, increased their claustrophobia and disorientation.

Their new living space lacked a bath. Annie, who had primarily used the flat as a pied-à-terre for meeting her language students and rarely spent the night there, hadn't felt it was necessary; somehow the Schnells had also made do without a proper bath. The Franks would have to as well.

Anxious to bring as little attention to themselves as possible, Myrtil, the de facto unit commander at number 14, instructed his wife and daughters to draw only the minimum amount of water necessary to clean themselves. 'Using a little bit of water to wash ourselves – only a little,' Flory recalled in 1979, shaking her head at the memory. 'It is something so unusual that one could live in such diminished circumstances.'

Myrtil, still thankfully in possession of his sense of humour, helped make light of the situation. 'I have overcome my inner *Schweinehund*!!!' he exclaimed as he emerged from one such washing.

Eventually, they all got used to it. Eventually, they got used to many things.

Perhaps the aspect which was most difficult for the Franks to get used to – especially Flory and Myrtil, who had been virtually estranged before the war – was the extreme togetherness of it all: suddenly they were a family again – a *close* family. Sometimes too close, particularly for Myrtil's comfort. Frequently, especially during the first few months of the dive, there were fights. But they were a family unit again, even if a family bound by ties not entirely of their own making.

Outside, beyond the contained world of number 14, the elaborate, half-planned, half-improvised process for making Holland *Judenrein* lurched into high gear, as the responsible officials at the *Zentralstelle* and IVB4 strove to fulfil the new imposed quota of 40,000 Jews which Eichmann and the other SS higher-ups in Berlin responsible for carrying out the Final Solution had set for the Dutch.

Elsewhere in the Reich, the Final Solution had already been in full spate for over half a year, most notably in Poland, where the Jewish population was isolated by then and the Germans were less concerned with wounding the sensibilities of the locals – many if not most of whom were anti-Semitic. Thus, as early as December 1941 – a month before the parameters of the *Endlösung* were decided at the Wannsee Conference under the leadership of Reinhard Heydrich – while Dorrit and Sybil were hanging out and listening to music with their friends in Hilversum and Dorrit was falling in love with Edgar, Polish Jews were already being gassed in sealed vans at Chelmno, the death camp the Germans had built in the western part of the country.

Now, in July 1942, high noon, as it were, for the Final Solution, the *Reichskommissar* and his colleagues were particularly keen to show that they knew what was needed to make the Netherlands *Judenrein*. Rauter, the SS chief, confidently predicted to Himmler that Holland's 'Jewish problem' would be largely 'solved' within fifteen months.

To be sure, even with the bulk of the Jewish population concentrated in Amsterdam, the process of simultaneously enforcing and masking the *Endlösung* in Holland would continue to be a nerve-racking one for Nazi officials, involving complex deliberations over which groups to grant exemptions, and then when to withdraw them. Then, too, there were such concomitant worries as what to do about Jews from friendly or neutral nations. 'My biggest headache is the concentration of the Jews,' Rauter confessed to Himmler in the autumn.

Nevertheless, the process went forward. Whatever was required – whether full-scale *razzias* and hostage-taking, or conveniently looking the other way when Jews from a neutral country were caught up in the Nazis' net and deported (as a group of Swedish Jews were) – the process went forward.

For the remainder of July, there were no headaches whatsoever. Thus, on 31 July, Otto Bene, the representative of the German Foreign Office in The Hague, was able to report with satisfaction to Seyss-Inquart that 'the deportation of the Dutch Jews has proceeded undisturbed. Today's trains bring the total of Jews so far deported up to 6,000.'

At one point at his trial in Jerusalem, Adolf Eichmann, the chief engineer of the elaborate extermination system who visited Holland himself in early 1943, would enthuse about the efficiency of the Dutch. 'The trains from Holland [to the death camps],' he explained in a macabre aside, 'went like . . . clockwork.'

The SS's gravest fear was a repeat of the anti-pogrom strike of the previous February, or some kindred resistance action to stymie the deportations as would later take place in Denmark when most of the country's 7,000 Jews were smuggled across the Baltic to safety in neutral Sweden (or in Belgium, in 1944, where one of the trains bound for Auschwitz was ambushed and some of its passengers liberated) – but these did not take place.

'Of course,' wrote Bene, noting the largely complacent attitude of the Dutch, 'the Dutch population has become aware of this measure and some temporary excitement [*sic*] was noticeable.'

One of those Dutchmen looking on as the grim process of collecting and deporting Jews went forward was Amsterdammer R.M. van der Veen. 'I came there, to the [train] platform, and there were twenty-four people – young and old, ladies, children,' he recalled a quarter of a century later in an interview for the 1974 television documentary *The World at War*.

Four Germans were there, three on one side, all with tommy guns, and one on the other side . . . I was alone, it was twelve o'clock in the midst of a city on a raised platform . . . what could [I] do? . . . If I could – by surprise – shoot down the three, then the other one would have a pistol and shoot you . . . But what if you got them all? What would you do with twenty-four people . . . in the middle of the day, after a shooting party in a place that's crowded with Germans? . . . You walk away . . . That is absolutely terrible . . . but if you have this experience you have a new stimulus to risk yourself for the few possibilities to save others [as van der Veen later did].

Pieter Gerbrandy, Prime Minister of the Dutch government-in-exile in London, dismayed at the initial reports of the deportations, had already on 25 July broadcast an appeal to his countrymen via Radio Oranje to assist the Jews, a theme he would continue in future broadcasts that year – including another one six weeks later in which he denounced the Germans' 'satanic plan', as he called it, for depopulating Holland of its Jews.

Apart from ad hoc groups that had begun to form to assist *onderduikers* (like the one that Annie had organised to help Myrtil and his family), the Jews of Holland knew that they were alone.

The four divers at number 14, still struggling to come to grips with their new circumstances, certainly felt alone – and afraid. Unsurprisingly, too, as the long days of their first summer in hiding passed, they felt quite bored.

Fear and boredom. Boredom and fear. Those were the Franks' new best friends. Sometimes they came alone, sometimes they came together, but always, every day, they came.

Little could be done to alleviate the fear, but Flory decided early on that something could be done about the tedium. To that end, she now set about instituting and supervising a daily regime of sewing, reading and cleaning, and a strict routine that would remain more or less in place for the duration until, at the end, the Franks' straitened circumstances caused it to break down.

First cleaning, as the family collectively set to work upon their inner *Schweinhund* before doing their best with the outer one, i.e., the apartment itself, getting down on their hands and knees to scrub the floors.

Next, a late brunch – if you could call it that – generally consisting of ersatz coffee, bread and, on the rare occasion when it was available, jelly.

Afternoons were devoted to group and individual reading and study. Some days, Flory would use the art books Myrtil had brought to number 14 to teach a self-styled history of modern art, with a strong emphasis on Impressionism and Post-Impressionism, her aesthetic standbys. The girls would do their own reading too. Ever the romantic, Dorrit buried herself in *Gone With the Wind* (alas, the small library the Schnells had left lacked Galsworthy) and pined for Edgar. Sybil pored over the scientific texts that Schnell, a chemist, had left behind.

Then the three women would talk. Quietly. Occasionally, they would cry. Quietly. Everything they did, as Myrtil had ordered, had to be done quietly. This included arguing. And so when the Franks argued, they did so quietly, making angry faces at each other. Sometimes the act of pantomiming their anger was so inherently ridiculous that they would laugh. Quietly.

Sometimes, in their fear and confusion, they would turn to prayer. As always, Flory was convinced that she had an interference-proof channel to God. He would get them through this, she assured her worried daughters as she knitted away. She tried not to think about what was happening to Leontine, now alone and above ground, sixty miles away in Amsterdam. Perhaps she would be all right, Flory told herself. Perhaps God would get her through this too.

Dorrit and Sybil, with less insight into His inscrutable will, weren't as sure, but they nodded their assent in order to keep their mother happy, while 'Til kept watch by the door, or just sat in his chair reading, trying to come to grips with the unreality of it all. Subliminally, all the Franks had begun to realise that if and when they survived this experience and resurfaced, they would be changed people.

If they survived. *When* they emerged. But when would that be? Surely no more than a few months. Longer was beyond their comprehension.

Like his wife, Myrtil tried to steer the girls away from dwelling upon such imponderables. 'He didn't let us think about the inevitable,' Sybil said of her father. Very soon, she added, the overriding question remaining with them throughout their time underground simply became: 'Can we get through *this* day?'

Above ground, in Amsterdam, the clockwork of the Dutch sector of the Final Solution became stuck. The fear and guilt induced in the Jews by the large seizure of hostages on 14 July and in subsequent raids had evidently worn off, and not enough Jews were answering their summonses to report for 'labour service'.

One solution, Aus der Fünten decided, was to clarify the penalties for refusing to report for labour service in Germany, and for not wearing and carrying proper identification. As usual he turned to the Jewish Council to spread the word. Thus, on Thursday 6 August *Het Joodsche Weekblad* published a special edition, and under the heading of *De Duitsche Autoriteiten* ('the German authorities announce'), warned:

> All Jews who do not immediately come forward for forced labour in Germany will be arrested and deported to the concentration camp in Mauthausen. This . . . punishment will not be meted out to those Jews who come forward at the latest on Sunday 9 August at 5 p.m. or who declare that they are willing to take part in the provision for additional work . . . All Jews not wearing a Jewish star will be deported to the concentration camp, Mauthausen . . .

'All Jews who change residence without permission from the authorities,' the fiat continued, referring to the growing number of Jews who had sequestered themselves in cellars, attics or hidden compartments around the city and elsewhere, 'will be deported to the concentration camp Mauthausen.'

Now, any *onderduiker* or potential *onderduiker* knew exactly where he or she stood: they were enemies of the Reich.

Whether the notice had the intended deterrent effect is unclear. Some Jews still dived under, or – like the van Pels (or the van Daans, as they are called in the revised version of Anne Frank's journal), the Jewish couple whom Otto Frank invited to share his hiding place and who arrived at 263 Prinsengracht in November 1942 – joined others who had already done so. Others shrank from the thought of hiding, the idea of breaking the law too difficult for them to countenance. Or if they did consider it, perhaps they were reluctant to leave their loved ones above ground – as Dorrit was before submitting to her parents' decision. Yet others hovered and remained in their homes, paralysed by fear and indecision.

In any case, not enough Jews had reported. The process had bogged down. On 13 August, at his offices in The Hague, Bene, the studious Foreign Office representative, sent an anxious memo to Seyss-Inquart, several blocks away – like bureaucrats everywhere, the Germans enjoyed putting things on paper when they could have phoned instead. Since his report of 31 July, Bene reported, 'The situation [regarding the Jews] has considerably changed. After the Jews found us out and *got to know what is behind the deportations and labour service* [author's italics], they no longer report for the weekly shipments. Of 2,000 Jews called up for this week only 400 Jews showed up.'

What *did* the Jews know at this point – or more precisely, what *could* they have known?

There were, of course, rumours already, some of them possibly propelled by bits of correspondence left behind by the initial deportees from Westerbork. At some point that year, according to the harrowing Westerbork archives, Dutch deportees began to realise that the same trains were being used continuously to transport 'Jewish material' to 'labour service' in Germany, and left notes on the trains.

In one such extant note the author writes that his carriage is full of people and that it is suffocating inside. 'The atmosphere is horrifying and everyone is picking fights with everybody else.' Another relates: 'Thanks to some funny remarks from a true-born Amsterdammer, the mood was quite good, but the closer we came to the border, the quieter people became.'

Not all of the notes left behind are as black; a few are jovial. Thus one writer notes that there was an 'outstanding' atmosphere as a result of the 'cabaret' that was organised in her carriage on the evening of the first day of her enforced rail journey.

A number briskly kept on writing right up until the moment when the screws holdings the doors of their carriages were unwound and they were ordered to jump out. 'We have stopped at Auschwitz,' says another assiduous correspondent. 'We have to get out. It is a large factory city, because you can see a lot of chimneys.' Another comments: '. . . in the distance there is a building which is lit'.

These 'postcards' from the edge of hell, recovered when the trains returned to Westerbork, might have been the source of the rumours that had begun to circulate, especially since it was still possible for an exempt Jew to visit Westerbork and return with news.

The BBC first broadcast its informed opinion about what was really taking place in the camps in October. Many Jews with access to illegal radios heard it. One of them was Anne Frank. 'The British radio speaks of their being gassed,' she duly recorded on 29 October 1942.

If Myrtil heard this, or heard of it from his friend L., the art dealer, who owned a radio set, he didn't pass it on: his consistent policy was not to allow his wife and daughters to dwell upon the inevitable. In this respect, the Franks' lack of a radio – or at least a radio with which they could listen to the BBC – was probably a blessing.

In any case, neither Sybil nor Dorrit recalls any discussion about what was behind the meaning of 'labour service'. 'I am sure that he knew much more than he let on,' said Dorrit.

It was now The Hague's turn to make its first 'contribution' to the process. On 18 August 1942, deportation notices for 4,000 Jews living in The Hague and Scheveningen were sent out.

The Hague was the the seat of government and the Germans were particularly eager to rid it of its resident Jewish population. Aside from the 2,000 foreign Jews like the Franks who had originally been forced to move away from the coast, the Jewish population there remained largely in place and ready to be shipped, or 'relocated', in the German bureaucratic parlance.

Rauter instructed his colleague Willy Zopf, who was in charge of the deportations from The Hague, to make especially sure that *Den Haag* was *Judenrein*. After all, the *Reichskommissar* lived there. Then there were 'security' concerns. With so many Jews still situated so close to the coast, he felt, German interests were not safe.

In Zopf's absence, the task of expediting the deportations fell to his subordinate, Franz Fischer. Described by historian Bart van der Boom 'as both a brute and a bureaucrat at the same time', Fischer was evidently very glad to take on the job. After the war, he readily owned up to his responsibility for his 'sector' of the *Endlösung*. His pride in his work impelled him to personally see off each trainload of Jews from Station Staatsspoor for Westerbork, just like the officials at Westerbork who felt duty-bound to see *their* Dutch charges off on the twice-weekly shipments to the East.

As in Amsterdam, the first call-up was something of a disappointment: only 1,200 of the 4,000 who received summonses reported. Zopf's and

Fischer's response was to launch a *razzia* against the Haagse Jews. To Fischer's consternation, that didn't quite work either. Equipped with an inaccurate list of addresses, the flustered raiders found themselves knocking on Gentile doors rather than Jewish ones.

Enter Henri Edelsheim, the head of The Haagse *Joodsche Raad*. No less proud of his powers than was his German counterpart, Fischer, Edelsheim supervised the only branch of the *Raad* that had effective control over the lists of those who were called up for deportation. A lawyer, and the son of a distinguished Jewish family, he was made from the same accommodationist cloth as his superiors in Amsterdam, Asscher and Cohen. Meeting with Fischer, the *Raad* official offered to make up the requisite list, even volunteering four of his own staff to help type it up.

Thanks to the updated list, Fischer and his scrupulous colleagues decided on a somewhat different collecting procedure than had been employed in the past. Mass 'actions', the IVB4 official decided, were out. From now on, at least in The Hague, Jews were ordered to stay at home, from where they would be collected by Jewish policemen. It was found that this facilitated a quick transport. Curiously, this new method, which included some warning time, did not cause large additional numbers of Jews to go into hiding. Nor, so far as is known, was the 'temporary excitement' that Otto Bene said had occurred in Amsterdam after the deportations there replicated in The Hague. An estimated 1,500 to 2,000 Jews *did* decide to become *onderduikers* (an even lower proportion than in Amsterdam and Rotterdam) but for the rest it was almost as if they had had their power of volition removed. They obeyed the law, not so strange an impulse, perhaps, in a city whose populace was exceptionally conservative and law-abiding. In any event, Fischer decided, the yield from this new, improved method proved satisfactory.

A template for cooperation had been set up. As Bart van der Boom, a chronicler of the war in The Hague, has written, 'when [Fischer] ordered the Jewish Council to provide him with a list of 100 names, the Jewish Council never complained or protested but had a list made of one hundred persons who could be arrested. Their names and addresses were always accurate.'

Amongst those names and addresses, on a meticulously typed page from the final deportee manifest put together by the Westerbork staff in 1944 (presumably by one of the German-speaking inmates who had not yet been shipped out), a few lines under the entries for Edgar Reich and his parents, was a Jewish family named Reichmann who lived at number 38 Pieter van den Zandestraat, a few doors down from the Franks.

According to the meticulously kept records, two members of the Reichmann family, Anna and Theodor, were caught up in the first wave of round-ups in The Hague during the first week of August 1942 – about a month after the Franks surreptitiously moved next door – while another two, Berta and Markela, remained above ground and joined the rest of their kin at Westerbork later.

Why did Anna and Theodor Reichmann wait to receive their letters from the Jewish Council? Why did Berta and Markela wait to get picked up? Why did the Reichmanns not try to dive under? Perhaps they lacked the means and the will to do so.

Perhaps they had the means to go underground but were reluctant because they felt that by doing so they would be disobeying their religion, as did two friends of the Franks' fellow *onderduikers* Herbert and Hilda Boucher. 'Amy and Nico Herschel were two of our dearest friends,' Boucher recalls in his 1996 memoir, *Miracle of Survival*. 'They had no children and we advised them in no uncertain terms that they should not answer the call but go into hiding. We also told them in detail that we were planning to do the same.

'Their answer amazed us,' said Boucher, who dived under with his wife shortly afterwards. 'They said that according to the Bible, Orthodox Jews must obey the decisions and commands of the government. No matter how much we remonstrated with them, they would not waver from this attitude. I have to believe they were psychologically unable to face the strain of a life in hiding.'

'A few months later,' Boucher writes sadly, 'their call came and they went, literally, like sheep, and never returned.' Perhaps it was this way with the residents of number 38 Pieter van den Zandestraat. Perhaps the two Reichmanns who stayed above ground deliberately waited to be called up so that they could join the other family members. Those who dived under, it must be stressed, did not have a monopoly on courage. Some of those who knowingly answered the call-ups had both the means and the will to dive under, but chose to go along with the process nevertheless, despite knowing, or at least strongly suspecting, that they were going to their deaths. Amongst this brave group was the chief rabbi of Rotterdam, who refused a chance to dive under because he felt that he had a moral obligation to remain with his congregants.

Perhaps Berta and Markola Reichmann belonged to this heroic group.

Later, Flory would recall that when the Franks moved into number 14, they occasionally saw a Jewish man wearing a yellow star walking down the street, a sight that understandably perturbed her. 'I thought that as long as that man is here, or near here, I am not very safe,' she said.

Then, after a few weeks, he was gone. Was that man Theodor Reichmann? It is possible. In any event, Flory never saw that Jew, or any other Jew (at least not one wearing a star) walking along Pieter van den Zandestraat after the summer of 1942.

Somehow, this made her feel safer, she said – or at least less vulnerable. Of course, she knew it was an illusion. But people in hiding need their illusions.

And so, guided by local Nazis like Fischer, aided by 'accommodationist' Dutch police overseen by P.M.C.J. Hamer, the capital's flamboyant collaborationist police commissioner, and abetted by Jewish 'accomodationists' like Edelsheim, the process went forward of making The Hague, like the rest of Holland, Jew-free. Just as did the tandem processes of making France Jew-free, and Belgium Jew-free, and Norway Jew-free, and so forth, subject to the varying capacity of Auschwitz and the other extermination camps and the timetables and quotas imposed by Eichmann in Berlin.

By the autumn of 1942, the outlook for Holland's contribution to that process was looking excellent. This was due in part to the success of the August 'collections', as well as to Seyss-Inquart's utter determination to see the process through. If anyone doubted the *Reichskommissar*'s will in this matter, they were disabused on 7 September, when all Dutch Catholics of Jewish origin were arrested and sent directly to Auschwitz via Westerbork, amongst them the famed philosopher Edith Stein. This was in response to a letter of protest Seyss-Inquart had received from the Dutch churches – which, like previous such letters, had, to his annoyance, been read out in the Catholic churches.

Thus, on 11 September 1942, Otto Bene was able to report to Seyss-Inquart that 17,603 Jews had been successfully deported, 15,603 to Auschwitz – including the recent group of 700 Catholic Jews – and 2,000 to Mauthausen.

'About 46,000' – approximately one third of the estimated total of 140,000 'full' Dutch Jews[*] – 'are *for the time being* [author's italics] being

---

[*] According to the Nuremberg racial laws, which had also been imposed in Holland and the occupied territories, a 'Full Jew' was the child of two Jewish parents.

exempted from deportation,' Bene went on to report, 'because they live in mixed marriages, work in the armament industry and in the diamond trade or because they are "protected Jews".'

All in all, the Foreign Office's representative felt that the situation was well in hand. Nor was he unduly concerned by the subsidiary *onderduiker* problem: 'It is estimated that about 25,000 Jews are in hiding inside the Netherlands.'

Bene summed up: 'The figures scheduled for the shipments [from Holland] have so far been reached,' adding, 'Various measures are in preparation to secure these figures in the future.'

Amongst the measures that Bene referred to were a number specifically aimed at flushing out the problematic Jewish *onderduikers*, who collectively represented a new front of the war between the Germans and the Jews. These measures included the offering of monetary bounties ranging from five to seventy-five guilders for information leading to the capture of Jewish *onderduikers*. There was now a financial incentive for nosy Gentiles to turn in suspected divers – a measure that would lead to the betrayal and capture of hundreds of Jews, including, very likely, the family of Otto Frank, who were given up by a still unknown party in August 1944, two years into their dive.

Additionally Rauter decreed that Dutch policemen no longer needed authority from *Zentralstelle* or IVB4 to arrest a suspected Jewish fugitive. Henceforth they could act on their own.

The Dutch institution most greatly damaged by its collusion with the German authorities during the occupation was the Dutch police. It was later ashamed of its record, although there had been many individual acts of bravery, like that of the Amsterdam policeman who hid the young Leo Ullman, mentioned earlier.

In the Jewish Museum in Amsterdam there hangs a photograph in which you can actually see this shame. The photo is of the first postwar service at the Portuguese-Jewish Synagogue of Amsterdam, in June 1945, for the remnants of the decimated congregation, who were still in the process of returning from the camps, as well as from their hiding places. The focus of the photograph is the head rabbi, as he leads the service. In front of the altar are three Dutch policemen, standing guard, facing the unseen congregants, some of whom had doubtless been arrested by these same policemen's colleagues, or perhaps even these men themselves. They look petrified.

'The Dutch police behave outstandingly and catch hundreds of Jews day and night,' Rauter told Himmler. 'We would not have been able to arrest ten per cent of the Jews without their help,' Rauter's lieutenant, Willy Lages, said after the war.

Christopher Browning takes special note of the cooperativeness of the Amsterdam police in his authoritative study, citing the Germans' installation of the pro-German Sybren Tulp as chief constable of the force, and Tulp's efficiency and ruthlessness, and those of many of the men under him, as making a major contribution to the persecution of the city's Jews, particularly during the first years of the occupation. 'It was Tulp's Amsterdam police, not the Germans,' Browning notes,

> who in June 1941 arrested the 300 German Jews who composed the second group of 'hostages' sent from the Netherlands as a retaliation measure. And it was Tulp's police who enforced the German measures expelling Jews from public life in the fall of 1941.

This was an exaggeration, of course, but not by all that much. The police in The Hague, under the command of their commissioner, Hamer, also 'behaved outstandingly' in this regard. To see a lone Dutch policeman through the curtains investigating some matter or another, as the Franks very occasionally did on their tiny street, was just as much a cause for fear as the sight of a German soldier.

The new measures taken by the Germans to defeat *onderduikers* significantly raised the fear level within the Franks' little diving capsule. Since they were residing at an address that was listed as belonging to a Gentile, they were less concerned about being given up by the *Joodsche Raad* – which still had them on record as having moved to Amsterdam – than they were about being betrayed by their neighbours.

The Franks remained essentially visible and vulnerable to betrayal and arrest, the thing that had bothered Myrtil most during his initial reconnaissance. Unlike most *onderduikers*, they were not sequestered behind a false compartment, as Otto Frank's family, or in a cellar or roof, like the Jews who reportedly hid beneath the roof of the nearby Hotel des Indes where it is said they ate their fellow residents, the pigeons. The illegal residents of 14 Pieter van den Zandestraat were, in effect, hiding in plain sight.

Surely, they thought to themselves, as they marked their first hundred days in hiding, surely *someone* on their little street must be wondering about the strange activity at number 14, the comings and goings of their Dutch friends and of the 'German-Swiss doctor' who reputedly lived there with his mad wife. Despite Myrtil's orders to his family not to touch the curtains in the front window, surely someone must have also glimpsed two young women as they passed by – perhaps they could see Dorrit's and Sybil's silhouettes through the back window. 'Remember, this was a street where everyone knew each other's business,' said Sybil. 'And the Dutch are *very* nosy people.'

Once bounties were placed on Jewish heads, those same neighbours who had such suspicions might well claim a reward for reporting them.

Yet none did.

And what if a Dutch policeman or a German soldier *did* come to number 14? They were done for.

Such were the parameters of the Franks' new subterranean existence.

In October the family learned that the Germans planned to evacuate the Dutch coast, including a large part of The Hague and Scheveningen.

The rumours were true. The Second Front and the invasion of occupied Europe were, even by the most optimistic Free Dutch predictions, at least a year off. The 'exploratory' raid by Canadian troops on Dieppe, in occupied northern France, a fiasco that had resulted in many Allied casualties, as well as a major propaganda coup for the Nazis, had underscored that downbeat assessment.

Still, the German High Command was sufficiently concerned to begin work on what would ultimately become the Atlantic Wall, a heavily mined and fortified defence extending the entire length of the English Channel on the Axis side, from northern Holland all the way down to Normandy. This entailed evacuating the immediate area behind the sea fortifications for a distance of at least a mile. The Dutch part of the wall included five strongpoints, including *Festung Scheveningen*, which encompassed most of the northern part of the city along a broken line up to a mile inland and all of the strategically important beach resort itself (including the Franks' former home).

By 1944, before the actual D-Day, the Germans would discount Scheveningen – technically the closest landing beach to England – as a future site for an Allied invasion, and would correctly focus their attention southward, on the French coast. A number of factors caused SHAEF (Supreme Headquarters Allied Expeditionary Force) to eliminate the Dutch coast from their plans, most notably its relatively genial nature and lack of natural obstacles, in contradistinction to the French beaches; as well as the dense Dutch road network, which made it too easy for the Germans to bring up reinforcements to repel a seaborne landing force.

If for some reason the Allies did land at Scheveningen, General Christiansen, the *Wehrmacht* commander in the Netherlands, could have several divisions on the scene immediately. Why, he could even send them by tram.

But in the autumn of 1942, the Germans felt that Holland was a likely target. In early October, as had previously been rumoured, thousands of residents of Scheveningen and a large adjoining swathe of The Hague were evicted from their homes and ordered to find accommodation elsewhere. With housing in The Hague now at a premium, officials were determined to make full use of all available stock in the unevacuated neighbourhoods of the city, including the central district encompassing Pieter van den Zandestraat.

Under these circumstances, Annie, as the tenant of two apartments, her primary residence in the *Bezuidenhout* neighbourhood south of the Haagse Bos – the Hague Woods – and her pied-à-terre at 14 Pieter van den Zandestraat, would be hard put to explain why she needed two dwellings. Perhaps someone in authority might want to see this second apartment for himself: on-site inspections of extant housing stock were quite normal.

For weeks the Franks watched and waited for a knock on the door from a city housing official. Yet none came. Somehow Annie was able to defend the pied-à-terre at number 14 without having to suffer such an inspection.

Perhaps this is not so surprising in the light of the other surviving tales of this formidable Dutchwoman's persuasive powers; witness the charged meeting she is reported to have had with a German official regarding her main means of transportation, her bicycle: the Germans had recently launched a campaign to collect privately owned bicycles in The Hague and Rotterdam, an effort which they eventually abandoned because of the resistance of people like Annie van der Sluijs. Annie, who relied upon her bicycle for her visits to the Franks (amongst other things), insisted in her meeting with the flustered German official that she needed her velocipede to assist her 'students'. The official was convinced. Annie kept her bike – and her pied-à-terre.

Through all this, Myrtil continued with what his neighbours must have found mystifying comings and goings. It seems extraordinary that a Jewish *onderduiker* could have walked around the neighbourhood without proper papers and identification.

'He was not boasting about it,' Jeanne recalled. 'It is like this. 'Til could do it and he did it.'

Moore writes that it was not unknown for some *onderduikers* to go outdoors. Myrtil needed to make those dangerous trips in order to supplement the Franks' often inadequate supplies: what their friends brought them sometimes just wasn't enough.

So out he went. Sometimes he went up the street to the corner store to stock up on food with one of the illicit ration cards he mysteriously obtained. ''Til took care of the food situation,' said Jeanne. Other times he would visit his friend L., the art dealer on the Zeestraat, or another friend, a sympathetic florist married to a Jewish woman who had a shop called Ixora on the Noordeinde, just a few blocks away. During these visits 'Til would stock up on such other items and stores as he could obtain, or he would listen to the BBC on his friend's illegal radio set. Or he would just hang out. The truth was, as much as he loved and admired his wife – and came to admire her more underground – there was only so much he could stand of being cooped up with Flory. *Schnapps* still didn't mix with *Dubonnet*, especially underground.

Sometimes the roving commander of number 14 ranged further afield. Generally he was silent when he returned. His wife and daughters were terrified during these sorties into the unknown. They should have been. On one occasion that he only told his family about later Myrtil contrived to run an errand for L. to German police headquarters, where he managed to swipe a piece of official stationery for later use. Inevitably, one night early into the dive, Myrtil was caught outdoors during an Allied bombing raid and had to seek shelter, leaving his wife and daughters in sheer terror until he reappeared, flashing his familiar killer smile.

Some time later, probably in early 1943, 'Til had an even closer shave when he was stopped by an inquisitive German policeman and asked for his papers. Whereupon, as he later recalled for his agog family, he went into high thespian mode.

'What do you mean by stopping me?' the fugitive brazenly responded. 'I am a German doctor!'

Duly impressed, the policeman let him pass.

The destruction of Dutch Jewry proceeded. The revised collection procedures were working wonderfully, Bene noted in his secret report to the *Reichskommissar* of 12 November 1942. So were the new counter-measures taken to defeat those in hiding. Whatever the Jews believed or didn't believe about what was really happening in the East, Bene declared, the overall quota was being met, timetables were being fulfilled, and deportations were proceeding 'without incident'. That month, as Bene had predicted, Dutch-Jewish armament workers had their exemptions rescinded, bringing the total of Jews deported to 25,000. By the year's end the total number of deportees would stand at 38,500 – or roughly one third of the total pre-war Jewish population.

Still, Seyss-Inquart and Rauter were not satisfied. They would do better next year, they vowed, as winter approached.

It was still possible to dive under. *Onderduikers* with the will and the means to support themselves continued to do so. They needed valid ration cards or the funds with which to purchase them, and the cash to pay rent to those Gentiles who were willing to take them in. Some good Samaritans, such as Annie, did not charge rent, and others voluntarily paid rent to help their Dutch friends. On 11 November 1942, according to the diary of Anne Frank, the group of six Jewish fugitives already sequestered at 263 Prinsengracht were joined by the Pels ('van Daans'), after Otto Frank made it known that he wished to take two more people into their *achter-huis*. Then the hatch to his hiding place closed.

The *Joodsche Raad* continued to advise people not to dive under. Unless everyone could do it, the Council insisted, no one should. In the increasingly depopulated Jewish quarters of Amsterdam, The Hague and Rotterdam, life of a crazed, self-deluded sort went on. Engagements and weddings continued to be reported in *Het Joodsche Weekblad*. Advertisements were placed, business solicited. '*Not travelling?*' one announcement read, alluding to the ban on Jewish travel (except to Westerbork, of course). '*You can still keep in touch with your clients with well-written business letters.*'

On Christmas Day 1942, there was great rejoicing at the main offices of the Council, as the staff, still secure in their exemptions, celebrated the sixtieth birthday of Professor Cohen, the pipe-smoking *Raad* co-president. A Jew could still act like a fool, if he or she wished. Or worse. Herbert Boucher bitterly recalls several instances in which some of the less self-deluded members of the local *Raad* advised other non-exempt Jews not to dive under, whilst preparing to do so themselves. By now, some Jews had taken to calling the Council *Joodsche Verraad*: Jewish betrayal.

Meanwhile, as the vast machinery of the *Endlösung* continued to gather force around them, pulling in Dutch, French and Belgian Jews, Jeanne, Annie and her sisters continued with their brave sorties to number 14, bringing additional supplies, news, hope, encouragement, and company.

'It was just girlfriends visiting each other,' Jeanne would put it later, in the same self-effacing way that many such helpers and rescuers would describe their efforts. 'There were no heroic acts.'

Then, one horrible day in early December, Jeanne brought something else with her on her visit to number 14: a package for Dorrit from Edgar, posted from Westerbork, containing a sketch pad of his. This included a number of deft drawings the artist had done following Dorrit's visit to the camp that May. One showed the couple dancing to 'Ole Guappa', their old favourite from the Hilversum days. Another especially heart-tugging one depicted the two strolling arm in arm through the snow-covered fields outside Hilversum, as they had done the previous winter, before Edgar and his family had been shipped to Drenthe. A final drawing, limning the beginnings of a scroll of some sort – a love screed, no doubt – was unfinished. Perhaps Edgar had been at work on it when he had been picked to board the first train to Auschwitz on 15 July, the day after the Franks dived under.

The moment Dorrit opened the sketchbook, she *knew*.

She was inconsolable. Morale at 14 Pieter van den Zandestraat plunged to a new low, as the four fugitive Jews struggled again not to dwell upon the inevitable, or what had actually happened to Edgar, or what was to happen to Leontine and the rest of their friends and loved ones still above ground. They struggled, in their own way, to pretend and not to face the parlous reality of their situation.

On New Year's Day, the imprisoned foursome – 'Til had decided to stay in on this grim 'holiday' evening – listened to the òne official channel they could get on their radio set, a primitive device that only allowed them to hear the Nazi-controlled Radio Hilversum, with feeds from its parent station, Radio Berlin. They sat in despair as the Radio Berlin announcer hailed the 130 million people of the new, greater, ever-expanding Reich and its territories, 'stretching all the way from the Caucasus in the east' – the *Wehrmacht*, advancing through the Russian steppes, had now reached the distant mountain range – 'to the Atlantic'.

'When I heard *that*,' Flory said years later, 'I thought, "*Now* they have everything!"'

CHAPTER 8

'My Name is Toni Muller'

'Tension in the Netherlands is greater than at any time since the German inva-
sion. The coastal region is being heavily fortified,' the spokesman [for the Dutch
government-in-exile] said. A huge wall of concrete and steel is being erected
between the sea and the villages . . . It was reported that 25,000 houses had
been demolished by the Germans in The Hague alone . . .

From a London dispatch in *The New York Times*,
3 March 1943

The scene: an operating theatre in Bronovo Hospital, The Hague. The date: spring 1943.

The patient is a seventeen-year-old girl who was listed on the form attached to her cot as one Toni Muller of The Hague. The operation, for a rare uterine condition, is a serious one – the girl had been blue in the face when she had been escorted to the hospital by a friend the previous day. If she had come in any later, the doctors agreed, the situation would have been even more serious.

The Dutch doctor who was to perform the operation was very reassuring. (Tine had checked him out to ensure that he was not a German sympathiser.) They didn't do this sort of procedure every day, he said, but everything would be fine. In a few weeks, they promised the young woman, she could go back to her family and return to her normal life.

Normal life, 'Toni' said to herself sarcastically. If only they knew.

In fact, 'Toni Muller' was Sybil Frank. This was not to say Toni didn't exist; Toni Muller was the name of a Dutchwoman who had agreed, via Annie, to lend her ID card to Sybil before she was brought to the hospital for the hastily arranged operation. Sybil had to remain focused; she was, after all, in danger – and was soon to be in greater danger. The physicians reminded her that she would have to go under an anaesthetic for the lengthy operation. What if she forgot who she was, or who she was supposed to be, while she was unconscious? What if she accidentally gave herself and her family away?

The safety and well-being of the Franks rested on her shoulders. The thought made Sybil feel faint.

Then she got it: self-conscious autosuggestion, the psychological fad that Flory had briefly espoused in the 1920s. Perhaps she could 'harness the power of the imagination' to make it believe that she was someone other than her real self – Sybil Frank, *onderduiker* – at least while the anaesthesia was taking effect, prior to going under the knife. At least it was worth a try.

And so there Sybil was on the operating table, a little while later, transmitting the urgent message to her subconscious by repeating to herself: 'I am not Billy – my name is Toni Muller . . . I am not Billy – my name is . . .'

Radio Berlin had been wrong. The Germans did not have everything. Strategically they had begun to lose the war in late 1942 and early 1943, suffering pivotal defeats in North Africa and Russia. The first major setback for the Reich had occurred in early November, when, at the Battle of El Alamein, Field Marshal Bernard Montgomery had led the British Eighth Army in an important strategic victory against Italian troops and Field Marshal Erwin Rommel's Afrika Korps. At the same time, on the far western part of the North African coast, the Allies successfully launched Operation Torch, a seaborne invasion of German-occupied Morocco and Tunisia. Within months, British and American forces would succeed in pushing the *Wehrmacht* completely out of Africa.

In England, which had already weathered the worst of the blitz, church bells were rung after Montgomery's feat of arms. It wasn't the end, Churchill declared in a speech he delivered in November 1942, nor even the beginning of the end, but perhaps it was the end of the beginning.

Then, on 2 February 1943, the normally self-satisfied tones of Radio Berlin gave way to the solemn announcement that the German troops at Stalingrad, engaged in an epochal struggle with the Russians since mid-November, had surrendered.

The death knell for the German forces, under the command of Lieutenant General Friedrich von Paulus, had already sounded in

November after Russian forces to the east and west of the city had linked
up, sealing the Sixth Army's doom. Von Paulus requested Hitler's permission to break out.

Permission was refused. Instead Hitler promoted Von Paulus to the
rank of field marshal, under the illusion – for the *Führer* too was a great
believer in the power of self-conscious autosuggestion – that by so
elevating the besieged general, the positive suggestion would penetrate
his imagination, as well as those of the freezing, demoralised troops under
him, in such a way as to allow them to surmount the incontrovertible
reality of the battlefield situation. After all, Hitler could assure himself,
no field marshal in German history had surrendered: Von Paulus wouldn't
dare do so now.

But he did.

Berlin reeled, but not for long. While the *Führer* sulked in his tent,
his Propaganda Minister, Goebbels, perversely inspired, seized on the
reverse as an opportunity to motivate the German people and to inspire
German troops to greater sacrifice. In this effort, he was aided by the
decision of the Big Three – Roosevelt, Churchill and Stalin – at that
month's Casablanca conference to accept nothing less than Germany's
unconditional surrender, which, as writers such as Hanson Baldwin,
the former military editor of *The New York Times* and others have
argued, undercut those elements in the German armed forces which
might have been prepared to accept less: after Stalingrad and Casablanca
many Germans felt that they had no choice but to fight on as Goebbels
wished.

Yet a milestone in the war had unquestionably been reached. Although
German forces would remain in the Caucasus for another year – as the
Radio Berlin commentator had boasted in the broadcast that had so chilled
Flory – and even win some scattered victories, the tide had indeed turned.

The shockwaves from Stalingrad rippled throughout the Greater Reich,
including occupied Holland. Some Dutch blackshirts began to hedge their
bets: a February 1943 photograph shows a group of Haagse NSB
supporters at the funeral procession of H.A. Seyffardt. Amongst the line
of stern-faced mourners with right hands dutifully raised, one can be seen
attempting to cover his face with his hat. Evidently the man didn't wish
to publicise his appearance at the funeral. Perhaps he was thinking ahead,
to the time when he and his friends would have to justify their support
of the *moffen*, the derogatory word for the Germans. Another Dutchman
who evidently began having doubts at this time was Hamer, the hitherto

enthusiastically cooperative head of the Haagse police, who was no longer quite as enthusiastic about following Nazi orders after early 1943.

No doubt others who had chosen the Nazi side, both in the Netherlands and elsewhere, began making similar calculations at this time.

Still, to the Franks, trying to get through each day, the Allied victories in North Africa and Russia didn't amount to very much.

'I remember hearing something about North Africa,' Dorrit recalled later. 'But it seemed very, very far away.'

The winter proved an especially long and wet one, with bitter temperatures lasting until April. For days on end, when they peeked through the curtains, the Franks saw nothing but grey. The picturesque snow which often sets off the dreariness of the Dutch winter and provides a backdrop to village ice-skating meets and contests, like that depicted in Hendrik Avercamp's 1634 painting *Enjoying the Ice* that hung in the Mauritshuis, did not fall that year.

'At a certain point in 1943,' Sybil said, 'we realised that this . . . experience' – the German occupation; the ordeal of being an *onderduiker* – 'was never going to end.' If the Allies did manage to invade Europe and the Netherlands, the Franks feared it would be too late.

Across *Festung Europa*, as SS officials around the Reich raced to meet or surpass their quotas and timetables, other Jews decided to take matters into their own hands.

The three million Jews of Poland, persecuted by the Germans virtually since the day the *Wehrmacht* had invaded four years before, often with the encouragement of the anti-Semitic population itself, were under few illusions as to what was really happening in the East. In July 1942, Adam Czerniakow, an official of the *Judenrat* – the Polish counterpart of the *Joodsche Raad* – committed suicide after the Nazis ordered him to help arrange the deportation of 9,000 Jews from the Warsaw ghetto.

That month, the gas chambers of Treblinka, an extermination camp built for the express purpose of 'solving' Poland's 'Jewish problem', received their first Polish 'material'.

Nine months later, having seen their friends, family and neighbours transported to what was widely assumed to be their deaths, the Jews remaining in the Warsaw ghetto took up such arms as they could find. These Jews, they vowed, would not go so willingly to their deaths. On 19 April, in the first engagement of the Warsaw Ghetto Uprising, small groups of Jews fanned out through the occupied city and began attacking

(*Above left*) In London, Queen Wilhelmina observes the first anniversary of the German invasion in exile. On her left is Gerbrandy, the stalwart Dutch prime minister, on her right, her son-in-law, Bernhard. (*Above right*) Seyss-Inquart, Nazi Reichscommissar. Forced to leave the coast, the Franks moved to a new house in Hilversum, and, despite increasing restrictions, life went on. (*Below left*) Dorrit looks happy in this photo, shot in late 1941, but Myrtil is clearly worried. (*Below right*) New Year's Eve 1942. A group of young Jews, including Dorrit (top row, second right) and Sybil (middle, right) celebrate at the Franks and hope for the best. At bottom is Dorrit's boyfriend (and soon to be fiancé), Edgar Reich. Soon all would be dead or in hiding.

Lost love. Deported to Westerbork – the then Dutch-administered work camp, soon to convert into an SS-run transit camp – in February 1942, Edgar, a talented artist, limned scenes from his romance with Dorrit in a sketchbook. In May 1942, Dorrit received permission to visit him at Westerbork. It was the last time she saw him. (*Below left*) On July 15 1942, Edgar was put aboard the first train from Westerbork to Auschwitz, as the Nazis' scrupulous records show. (*Right*) A photo of Edgar taken at Westerbork. In December 1942 Jeanne delivered the package, which included this photo of Edgar, to Dorrit, by then in hiding. She knew then that he was gone.

van Aaa	Bowaja	7.3.72	Arnhem,	de Wilstr.62	18.5.43
Regensberg-Johansje	Dina	21.1.84	A.dam	Maritstr.24	26.7.43
Regensberg	Ida	26.6.13	A.dam	Maritsstr.24	20.7.43
Regensberg	Moritz	30.5.81	A.dam	Maritsstr.24	20.7.43
Regensberg	Grietje	2.9.83	Haak,	Zuid.Waal	23.2.43
Ingenaulig	Jaques	14.5.89	Haag	J.v.Pisbegkstr.112	4.8.42
Regensberg	Philipp	10.12.04	Groningen	Stiltorstr.20	81.4.43
Legestein.M.A	Sara E.	30.7.95	Harlem	Nw. Gracht 62	26.4.43
Lodfer	David	19.10.41	A.dam	Rebukersgrt.17	onto 30.7.43
Leifel	Rosa	15.9.59	A.dam	Dr.Willingpl.17	24.6.43
Laufter	Herta	21.5.07	A.dam	Mijnaplatko	8.4.43
Laufter	Alfred	18.5.77	A.dam	Mijnaplatko	8.4.43
Linc	Alfred	19.11.04	A.dam	Oostgarten Ak	8.10.42
Linc	Amelia	7.10.97	Eldsant	Ruckilstr.18	11.4.41
Linc	Roppi	13.7.48	A.dam	Nw. Uileabrgstr.18	20.7.43
Reich.Freund	Betina	13.7.68	A.dam	Zaturdatr.50	20.4.42
Reich.mother	Amelé H.	35.5.97	A.dam	Mortusplaats.nr7	20.7.43
Reich	David	1.11.81	A.dam	Lepelstr.18	13.11.42
Reich	David	5.1.23	A.dam	Kerwedagl.37	5.7.43
Reich	Edgar	19.8.23	Lagerwesterbork		15.7.43
Reich	Eliat	12.6.07	A.dam	Persuplanaoct	26.7.43
Reich	Frederik	13.15	A.dam	Lepelstr.88	16.11.42
Reich	Hendrina	26.2.81	A.dam	Nw. Uileuirgstj.18	11.6.43
Reich	Herman	28.5.81	A.dam	Mortusplansen7	26.7.43
Reich	Henriette	2.9.17	Utrecht	Nw.Balletstr.13	28.8.42
Reich	Bertha	14.6.15			16.7.42
Reich	Juda	29.4.11	A.dam	Nw. Uileubrgstr.18	11.6.43
Reich	Luuka	9.11.37	A.dam	Nw. Uileubrgstr.18	11.6.43
Reich	Jeisach	13.2.25	A.dam	Mortusplansen7	20.7.43
Reich	Philip	14.8.95	A.dam	Hohendiepatr.15	8.6.43
Reich-Achtienriboen	Rachel	3.10.10	A.dam	Lepelstr.88	13.11.42

Pieter van den Zandestraat, as photographed by the author in 1965 on the first of many pilgrimages he would make to the tiny street. On the left is the corner store where Myrtil planted the rumour that his wife was mad and later shopped with illegal coupons. 'If we had known we would be there for *3 years*,' Flory said, 'I am sure that we would not have undertaken that.'

By spring 1943 the Germans had succeeded in deporting the bulk of Holland's Jewish population to the East. (*Above*) A group of Amsterdam Jews await their fate after one of the large round-ups, spring 1943. (*Right*) Hans Albin Rauter, standing below a portrait of Hitler, oversaw the Jewish 'removal' campaign, the most 'successful' in Nazi-occupied Europe outside Poland. The Dutch executed him in 1949.

Unknown to Dorrit or Sybil, Myrtil had been preparing to 'dive under' with the aid of Annie van der Sluijs, Dorrit's former Dutch teacher. Annie agreed to let the Franks hide out in a small flat she rented in The Hague. First though, the Franks, then living in Amsterdam, had to get there. The bravery of Annie and others was in contrast to the apathy and passive collaboration of some of the Dutch. Here she stands in her doorway with an unidentified friend.

On July 14 1942, after surviving the dangerous and illegal train journey from Amsterdam, the four *onderduikers* entered No. 14 Pieter van den Zandestraat.

The Franks were nearly discovered during a house-to-house slave labour raid in November 1944.

(*Above*) The aftermath of the raid; by this time over 300,000 Dutch people – including some 25,000 Jews – had dived under.

(*Left*) Misfiring V-2s, launched from The Hague, were a constant threat.

The Franks barely survived the *hongerwinter* of '44-'45. Over 20,000 people died in western Holland, including many *onderduikers*.

(*Left*) In March 1945 a misdirected RAF bombing raid killed over 500 Hagenaars. The Franks could see the fires from their window.

(*Below*) Jubilant Hagenaars greet the Allied 'foodlift' in April. The Franks, still in hiding after 1,000 days, had to stay inside, but they knew the end was near.

The New York Times.

THE WAR IN EUROPE IS ENDED! SURRENDER IS UNCONDITIONAL; V-E WILL BE PROCLAIMED TODAY; OUR TROOPS ON OKINAWA GAIN

(*Below*) On 8 May 1945, nearly 5 years to the day after the Germans had invaded, Holland's ordeal was finally over. Several months later the Franks posed for an 'official' photograph that they sent to family and friends, many of whom had assumed that they perished. 'The Frank family after liberation', it read.

(*Left*) In April 1947 Myrtil and Julius visited their sister Lisbeth and her children in Palestine. Shortly afterwards, their 87-year-old mother, Johanna, who had held on to see them, died. (*Right*) In July the diary of Anne Frank was first published in Holland. The Franks were startled by the coincidences between their story and that of their namesakes.

(*Left*) Last leg. In August, Sybil and Dorrit boarded a freighter bound for New York City. They were amazed by the contrast between battered Europe and booming America.
(*Above*) In 1948 a radiant Flory sailed to New York.

Happy ending.

(*Left*) In September 1949, Dorrit married Kurt Sander, a naturalized German Jew and decorated U.S. Army officer. Here they are photographed at Riverside Park, New York, in 1950.

(*Below*) Flory at an art show, *c.*1956. Using her taste and Myrtil's business savvy, the Franks became art dealers.

(*Left*) In 1966 three generations of Franks gathered at Sybil's home in New Jersey. Myrtil died in 1968. Flory in 1981.

(*Above*) Dorrit on a visit to No. 14 in 2000.

German troops with rifles and hand grenades. Shortly their number grew into the thousands. The resisters knew they were doomed before the start. It didn't matter. They fought on. This was how Hitler had secretly hoped his trapped soldiers at Stalingrad would fight – to the death, like Maccabees.

It took nearly a month and the efforts of an entire division of German troops before the last Polish-Jewish guerrilla gave up or was killed. Then, in the German tradition, Jurgen Stroop, the commander of the German police, ordered the entire ghetto razed.

Observing the carnage in Warsaw with approval, Rauter, Stroop's Dutch-based SS colleague, pronounced himself 'inspired' by his example and vowed to carry on his own anti-Jewish campaign in the same spirit.

December had been an 'off month', as far as deportations from the Netherlands were concerned, with a mere 2,496 Jews transported to Auschwitz from Westerbork. This was the lowest monthly total since the deportations had begun five months before. Rauter and his cohorts at the *Zentralstelle* and IVB4 redoubled their efforts in January when 3,594 more were dispatched. This included more than 300 Jews picked up in a Rauter-approved raid on Amsterdam's Jewish invalid hospital, *Joodsche Invalide*, most of them sick, old or disabled, together with 900 taken in a raid that month on the *Apeldoornse Bos*, a home for the mentally ill. This exploded the convenient fiction that the Germans were only interested in drafting healthy Jews for 'labour deployment'. These latest unfortunates, dragged to the Apeldoorn and Amsterdam train stations like so much baggage, were not qualified for any sort of constructive work.

In February, the pace continued to pick up, with 4,283 more Jews transported, including some of the 780 Haagse Jews who departed Station Staatsspoor under *Reichssicherheitshauptampt* Franz Fischer's watchful eye.

The Jew-killing process had achieved synchronicity by now. According to the Germans' meticulous records, on 11 January 1943, a train from Westerbork carrying 750 Dutch Jews left for the East. This was followed the next day by a train carrying 1,000 of Berlin's remaining Jews from the German capital to Auschwitz and Treblinka. After that, on the 15th, two trains, with complements of 948 and 612 Jews, respectively, departed the transit camp at Malines, Belgium; the Germans had not made such high figures in Belgium, thanks in part to the relative moderation of the military commander, General Von Falkenhausen, who baulked at enforcing the yellow star edict. Belgium would ultimately lose approximately 25,000 of its Jews, out of its registered Jewish population of 56,000. This was considerably less than Holland, with its harsher civil administration, which would ultimately lose over three quarters of its Jews.

On 18 January, another train from Westerbork, carrying 748, left. Further, on 9 February, a transport containing 1,184 Jews left Westerbork, followed the same day by a trainload of 1,000 Jews from France, then two more trainloads from France, on the 11th and 13th, carrying 2,000 more. These, in turn, were succeeded by the next train from Holland, on the 16th, bearing an additional 1,108 for the Germans' extermination complex. And so on.

In its own way, the *Endlösung* was a work of logistical genius, a masterfully timed and coordinated example of what is today known in the corporate world as an extended enterprise, the enterprise in this case being the destruction of European Jewry.

The end point for Dutch Jews changed in March 1943, when the Germans, instead of Auschwitz, which was supposedly full, started directing them towards the newly opened camp at Sobibor, in Poland; a typhoid epidemic at the latter camp persuaded Eichmann's technicians to continue with this arrangement through the summer, after which trains from Holland were once more routed back to Auschwitz.

Unlike Auschwitz, which housed a 'real' factory, employing some of the 'luckier' Jews as slaves, in addition to its on-site death factory, Sobibor was a death camp pure and simple. New arrivals were given a polite welcome, allowed to write a postcard home signifying their arrival in good health, and unceremoniously killed. Between March and July 1943, over 35,000 Dutch Jews were sent to Sobibor, out of the estimated quarter of a million European Jews who were dispatched and liquidated there. A total of nineteen survived.

Demonstrably proud of his efforts, Rauter sent a smug secret report, which was later presented as evidence at his postwar trial, to Seyss-Inquart in The Hague on 26 March 1943, which stated: 'In the course of the deportations from Westerbork which have now been carried out for eight months without interruption and disturbance, altogether 50,000 Jews have been deported from the Netherlands to the East.'

Evidently some of the doomed Dutch Jews had offered resistance to the police who came to rout them out, some reportedly with guns. 'Sometimes we heard gunshots in the night,' Dorrit said, evidently referring to the then ensuing *razzias* taking place in The Hague. 'We wondered if someone had been picked up.'

But such 'insolence', as Rauter termed it, was over now, another indirect effect of the Stalingrad shockwave, or the 'weakening of the Soviet offensive'. He continued:

> The Jews expect the next months to be the worst for them and are telling each other that the German authorities are planning on settling the Jewish question in the Netherlands completely by summer regardless of all hitherto valid exemption stamps. Accordingly all sorts of methods continue to be used and recommended to escape the round-up, and to keep going during the next few months till the hoped-for invasion starts.

The *onderduiker* war had also been going well: Rauter estimated the number of Jews in hiding at between 10,000 and 15,000, about half of Bene's estimate from the previous October. The search police had become expert at finding Jews. Corrie ten Boom notes that the SD's 'favourite technique' upon entering a house where Jews were reportedly concealed was to feel the mattresses for warm spots.

Regarding the aforementioned recalcitrants:

> The largest part of them has probably *submerged* [author's italics] in the western big cities . . . [W]hereas the rest is hidden in the provinces. In many cases their accommodation is prepared and carried out by small organisations, and couriers maintain communications between the single members of a family and procure food. Also unusual hiding places are resorted to, e.g., a mobile chicken house in the middle of a forest, which had accommodated five Jews [in Arnhem]. In Rotterdam a number of Jews [were arrested], who were living in the loft of a big business building, amongst them a former Dutch officer. In a large castle at Almelo, 18 Jews were caught, [including] a Dutch policeman mixed up [*sic*] in Jewish affairs.

This section of Rauter's report highlights the unusual aspects of the Franks' hiding set-up, some of which they shared with the Amsterdam Franks. At Pieter van den Zandestraat, the hiding place had been arranged by Myrtil himself and a few trusted friends, rather than with the aid of the organised resistance, which was more the norm – in much the same way as Otto Frank had arranged his *onderduikadres* on his own.

Moreover, as The Hague Franks were only too well aware, *their* hiding place wasn't really hidden.

Rauter was confident of victory. The side battle with the *onderduikers* – as well as those Dutchmen who 'out of pity or of gain' assisted them

– would be won. The police chief noted that the unexpected withdrawal from circulation of 500- and 1,000-guilder notes – a measure specifically aimed at the *onderduikers* – had been effective, 'render[ing] it more difficult for the underground Jews to pay their landlords and in this way to stay in hiding'. In one fell swoop the move invalidated a large portion of the concealed Jews' concealed assets. This may help explain why Myrtil's resources shrank at this time.

Yet more ominously, Rauter was pleased to report that 'an increasing number of fugitive Jews [are] being spotted by means of denunciations on the part of the [Dutch] population'. Whether out of loyalty to the Germans – an impulse that was demonstrably weakening – or from the sheer maliciousness of it, or simply for monetary gain, more and more Dutchmen were turning in Jewish divers. To Rauter and Seyss-Inquart, this was the most promising news of all.

Three days before Rauter sent his weekly round-up, on 23 March, Flory's mother, Leontine Marburger-Ullman, aged seventy-two, was removed from her pension in the River Quarter and dispatched to 'the penal hut' (as Rauter now called it) at Westerbork – via the Hollandse Schouwburg, the former theatre that had become the main assembly point for the city's Jews – and sent to Sobibor.

A small amount of footage of life at Westerbork, shot at the height of the deportations at the behest of the commandant, Albert Gemmeker, who had taken over from Erich Deppner, the man who had selected Edgar Reich for the first transport, survives to this day. The most harrowing part of the film, which is available by special request at the museum that now occupies the site of the camp, is that of a 'typical' transport being readied for the East, prior to being shipped out; evidently Gemmeker, who is pictured standing by the train with another group of his crew – including the by now experienced Jewish OD who personally delivered the selected deportees to the cars – wanted a proper record of his work.

The entire sequence, running to no more than five minutes, goes by too quickly to register more than the general horror of the scene and the efficiency of Gemmeker's minions. However if one slows down the film one can see at the back of the car a well-dressed elderly woman, sitting propped up against an equally terrified man in his seventies. The woman, struggling to retain her composure as the German camera crew continues to film, dabs her face with a handkerchief.

It is not Leontine. But it could have been.

There were more *razzias*. A Jewish woman, evidently exempt from the round-ups, writes about the effect the increasingly brutal raids were having on her mother.

> Shuddering with revulsion, Mother told how she sat in the dark in front of the window every evening while people were dragged away like animals, shivering with apprehension, because it could be her and father's turn at the moment; how large trucks brought in for the raids had waited there, loaded with people whimpering or shouting out loud with fear, of whom only a hopeless tangle of arms and legs had been visible.

The weekly shipments expanded. On 6 April a train carrying 2,020 Dutch Jews – the single largest transport yet – puffed its way out of Westerbork, bound for the crematoria at Sobibor; on the 13th, another with 1,204 deportees, followed by another on the 20th carrying 1,166, followed by another on the 27th containing 1,204, bringing the monthly total to 5,594.

The next month, May 1943, produced an even higher yield, with a total of 8,006 Jews shipped to the East.

Situated on their small, out-of-the-way street in the centre of The Hague, only a mile from Seyss-Inquart's offices on the Plein, the Franks did not see lorries roll up outside their window. Pieter van den Zandestraat was too narrow for a lorry. But what they couldn't see could be imagined.

Then another danger appeared: Allied bombing.

'At first,' Flory said, referring to the first six months the Franks were in hiding, 'I thought perhaps this [bombing] could be over. But then in early 1943 it started to get really bad.'

As the pace of the bombing offensive against the German industrial heartland increased, so, inevitably, did the collateral damage to the Dutch cities inflicted by the British and American Lancasters and B-24s. On 2 April 1943, in a replay of the horror of May 1940, 400 civilians were accidentally killed in Rotterdam. Two weeks later, on 16 April, another Allied mistake resulted in the destruction of a large area of Haarlem and 85 deaths.

The Hague also suffered its share of air raids and mis-targeted bombs. Sometimes the raids were preceded by an air-raid siren, sometimes not, but this didn't matter much to the Franks since they had nowhere to take cover.

'All we could do was huddle together under the table,' said Dorrit, 'and pray.'

And yet they took it.

One of the reasons The Hague Franks, like the Amsterdam Franks, were able 'to take it' relatively well is because, unlike many other *onder-duikers*, they had remained together as a family.

One of the misconceptions arising from the popularity of Anne Frank's journal is that most Jewish families remained together and in the same place for the duration of their dives.

As Bob Moore notes, nothing was further from the truth. 'For the vast majority [of *onderduikers*] remaining in safety usually involved moving around', in addition to splitting up. In this respect, the situation of Leo Ullman, whose parents placed him with a sympathetic Dutch policeman while they themselves dived under separately in the country, was far more typical. The Franks' fellow German-Jewish emigrés Hilda and Herbert Boucher also moved around considerably before winding up in the small Frisian town of Sneek; the Bouchers did not have to face the frequent, agonising dilemma of having to entrust their children to strangers.

For both Otto Frank's family and Myrtil's, the family unit itself proved the pillar of survival. If nothing else, Myrtil, Flory, Dorrit and Sybil could tell themselves, as the apartment resonated from the blast of another mis-guided Allied bomb, or when they heard shots and screams in the night and wondered when their number would come up – if nothing else, they had each other.

Indeed, when it came down to it, that was *all* they had.

Years later, there was no doubt in Flory's mind that this was one of the main reasons why they did survive the entire dive.

'We were one of the few who were not separated. I *insisted* on the family staying together,' Flory said in 1979. 'I think this is one of the things that saved us.'

Then one day, in spring 1943, to her parents' and sister's consternation, Sybil started to turn blue.

It was to be expected over the course of such a long dive, that the Franks would someday face a medical crisis. Anne Frank writes about illness at several points in her journal. People, after all, became sick underground, just as they did above ground. As resistance to German rule hardened, especially amongst the medical profession, which called a protest strike on 22 April, there were doctors, nurses and medical technicians who could be persuaded to help. The Christian-inspired rescuer Corrie ten Boom writes in her memoir *The Hiding Place* of arranging an emergency appendectomy with the aid of sympathetic physicians.

One such doctor – possibly Tine's fiancé Willem, who is known to have made occasional house calls to number 14 – was summoned via Jeanne's underground contacts in order to examine Sybil. His prognosis was dire: Sybil had developed twin uteri, a serious condition that required an immediate operation. If she did not receive that operation, the resistance doctor said, she would die.

With their confederates' aid, the arrangements for the 'illicit' operation were quickly made. Bronovo Hospital, a Protestant teaching hospital, was, it was decided, the one that was best suited. The head nun agreed to keep Sybil's true identity a secret, telling only a few of the staff.

And so there Sybil was in the operating room of Bronovo Hospital, repeating her mantra to herself: 'I am not Billy – my name is Toni Muller . . . I am not Billy . . .'

The message got through to her subconscious: she remained Toni Muller, anaesthetic notwithstanding. The operation was a success. But she still had to get through her two-weeks' convalescence while maintaining her alias.

In the next bed to Sybil was Pru de Monchy, the daughter of S.J.R. de Monchy, the pre-war mayor of The Hague, whom the Nazis had dismissed in 1941. With admirable sang-froid – a quality she apparently inherited from her father – Sybil chatted away in flawless Dutch to her neighbour, with whose still popular father's name she was familiar.

Several days later, one of the nuns, innocent of Sybil's identity, stopped at the seventeen-year-old Jewish girl's bed in the recovery room at the hospital and asked which psalm she wished to have read to her.

'That's all right,' the young fugitive replied breezily, 'you choose.'

By the time she was ready to be released, Sybil had come to trust Pru de Monchy; she had reached the point where she didn't feel like lying to her any more – after all, she figured, she *was* the daughter of a known anti-Nazi.

'Give me your address,' Pru asked as Sybil was packing. 'I want to visit you.'

'I'm not the person you think I am,' Sybil said. 'I can't give you my address, but give me yours.' She did. *

About a week later, with Jeanne's help again, Sybil was smuggled back to her grateful family. She told them of her surprise meeting with the daughter of the former mayor of The Hague. The thing that astounded her the most, Sybil added, was the sight of other Jewish patients at the

---

* Later, after the liberation, Sybil would use it to visit her astonished friend.

hospital, wearing the yellow star on their hospital gowns. They had not yet been called up, or perhaps held valid exemptions approved by the *Joodsche Raad*. Anyway they felt secure enough to remain above ground and to enter hospital openly.

The sight had made her dizzy. Surely there was something wrong with this picture?

But there wasn't. *Pretend as if nothing will happen, and nothing will happen . . .*

The Franks knew how much they owed Jeanne and Annie and the other members of their support group.

How often did the band of helpers actually visit them? The memories of Dorrit, Sybil and Flory would later diverge on this point, as they did on others; unlike the *onderduikers* at 263 Prinsengracht, whose daily comings and goings were faithfully recorded by Anne Frank, none of The Hague Franks kept a journal that could settle the matter.

Dorrit, the most romantic, and the one who was most attached to her adopted homeland, would later recollect that their friends came every few days. Flory, perhaps more objectively, estimated that they visited once a week. Sybil, the least dewy-eyed of the family, would claim that they came less frequently even than that.

But Jeanne and Annie and Ans and Tine *did* come.

Years later, Jeanne downplayed the significance of her visits to number 14. 'I don't remember any heroic acts,' she said. 'Of course, if the Germans had come while any one of us were there, there would have been trouble, but that was the chance we took.'

In fact, most Dutch harboured few illusions about the penalties involved in assisting Jews in the way that Jeanne and the others did.

Louis de Jong, the first great historian of the Dutch Holocaust, who managed to escape Holland after the invasion and went to work for the government-in-exile in London, writes, 'Every non-Jew who helped Jews expected that if found out, he would be sent to a German concentration camp.'

So, then, why *did* they come?

Ernst Sittig, the nephew of Annie van der Sluijs, who later lived at 14 Pieter van den Zandestraat himself, interprets his aunt's motives this way:

I think that the Dutch, like most people, can be divided into 'good ones' and 'bad ones'. The bad ones cooperated with the Germans, the good ones opposed them.

Both groups can be divided into active and passive: The active bad ones voluntarily joined the German army or joined the NSB, the passive bad ones simply tolerated or supported the occupation, as so many Dutchmen did, especially in the years immediately following the invasion.

The active good ones joined the resistance and went as far as assassinating Germans and committing sabotage and getting involved with the underground press, or they rendered courier services, or they helped *onderduikers* like Annie and the others did. The passive good Dutch simply disagreed with the occupation, but were afraid to do anything about it.

Annie and her sisters and Jeanne belong to the active good group. They were raised in an atmosphere of very strict ethical awareness, so it wasn't more than logical that they all did what they did. It was what they had been brought up to do.

Some of the 'active' Dutch who helped *onderduikers* ran extraordinary suicidal risks to save their fellow men. Amongst this group was Corrie ten Boom, who in 1942 opened her Haarlem home to what would become a torrent of Jewish fugitives, in total disregard of the risks involved.

'No, no . . . how can I turn them away?' she said at one point, when asked to harbour yet another *onderduiker*. 'Bring them tonight, we'll manage.'

Inevitably, Ten Boom's underground organisation was betrayed and she was dispatched to Vught, the prison the Germans maintained for 'political' prisoners on Dutch soil, and then to the Ravensbruck concentration camp for women in Germany, which she miraculously survived.

Joop Westerweel, another Christian-impelled rescuer of Jews, ran a network which successfully smuggled an estimated 200 Dutch Jews across the Pyrenees to Spain before he was arrested, tortured and killed by the Gestapo in 1944.

Long may their names live, as well as those of Jeanne Guthschmidt, née Houtepen, Annie, Tine and Ans van der Sluijs, who, through efforts such as Jeanne's selfless decision to escort Sybil to Bronovo Hospital for her operation were the rescuers of the Franks.

The family's joy at Sybil's successful operation and safe return to number 14 was short-lived. Soon Myrtil's money ran short. As food supplies dwindled, so did morale.

The danger of betrayal remained a real and palpable one. Who could know when someone on their short street might need to buy something essential and be tempted to claim the increasingly lucrative bounties? The number of such denunciations was rising.

Meanwhile, spurred on by a number of politically disastrous moves on the part of the Germans, the Dutch nation moved to the edge of open revolt.

On 4 April, *The New York Times* reported that Kurt Daleuge, Heydrich's former police chief, had been transferred from Prague in order to bring the increasingly restive Dutch into line.

'There is no animosity in our hearts,' Seyss-Inquart had vowed three years before. But now, angered by student protests against the Nazi regime, he demanded in March that all Dutch university students sign a loyalty oath.

The response was overwhelming: over 85 per cent refused.

Then, in a particularly self-defeating move, General Christiansen, commander of the *Wehrmacht* in Holland, ordered the re-internment of all 300,000 members of the Dutch army, cancelling the amnesty they had been granted after the invasion, which had helped pacify the Dutch at the time.

The reaction, particularly in Dutch rural areas, which had not yet felt the brunt of the German heel, was incendiary. Factories, farms, mines and other businesses fell idle. In Friesland, farmers stopped milking their cows. In Hilversum, the 15,000 plus workforce at the Philips factories once again walked out, as they had (or most had) during the February 1941 strike. Schools emptied.

With one act, the Germans had managed to unite city and countryside.

Recovering from their initial surprise, Rauter and Seyss-Inquart moved ruthlessly. Civil law was suspended. Rauter gave police permission to fire without warning on any assembly of more than a few persons. Martial law was imposed in five rural Dutch towns, including the largest, Hengelo.

Eighty strikers around the country were summarily executed. Ninety-five more were shot down in the street.

The Dutch government-in-exile, no less surprised by the strike than the Nazis, was silent. For months, Radio Oranje had been exhorting the Dutch to resist, but now, as the strike wound down, it lost its tongue. Gerbrandy and his cabinet thought that the strike was premature. Better wait for the Second Front, they felt.

The strike was suppressed. However, the months of April and May 1943 marked a watershed in the relationship between the Germans and the Dutch.

Meanwhile, in Germany the factories that made material for the

Wehrmacht continued to experience a severe manpower shortage, due in part to the reverses on the Russian front. More and more able-bodied German workers were drafted into the armed forces, leaving a vacuum which, it was decreed, would be filled by foreign workers. On 4 May, it was announced that all Dutchmen between the ages of eighteen and thirty-five would be required to register for placement in the German war industry.

Many, including former soldiers, refused and dived under, creating a second large wave of *onderduikers*.

A national organisation, the *Landelijke Organisatie voor Hulp aan Onderduikers* – the National Organisation for Help to Divers – commonly known as the LO, sprang into being. Founded at the end of 1942, the LO, which Rauter referred to in his 26 March memorandum, had already organised its first 'swap meet', where ration tickets, contacts and addresses were exchanged. Now there were more such meets – as well as more people willing to help out. By 1944, it had become the largest and most effective arm of the resistance, with over 15,000 workers assisting or sheltering an estimated 200,000 to 300,000 people, including thousands of Jews who had belatedly submerged.

Nevertheless, as Corrie ten Boom writes, it was still too late to help many prospective Jewish *onderduikers*: 'It was getting harder and harder to find safe homes in the country for the scores of Jews who were passing through our underground station by early 1943. Even with ration cards and forged papers, there were not enough places for them all.'

Many people were simply too frightened of the consequences. One of these, as Ten Boom writes in one of the most searing passages of her book, was the pastor of her local church.

'I confess that I too am searching for something,' Ten Boom had told the priest, after he walked into her shop-cum-underground-station with a watch for repairs:

> The pastor's eyes clouded. 'Confess?' I drew him out the back door of the shop and up the stairs to the dining room. 'I confess that I too am searching for something.' The pastor's face was now wrinkled with a frown. 'Would you be willing to take a Jewish mother and her baby into your home? They will almost certainly be arrested otherwise.' Colour drained from the man's face. He took a step back . . . 'Miss Ten Boom! I do hope you're not involved with this illegal concealment and undercover business. It's just not safe.'

Ten Boom was fifty and lived with her octogenarian father and a sister, Betsie.

> On impulse I told the pastor to wait and ran upstairs. Betsie had put the newcomers in Willem's [Ten Boom's brother] old room. I asked the mother's permission to borrow the infant: the little infant weighed hardly anything in my arms. Back in the dining room I pulled the coverlet from the baby's face. There was a long silence. The man bent forward, his hand in spite of himself reaching for the tiny fist curled round the blanket. For a moment I saw compassion and fear struggle in his face.

Then the moment was lost: 'He [the priest] straightened. "No. Definitely not. We could lose our lives for that Jewish child!"'

Ten Boom's father, who would later die in jail after the family was given up by an anonymous informer in February 1944, had the last word in this dramatic exchange:

> Father held the baby close, his white beard brushing its cheek, looking into the little face with eyes as blue and innocent as the baby's own. At last he looked up at the pastor. 'You say we could lose our lives for this child. I would consider that the greatest honour that could come to my family.' The pastor turned sharply on his heels and walked out of the room.

(It should be noted for the record that Dutch clergymen from both the Catholic and Protestant faiths were jailed for resistance activities, including assisting *onderduikers*, and that several dozen died in German concentration camps.)

In Holland, as almost everywhere else in occupied Europe, courage – or the willingness to do their Christian duty, as Ten Boom, Joop Westerweel and others like them saw their rescue work – was in limited supply during the Holocaust. Although individual acts of resistance against the deportations continued, there were no known mass actions after the February 1941 strike.

It was also in limited supply at the Council, whose original mission – to assist the Jewish community – had, inevitably, deteriorated. As Louis de Jong writes:

> The members of [the Jewish Council], dominated by the Jewish bourgeoisie, realised from the start that they were going to act in a situation of extreme

gravity. They were ordinary, law-abiding, well-to-do citizens, decently brought up, and they never realised what the Germans were up to.

Having decided to act as a sort of separate Jewish administration, they adopted as their principle that they would never help in carrying out activities which, they stated, were 'contrary to Jewish honour'. The path of collaboration, however, is a most slippery one, and after some time a different principle came to dominate the proceedings and the activities of the Council. This was a most human, but given the circumstances, a most fatal principle: self-preservation.

In May, just as Otto Bene, the Foreign Office representative, had promised in his secret memo of October, the Jewish Council was instructed to select 7,000 – nearly half – of its hitherto 'exempt' staff for deportation. In effect, the Council was being asked to cannibalise itself. 'Panic broke out' at the Council offices in Amsterdam, but the order was carried out.

The trains from Westerbork kept rolling; however, it should be noted that there were some Germans stationed in Holland, both uniformed and civilian officials, who secretly rebelled at their assigned roles in the *Endlösung* and tried to sabotage the process. Foremost amongst these was Dr Hans Georg Calmeyer, a Nazi offical attached to the *Zentralstelle* who was in charge of judging the numerous appeals from Dutch Jews who protested their designation as Jewish, and claimed they were actually of 'Aryan' descent – something that several hundred Jews, in their desperation to save themselves from the transports, did. Thanks to Calmeyer's 'wilful gullibility' – as Moore puts it – and what he felt as his moral duty to save as many Jews as he could, a significant number survived.

Not all Germans were monsters. One prison doctor manufactured an artificial medical condition in order to get Betsie ten Boom, incarcerated for aiding her sister in sheltering Jews, released from jail. Later, after her older sister, Corrie, was imprisoned at Scheveningen prison (not far from where the Franks used to live), a guilt-stricken lieutenant confessed to her: 'I hate my work.'

Nevertheless there was a sufficient number who were willing to follow orders and fulfil their roles in the process of making Holland *Judenrein* – whether it be the clerks dutifully clacking away at their typewriters in the offices of IVB4 in The Hague, or the *Ordnungspolizei* who participated in the *razzias*, or the *Wehrmacht* soldiers who guarded the trains to Westerbork – more than sufficient to get the job done more thoroughly and conscientiously than virtually anywhere else in the Greater German Reich. And there were adequate Dutch collaborators to help them.

The deportations reached their peak in early June, with all sorts of logistical milestones set, including the largest transport yet, 3,006, routed to Sobibor, on 1 June; a special shipment consisting only of children – 1,266, to be precise – entrained four days after that; and two trains holding 5,414 Jews, which together accounted for more than 1 per cent of the total pre-war Dutch-Jewish population, shipped out on one day, bringing the total number for the month to a full 9,686. After that, the returns diminished. There were fewer Jews to be found – at least above ground.

By July, with over 80,000 Jews accounted for and shipped out – a full two thirds of the pre-war Dutch-Jewish population – Hans Albis Rauter was well on his way to fulfilling the promise he had made to his superior, Himmler, the previous summer. The *Schwerpunkt*, the main thrust, of the war against the Dutch Jews was over. The rest would be more or less a mopping-up operation.

July 1943 saw three more transports from Westerbork to the crematoria at Sobibor, one on 6 July containing 2,417 Jews, another the following Tuesday, the 13th, bearing 1,988, and one more on the 20th, which ferried yet another 2,209 Jews to their deaths, for a grand total for the month of 6,614. Henceforth, until the end of the deportations the following year, the monthly totals would be half that or less.

Amongst those transported on 20 July was Henri Edelsheim, the former head of the *Joodsche Raad*'s office in The Hague.

On 14 July, the four Franks numbly observed the first anniversary of their self-imprisonment at 14 Pieter van den Zandestraat.

Could we possibly have been here a year? the four *onderduikers* asked themselves.

Could it possibly be?

CHAPTER 9

The Girl Next Door

It was taking much too long. The constant fear and waiting were unbearable.
                                        Herbert Boucher, *Miracle of Survival*

Four years ago today catastrophe and the Germans came to Holland. Since then the Dutch in Holland and abroad, their exiled Government and their Queen, have lived with but one thought: preparation for the day of liberation and restoration. As that day draws nearer, they are becoming increasingly aware of one fact: whether liberation be near or far, when it comes there will be little left of the Holland of May 1940.
                                        The Times, 10 May 1944

And so, to their collective stupefaction, the Franks began the tenth year of their odyssey of flight from the Germans – a journey that had begun when they had first arrived in The Hague from Berlin – and their second year as *onderduikers*.

Interestingly, Flory, Dorrit and Sybil would later remember few events from this middle phase of their submersion.

'It's funny,' Flory said, looking back. 'Those three years seem to melt together. You get used to the idea that the outside doesn't exist.'

Summer melted into autumn, autumn into winter. The basic routine continued: the Franks got up, did their exercises, sewed, read, laughed, argued, worried, went to sleep – when they could get to sleep – got up again, and tried to pretend that the outside world really didn't exist.

The occasional mis-targeted Allied bomb tended to shatter this illusion, of course.

Myrtil and their Dutch friends did bring news from The Outside, some of which was actually encouraging: in the Mediterranean, the Allies had invaded Sicily, then the Italian mainland. Mussolini had been ousted. But the Mediterranean was simply too far away. Unlike Anne Frank and other *onderduikers*, who obsessively followed the news throughout their time in hiding, her four kinsmen in The Hague cared only about when the Allies were finally going to invade Europe. However, Churchill and General Sir Alan Brooke delayed, wary of the casualties a premature operation would bring.

In Berlin, Joseph Goebbels told a German magazine in April that invasion of the Continent was 'a thing impossible'. The shock of Stalingrad had worn off. 'The Axis has a free hand in the East and commands all possibilities for the offensive,' he declared. Events on the 'periphery of the war' – by which the propaganda minister presumably was referring to the Russian front, where the *Wehrmacht* had largely gone on the defensive but still commanded large swathes of territory, and in North Africa, where the Germans had been completely evicted – were undergoing 'certain revisions'. But, he added, 'The centre is intact.'

As John Keegan notes, Goebbels's renewed confidence was not entirely misplaced:

> In midsummer 1943, a year before the Anglo-American invasion of Europe, Adolf Hitler's Wehrmacht still occupied all the territory it had gained in the blitzkrieg campaigns of 1939–41 and most of its Russian conquests of 1941–42. It also retained its foothold on the coast of North Africa . . . The Russian counteroffensives at Stalingrad and Kursk had pushed back the perimeter of Hitler's Europe in the east. Yet he or his allies still controlled the whole of mainland Europe, except for neutral Spain, Portugal, Switzerland, and Sweden. The Nazi war economy, though overshadowed by the growing power of America's, outmatched both that of Britain and that of the Soviet Union except in the key areas of tank and aircraft production. Without direct intervention by the western Allies on the continent – an intervention that would centre on the commitment of a large American army – Hitler could count on prolonging his military dominance for years to come.

The centre of Hitler's Third Reich, including the Netherlands and the other European countries Germany had overrun and annexed, was indeed intact.

Within the Frank household the tension and tedium of being in hiding were broken by the visits of Jeanne and Annie and her sisters. 'I don't think that I had dinner,' recalled Jeanne, who visited the fugitives after she finished work at a local bank. 'Anyway, that wouldn't have been proper, since the family needed its food for itself. They asked me what was going on in my life and what had happened to me, and I would try to tell them. Basically, I just tried to cheer them up.'

Sometimes, Flory recalled, Jeanne's chat about her life outside (where she had just become engaged) would have the opposite effect on Dorrit and Sybil. 'The girls would say, "Our youth goes," and I would say, "Be happy you are still alive." The girls would be envious of Jeanne, because she could still go out. And I would say, "Be happy you are still together. Other people are dispersed."'

Sometimes the Franks would allow their imaginations to wander into the past, back to the former days when they lived in a well-appointed apartment with a grand piano, a humming Chrysler at the ready, and a uniformed chauffeur named Schwann. But that wasn't a very constructive train of thought either. So the melancholy foursome would sit in the dark, distant from the world in which 'normal people' like Jeanne and Annie lived and loved or took strolls in the *Haagse Bos*, or along the Noordeinde, one of the main shopping streets of The Hague, which was located a few blocks away from Pieter van den Zandestraat; the world in which they could go to the cinema (though that meant having to sit through Nazi propaganda films these days); a world still firmly controlled by Arthur Seyss-Inquart, who lived on a great estate in *Clingendael*, near the Scheveningen dunes, with his devoutly fascist wife, Gerda, and his daughter; a world in which a joint German–Dutch team of detectives assigned to the offices of IVB4 were out hunting 'criminals' like the Franks at this very moment.

Myrtil, the commander and quartermaster of the cell, continued with his hair-raising sorties into The Outside, cautiously emerging from the flat, screwing up his features into his doctor persona before he opened the door, and swimming back with parcels of food and other items he somehow obtained from his friend L., the art dealer, or some other black-market contact.

It was always a shock – a welcome shock, of course – when he returned. For a moment he would decompress, re-adjusting to the dim light and rancid air of the flat. Then, like the proverbial hunter-gatherer, he would reveal his harvest.

'I remember once we got strawberries,' Sybil recalled. '*That* was an event.'

'Once 'Til brought back some baking chocolate,' said Flory, recalling another Santa Claus-like moment. 'We also had a little pastille to make tea. Of course, there was no coffee, just substitute coffee, but we were glad to have that as well.'

Sometimes, to supplement food supplies, Myrtil would also bring reading material: penny dreadfuls, old travel books, even American magazines, like *Esquire*; apparently L. was a subscriber. Flory recalled an advertisement in one of these which seemed to sum up both the pathos and the absurdity of their predicament. 'One of [the magazines] showed a cartoon of a girl staring at her naked boyfriend and saying, "Clothes certainly *do* make the man." I'll never forget that.'

Amongst the diverse reading material Myrtil brought back with him to number 14 was an old novel called *Juan in America* by Eric Linklater. By this time, the entire family had read or reread the book and were familiar with the *dramatis personae*, one of whom was named 'Crying Wonnie'. 'And now Crying Wonnie is going to sleep!' Myrtil said one night, as the four of them turned in, creating a much-needed spring of laughter, as well as a catchy *nom de guerre* for the Jewish swashbuckler. From that point on, Myrtil Frank was also known as Wonnie.

Humour didn't always work. Within their flat, the Franks had comparatively little room to move – certainly much less than, for example, their eight fellow *onderduikers* at 263 Prinsengracht, Amsterdam. Otto Frank's family were sometimes able to leave their 'secret annexe' and walk around his empty offices (which might ultimately have been their undoing). They had much more room to move and stretch out, as did the eight *onderduikers* Corrie ten Boom sheltered, who normally had the run of her house.

Everything is relative: some *onderduikers*, including ones who were wedged into spaces above toilets (as one Jewish Hagenaar was), had to make do with much less.

For some, the stress of prolonged indeterminate confinement, combined with the feeling that they were being watched (which all *onderduikers* had to assume), had physical side-effects. One Jewish boy was reported to have lost his power of speech after being left alone in a room for six months. Others suffered long depressive bouts. There were suicides. A few who felt that they couldn't take the strain of remaining underground even gave themselves up and allowed themselves to be deported. Some caused such difficulties for their hosts that they were forced to surface and look for other hiding places – or had to flee because their hosts themselves went mad with the strain; apparently this was what occurred to Corrie ten Boom's sister, who one day inexplicably went to the authorities to report herself for giving shelter to *onderduikers*. She was immediately imprisoned.

As Anne Frank records in *Het Achterhuis* – or *The Secret Annexe* – as her wartime journal was originally entitled, by their second year in hiding, the eight *onderduikers* at 263 Prinsengracht were beginning to get on each other's nerves. A major point of irritation was money – or the lack of it. In November 1943, their 'sublessees', the Pelses, exhausted the funds which they had brought with them, which led to considerable strife.

At 14 Pieter van den Zandestraat, money was also shrinking, but Myrtil still had some cash. He kept what he had with Annie, a precaution against thieves and robbers, another problem as the desperation of the general populace rose.

Mostly, however, there was simply too much togetherness.

'It was not easy to have three women living together the whole day,' said Jeanne. 'Flory was a dear – at least to me she always seemed a dear. But sometimes Dorrit and Sybil would get crazy.'

Sometimes pressures from outside the hiding place – fear of being watched, of betrayal, and of being bombed – combined with tensions from within to cause an explosion.

'Sometimes we were not sensitive to each other's feelings,' Sybil put it, diplomatically.

So the Franks bickered, or rather, pantomime-bickered, making contorted gestures with their faces to compensate for their necessarily muted voices, while above ground, the destruction of Dutch Jewry entered its final act.

On 29 September, the last large-scale round-up of Jews in Amsterdam took place. Over 10,000, including Asscher and Cohen, the leaders of the *Joodsche Raad*, were sent to the Nazis' 'model concentration camp' at Theresienstadt, before ultimately being shipped to Bergen-Belsen. The two would survive the war, but most of their staff perished.

A photo taken in Amsterdam at the pre-assembly point on the Polderweg, after one of the last *razzias*, captures the desperate mood of the deportees. Dated May 1943, it shows a large group of dazed and despondent people sitting with their luggage. A Good Samaritan nurse, perhaps from the Red Cross, is standing amidst this sea of despair with a cup of water, trying her best to help. And in the centre of the picture, a girl of seven or eight, a yellow star affixed to her dress, her hair neatly done up as if for a Sunday outing, faces the camera with a baffled look.

At Westerbork, fewer carriages were needed now. But still the trains continued to roll. September saw the last three shipments to Sobibor: on 7 September one with 987 'passengers'; on the 14th another with 1,005 – the last train carrying more than 1,000 deportees. One more on 26 September contained 979 of the condemned. Thenceforth – with the exception of the Theresienstadt train carrying Asscher and Cohen and other 'privileged' prisoners – trains from Westerbork would once more be routed to Auschwitz or Bergen-Belsen, where there was capacity again.

Rauter had fulfilled his promise to Himmler. The previous July he had assumed that the deportation of the bulk of Holland's Jewish population could be accomplished in fourteen months. By October 1943, some 90,324 Jews – close to 70 per cent of Holland's pre-war Jewish population – had successfully been deported to the camps.

In neighbouring Belgium, following one of the last *razzias* in that country, on 3 September 1943, 'such a significant protest erupted from civilian and religious leaders that the apprehended Jews were released', notes Gerald Reitlinger in *The Final Solution*, one of the first major postwar studies of the Holocaust. In November 1943, as previously noted, in a truly inspiring episode of resistance, large numbers of Danes banded together to rescue the bulk of Denmark's small population of 7,000 Jews and smuggle them across the Baltic to neutral Sweden, directly under the Germans' noses, thus providing one of the few 'happy-ending' stories of the Nazi genocide.

But there were no such happy endings in Holland.

As the Dutch journalist Geert Mak writes in *Amsterdam*, his popular biography of the city, the Dutch had become numbed to the sight of the trucks and trains taking Jews away: 'The shock had dissipated.' Just as during the French Revolution, 'the first tumbril on its way to the guillotine had been an event, the tenth no longer attracted comment'.

On 5 October, Seyss-Inquart issued instructions for the treatment of those Jews who had not been deported, including the 8,610 Jews in mixed marriages – many of whom would soon be deported nevertheless – plus those with 'exotic exemptions', amongst them a German-Jewish Olympic champion, and the son-in-law of the former royal librarian. Holland's 'Jewish problem' had been reduced to a manageable size.

That left the estimated 20,000 Jews who had dived under and who had not been discovered or betrayed. However, given the excellent progress that had been made as the temptation to claim the bounties on Jewish fugitives increased, the Germans were confident that they would ultimately succeed on that front. Most of the recalcitrant members of that group would either be discovered and deported, or would perish underground because their supplies had run out.

The Germans also reported success in apprehending those who helped them. Corrie ten Boom had been betrayed and arrested in February 1944, though the eight Jews she was sheltering at that time miraculously escaped detection. All in all, the German authorities were pleased with their progress in this area as well.

The harrowing silence in the former Jewish areas of Amsterdam, including the River Quarter, where both Frank families had once lived, where entire streets which once had teemed with life stood deserted, bore mute testament to the Germans' outstanding success. Grete Weil in her book *Tramhalte Beethovenstraat* (*Tramstop Beethovenstraat*) described just such a street, now inhabited only by a handful of *onderduikers* or Jews with false ID:

> In the Beethovenstraat the nights were still. Now and then a car passed by, sometimes [the *onderduikers*] heard footsteps and pricked up their ears. If this was the sound of jackboots, they crouched motionless. Often there was an air-raid warning, the crack of anti-aircraft guns, the bombers on their way to Germany overhead. Then again the sirens and the silence. The silence drove away sleep, just the silence.

By now, there were also equally haunted streets in the former Jewish section of The Hague. What had happened to the people who had once lived there?

The absence of news from the deportees spurred fears that they had come to an untimely end. At Westerbork, where Dorrit's friend Gerda Buchsbaum was still incarcerated with other members of her family, there was now a clearer picture of what awaited them and their fellow prisoners once the doors of the cattle cars were opened at Auschwitz, thanks to the descriptive notes some deportees left behind and which were then sent back to Westerbork. The inmates now knew that there was a large chimney that belched a greyish smoke, according to the postwar memoir of Gerda's brother Norbert, *Fotograaf Zonder Camera* (*Photographer without a Camera*).

Still, as Greda's brother writes, the inmates had trouble putting it all together. Why, when the Germans had so many other things to be concerned about, would they be going to so much trouble and expense to exterminate the Jews? It couldn't be. It just didn't make sense.

In London, a similar attitude of denial prevailed amongst the Dutch government-in-exile, despite the increasingly disturbing reports about the camps in Germany and Poland (already well documented by Allied aerial reconnaissance). A year before, at the start of the transports, Prime Minister Gerbrandy had blasted the Germans' 'satanic' plan for deporting Holland's Jews. However, as his aide Louis de Jong recounts, when presented with documentation indicating just how diabolical that plan was, the Dutchman became sceptical. Several months before, Gerald Riegner, the representative of the World Jewish Congress in Geneva, had transmitted reports on the actual conditions of the camps. Additionally, De Jong had been informed by the Red Cross that his own father, mother and sister had been deported.

'I had but little hope that I would see them again, for I was one of the very few people in London who was convinced of the truth of what Riegner had reported,' De Jong, who would go on to publish the magisterial *History of the Netherlands in the Second World War*, told a Harvard audience forty-five years later.

> The Dutch Prime Minister, to name one, was not. In November 1943, he asked me to accompany him for a weekend stay in a cottage outside London. I put the Riegner papers in my bag. On the first evening, I said: 'Sir, I want you to read this.' He did. He looked at me in complete amazement. 'De Jong,' he said, 'do you believe this to be true?' I said: 'Yes.' Did I convince him? I am not entirely sure.

By way of showing why both Jews and Gentiles refused to believe such evidence of the genocide then already long under way, De Jong explained:

> Everyone knew that human history had been scarred by endless cruelties. But that thousands, nay millions, of human beings – men, women and children, the old and the young, the healthy and the infirm – would be killed, finished off, mechanically, industrially, so to speak, would be exterminated like vermin – that was a notion so alien to the human mind, an event so gruesome, so new, that the instincts, indeed the natural reaction of most people was: *it can't be true*.

Anne Frank believed it to be true. Another who believed the reports was Myrtil's brother, Julius. Still living in London, he had not heard from the Franks for four years, and had long since concluded that his brother, sister-in-law and two nieces had met a horrible fate at the hands of their former countrymen.

The Franks braced themselves for their second winter in hiding, busying themselves, finding solace in their routine chores. The numbing ritual of doing the laundry – 'I remember standing there with this plunger and doing the wash over and over in cold water,' Sybil said – the sullen meals, the sudden, explosive fights all continued. So did the sewing bees. In anticipation of the cold, the girls knitted sweaters, then unravelled them, then knitted them again.

They also continued to devour – and redevour – their small, motley and much-coveted library. While Dorrit read and reread the dog-eared copy of *Gone With the Wind*, Sybil devoted herself to her new passion: chemistry. The previous tenant Alfred Schnell, a former chemist, who was now in hiding with his wife near Zwolle with Annie's help, had left behind a number of his professional texts. For Sybil, with her propensity for 'practical' subjects, the cache of chemistry books was a welcome diversion from life underground and a beacon of hope for a possible future as a chemist herself.

'I started worrying what I was going to be,' she said, 'and there were these books. We had no control over anything else but this was something that involved planning. This was the only part of my destiny I could control. I thought I wouldn't have a chance without a career.'

Lights-out for the Franks was generally about 8.30 p.m., or just before the citywide blackout. Occasionally, as they looked outside, they could see someone walking by with a torch with the mandated blue filter.

Then they went to bed.

Sometimes Sybil would take her manuals with her, reading the pages as best she could with a torch that she aimed through a small hole in her blanket. Dorrit tossed and turned, while her parents, who had long before the war stopped sharing a bed, fitfully became reacquainted with each other.

The front window of number 14 provided additional diversion as the war went on. The girls were under strict instructions not to touch the opaque muslin curtains, but after fifteen months of peering, they could see right through them.

No more than a hundred souls lived on the cobblestoned street and there was so little pedestrian traffic that seeing anything or anyone was an event.

'We would memorise every mannerism of every person who passed by,' Sybil recalled. 'We gave pretend names to them. One of our neighbours we called Slimmy, another Blond. Then there was the lady across the street who came with a bucket of water to clean the pavement. We used to be able to tell the time by her. Every Friday, come hell or high water, she would pitch the water out, like a good Dutchwoman, and then retreat into the house. This was a very big deal for us.'

Less diverting was the sight of the girl across the street and the disturbing company she kept.

'We always saw her bringing home German soldiers,' said Dorrit. Sometimes, she recalled, when the visitors were officers there would be a German staff car waiting outside. Evidently their neighbour was selective about the company she kept.

With food and necessities in increasingly short supply, there were many Dutchwomen who were willing to thus lend themselves to the occupiers for a night or more. Or perhaps the girl across the street was one of Mussert's followers, who believed – as the faux-Napoleon put it in a speech – 'that the Germanic tree [had] many branches'. Neither Dorrit nor Sybil cared. They knew that that NSB woman, or whatever she was, was a danger.

Then, one day in December, the sisters looked out of their window and saw snow. Another winter had come.

Collaborating with the Germans was becaming a dangerous business by 1943. The Dutch fascist Seyffardt was assassinated, followed by the NSB propaganda chief, H. Reydon. More garden-variety quislings were also gunned down. Among the more graphic images from the period is a police photo, dated 29 September 1943, showing one such turncoat, evidently surprised while he was bicycling, sprawled face down on a *Benoordenhout* street, blood running from his head. Another, from March 1944, depicts an assassinated *V-mann* – as the Germans' Dutch undercover men were called – by the name of Peter Mansen lying on another Haagse street after a similar attack.

The reckoning was beginning.

The question of collaboration and retribution was increasingly on the mind of the Dutch government-in-exile, just as it was on the minds of the French, Norwegians, Belgians, Poles and Czechs.

Who exactly *was* a collaborator? an article in *The Times* of 10 May 1944 asked. The newspaper divided collaborators into three types, similar to the basic distinctions the Dutch government would draw. 'Some civil servants,' it pointed out, 'have collaborated with the occupying power for the good of the people.' Those who helped enforce the country's rationing system, for example, fell into that category. 'But,' the correspondent continued, 'there have been weak men who went beyond what was necessary. And there have been collaborators who have given their wholehearted support to the enemy.'

Ultimately every occupied European country would define these categories differently. The Dutch government-in-exile, with its relish for organisation, set up a special postwar juridical authority in 1943, a full year before D-Day. The authority promised to be a harsh one; contrary to established Dutch practice, it was slated to include military officials. A new set of laws was enacted for the prosecution of German high officials, and those Dutchmen who fitted into the third, 'wholehearted' category of collaborators and could be adjudged as war criminals.

Thus at least a year before the three major Allied powers – the US, Great Britain and the Soviet Union – had laid the groundwork for the postwar crimes tribunal ultimately known as the Nuremberg trials, the Dutch had made preparations for their own private reckoning.

Nevertheless, the pool of Dutch fascists willing to give the occupying power their wholehearted support remained strong. In February 1944 the Germans established a new police academy in Schalkhaar in order to train a newly recruited, ideologically committed corps of Dutch policemen willing to fight for the new order in the Netherlands and combat the increasingly brazen but disorganised forces of the resistance.

In February, Heinrich Himmler made his second and last visit to Holland. One of the highlights of the SS *Reichsführer's* visit was his attendance at the inauguration of the new police academy. A photo of his visit shows him receiving the crisp salute of a group of newly minted Dutch police. Accompanying him are Rauter and Seyss-Inquart.

In 1942, *The New York Times* had prophesied that Himmler would become Holland's modern-day equivalent of the Duke of Alva, Philip II's cruel Dutch proconsol. Two years later, Himmler, and Rauter, his chief adjutant in Holland, had already fulfilled that bloody prophecy. Thousands more Dutchmen had died, including both resistance fighters and innocent Dutch hostages, and tens of thousands of Dutch Jews had already been murdered or were soon to be in the SS extermination camps in the East. Himmler's name was now second only to Hitler's on the list of war criminals the Allies had already drawn up.

Nevertheless, to judge from Himmler's confident look in the photograph, the year could still be 1942. Only the careworn expression of *Reichskommissar* Seyss-Inquart, exhausted and preoccupied with worries about the now imminent Allied invasion, indicates that the photograph was taken in 1944.

Several weeks later, in March, Seyss-Inquart gave his blessing to yet another new Dutch Nazi grouping, the *Landwacht*, a group of home-grown Nazis who, with no formal training, agreed to act as an auxiliary police force. Committed to act against their countrymen as the eyes, ears, legs and arms of the Germans, this untrained but enthusiastic group of uniformed hooligans was responsible for numerous atrocities during the last two years of the war. In the last phase of the *onderduiker* war the *Landwacht* also helped out with the large-scale manhunt that Rauter launched later in the year in the *onderduikersparadijs* – underground paradise – which was reputed to exist in the *Noordoostpolder*. This was the same polder that Dorrit had gazed out on en route to visit Edgar in Westerbork two years before. Scores of divers, including Jewish divers, were successfully flushed out.

The trains from Westerbork continued to run. On 3 March, a train-load of 240 was sent to Auschwitz and immediately dispatched. On 23 March, the next train, with 599, was sent to Bergen-Belsen. In March 1944, Rauter proudly informed Himmler that 'in ten days' time the last pure Jew will be sent East from Westerbork'. As far as the Jews of Holland were concerned, the SS had met its objective, or very nearly so.

That just left the *onderduikers*. Bounties were raised in order to assist the searchers. Earlier, after the first great wave of *onderduikers* dived under, a worthwhile tip phoned into the local Gestapo headquarters might net the successful informer five guilders; now, in 1944, a productive lead was worth as much as seventy-five guilders, no mean sum in poverty-stricken Holland. For a few enterprising, cold-blooded types – including one Jewish woman in Amsterdam who gave up several dozen of her fellow Jews – collecting bounties became a lucrative business.

On Sunday 5 March 1944, the Franks spent their six hundredth day in hiding.

They had many more to go.

PART FOUR

THE HUNGER WINTER
HOLLAND, 1944–45

CHAPTER 10

The Raid

[We must] demonstrate to the Dutch population that the Security Police is acting with special vigour under the present circumstances . . .
From a directive from German Security Police
Chief Karl Schoengarth, autumn 1944

The weeks before us will be the most difficult in the existence of our nation.
Radio Oranje broadcast, September 1944

No country has such claims on the Germans after the war as the Dutch.
The New York Times, 24 April 1945

'Take heart, downhearted Dutchmen, Belgians, Luxemburgers . . . deliverance is sure,' Winston Churchill had exhorted the countries of occupied Europe in a stirring BBC broadcast he made back in August 1941. Many had taken heart, but had lost it once more after the invasion of western Europe was postponed in favour of the more circuitous route of liberating the Continent via Sicily and the Italian boot. It was not until September 1943 that Allied forces finally landed on the European mainland at Salerno. In the winter of 1944, reports of the invasion force assembling across the Channel drifted westward and the rumours and hopes began again.

'Invasion fever is mounting daily throughout the country,' Anne Frank wrote on 4 February 1944.

In Haarlem, Corrie ten Boom, whose underground network was still in operation, had also caught invasion fever: 'There is a revolution in Europe!' she and her friends rejoiced. 'The war cannot last three weeks!'

Flory and Myrtil were sceptical, as were Dorrit and Sybil.

Myrtil first overheard the invasion rumours at the corner grocery shop during one of his increasingly infrequent sorties outdoors that winter. Could it be? After all those delays, were the Allies finally coming?

The RAF and the USAAF struck hundreds of targets along the Channel coast including many near The Hague, scaring the Franks and their neighbours, legal and otherwise, out of their wits, while again raising their hopes. Maybe, they thought, as they emerged from under the living room table after yet another raid, maybe this time there was something to the rumours.

At the Big Three summit at Tehran in November, Roosevelt and Stalin had combined against the yet reluctant British to force the adoption of May 1944 as the unalterable date for the invasion of Europe. Eventually the date for Operation Overlord, as the combined assault by British and American forces was now called, was postponed one more month, to the first week of June.

With even the Germans conceding that a cross-Channel attack was imminent, the principal remaining mystery was where on the Continent the long-anticipated blow would fall. The best guess of German intelligence was that it would come somewhere in France, probably in the Calais area, while Normandy remained a possibility. Seconding that opinion, Hitler, with the concurrence of the German High Command, moved his strongest forces to the Calais area.

The mid-Dutch coast, closer to England than Normandy, remained a possibility, albeit a more remote one. Still, the Germans couldn't afford to discount it. As the English magazine *Travel* noted in a feature about Holland published in June:

All those parts of The Netherlands, Belgium, and France that are accessible to an Army invading by water while protected overhead by fighter airplanes constitute the so-called invasion coast. Obviously it will be much simpler for the Germans to hurry their reinforcements to any point than it will be for the Allies to get men and heavy equipment across the Channel, whose notoriously bad weather is an added hazard . . .

Free Netherlands reports from London have included information that the approaches to The Hague, as well as many buildings up and down the coast immediately behind the high sand dunes, have been razed by the enemy to clear away obstructions and provide elbow room for fighting.

The Free Netherlands reports were true. Having already turned Scheveningen and the northern part of The Hague into a giant tank trap, under the supervision of Erwin Rommel, now commander of the Atlantic Wall, the entire area around *Festung Scheveningen* continued to be reinforced through the late spring. Large areas of western Holland were flooded and additional flooding was prepared by mining the dykes and pumping stations that helped keep low-lying Holland dry.

Like most Dutchmen, the Franks feared what would happen to their country if it became an invasion zone. And yet there was something exciting about the idea of the Allies storming ashore at Scheveningen.

In The Hague, as well as elsewhere in the western part of their small country, long lines of silent people waited for their increasingly meagre rations at bakers, butchers and greengrocers, while other shops, bereft of anything to sell, displayed empty wrappings instead of goods. Even though the Germans might well have failed at their original goal of absorbing Holland into the Reich, Seyss-Inquart and his colleagues had clearly succeeded in looting its economy.

Now it was the Nazis' turn to reap the whirlwind. Like his colleagues in occupied Belgium and France, Seyss-Inquart, ensconced in Wilhelmina's confiscated estate in Wassenaar and one of the last legal residents of evacuated, fortified Scheveningen, anxiously peered out to sea, trying to divine the Allies' intentions.

The blow, the Allied planners at SHAEF soon decided, would fall in France. Pas-de-Calais. Hitler was sure of it. So were Rommel and most of the rest of the German High Command. SHAEF's massive pre-invasion aerial campaign involved two thirds of the 195,000 tons of bombs being dropped outside the actual invasion area, including on Belgium and Holland. Allied deception technique also included creating a 'phantom' army based in south-east England under George S. Patton.

And so, early on the morning of 6 June 1944, as Cornelius Ryan memorably records in *The Longest Day*, Major Werner Pluskat, a battery commander defending what the Allies knew as Omaha Beach, the principal designated leading beach for American assault forces at Normandy, wearily scanned the horizon with his binoculars:

He reached the dead centre of the bay. The glasses stopped moving. Pluskat tensed, stared hard.

Through the scattering, thinning mist the horizon was magically filling with ships that casually manoeuvred back and forth as though they had been there for hours. There appeared to be thousands of them. It was a ghostly armada that somehow had appeared from nowhere. Pluskat stared in frozen disbelief, speechless, moved as he had never been before in his life. At that moment the world of the good soldier Pluskat began falling apart. He knew that [he later told Ryan] that in those first few moments he knew, calmly and surely, that 'this was the end of Germany'.

Transfixed, Pluskat dutifully telephoned regimental headquarters with the news. 'Block,' he informed his commander, 'it's the invasion. There must be ten thousand ships out there.'

Block was sceptical: 'Get hold of yourself, Pluskat!' he snapped. 'The Americans and British together don't have that many ships!'

Hitler was also sceptical. Convinced that the landings were a diversion from an even larger invasion of Calais, the master strategist of the German armed forces refused to release the reinforcements needed for a counter-assault at Normandy. Despite a near-disaster at Omaha, the invasion, the largest amphibious assault in history, was a success. By nightfall on 6 June British and Americans troops had successfully overcome opposition at all five landing beaches and had linked up with paratroops to create a bridgehead on German-held soil. The bridgehead was widened.

At 9.33 a.m., Eisenhower's press aide, Colonel Ernest Dupuy, broadcast the announcement that Europe and the world had been anxiously waiting for: 'Under the command of General Eisenhower, Allied naval forces began landing Allied armies this morning on the northern coast of France.'

Morning had come to occupied Europe.

Lacking a proper radio, the Franks did not hear Dupuy's dramatic announcement, but they did hear about the Normandy landings from Jeanne.

Like all freedom-loving Dutchmen, they cheered the news of the Allies' breakout from the Cotentin peninsula in late July, the virtually unopposed Allied landings in southern France in early August, the ecstatic liberation of Paris on 21 August.

The summer of '44 was the hottest summer in recent Dutch history. Unable to go outside like their neighbours, the Franks baked inside their diving bell. But they didn't mind. Deliverance was near – and it seemed to be drawing closer by the day.

On 10 June, four days after the invasion, Anton Mussert, who in 1942 had been given by Hitler the meaningless honorific title Leader of the Dutch

People, told an Amsterdam meeting of the NSB that the moment Allied troops set foot on Dutch soil he would enlist in the *Wehrmacht* as a private, a statement which purportedly moved those in attendance 'to tears'.

On 7 July 1944, a month after D-Day, in one of the most remarkable precision-bombing raids of the war, a group of British fighters suddenly swept in from the North Sea and made a run at The Hague city centre. Their target was the Central Population Registry. Housed in the former Kleykamp Gallery near the Peace Palace, just a quarter of a mile away from Pieter van den Zandestraat, the registry was one of the Germans' main repositories of information on the resistance. The raid, which the Franks heard from their hiding place, was a complete success. The gallery-turned-archive was destroyed, considerably hindering the German anti-resistance effort, while causing virtually no collateral damage to other nearby buildings. This impressive proof of RAF marksmanship showed the improving coordination between the resistance and London, and was an exciting omen.

In late July came word of the attempt on Hitler's life by a group of German officers at the *Führer's* so called Wolf's Lair near Rastenberg. Now even the *Wehrmacht* – or at least elements of it – were in open revolt. That was another good omen.

The scent of victory and of imminent liberation continued to hang in the air over Holland through the last two weeks of August and the first week of September, as Montgomery's 21st Army Group, spearheaded by George Patton's fast-moving Third Army, wheeled eastwards from Paris and poured into occupied Belgium, easily pushing aside the resistance offered by the stunned German defenders.

There was promising news from elsewhere in once impregnable *Festung Europa*, as the pillars of the Third Reich began to buckle. On 23 August Romania, which had suffered its own reign of terror under the Iron Guard, a particularly vicious indigenous quisling group, also capitulated. Adolf Eichmann tried to organise the deportation of Romania's 400,000 Jews, but was frustrated.

That same month, Finland, which had joined Germany as a co-belligerent against Russia in 1941 in hopes of regaining the territory it had lost after the Winter War and which, to both Eichmann's and Himmler's fury, had refused to give up its tiny population of Jews to the SS – put out feelers for a second and final armistice with the USSR, and prepared to swing its guns against its German friends.

Meanwhile the Allies had begun to uncover evidence of the *Endlösung*.

On 24 July, the Russians, advancing into Poland, overran Lublin and liberated the Nazi concentration camp at Majdanek. On 23 August, Drancy, the French equivalent of Westerbork, where 60,000 of France's 300,000 Jews had been processed for 'labour deployment in the East', was freed. But it would not be until spring of the final year of the war that the major extermination camps were liberated and the full truth of the *Endlösung* would be known.

The Gerbrandy government, which had begun plans for the repatriation of its citizens – including Jews – from the East, remained in denial about the camps in Germany and Poland. According to Dienke Hondius, as late as May 1944, Dutch officials expected to repatriate at least 60,000 Dutch Jews – most of those deported – out of an expected total of 700,000 repatriates. They discounted information about conditions in the camps from one of their own agents, H. Dentz. As Hondius notes, Dentz, a well-connected tobacco merchant who conducted an investigation of the situation, 'wrote frankly of mass murder, providing data which later proved highly reliable but was rejected by many at the time of its release as unimaginable or unbelievable. So unimaginable that Ferwerda, his direct superior, scrapped a number of stories of events in the Polish concentration camps.'

The optimism of the government notwithstanding, in March 1944 Dentz asserted that 'not many' Jews would ultimately return to Holland. But even he was not prepared for how few Dutch Jews would emerge from Auschwitz and the other camps to which they had been deported.

Montgomery's *blitzkrieg* rolled on. On 3 September there were wild scenes in Brussels as the Belgian capital was liberated. The following day, the 4th, it was Antwerp's turn. 'Peoples of Norway and Netherlands,' proclaimed an ebullient Eisenhower, directing his comments to the next two countries he expected to be freed, 'be confident that your day of liberation approaches.' Churchill added to the sense of anticipation around the country with his own rousing pre-liberation announcement.

In London, Queen Wilhelmina did her part to enhance the general high spirits by announcing that the Dutch resistance forces would henceforth be known as the *Binnenlandse Strijdkrachten* (BS), the Dutch Forces of the Interior. Inspired by the example of the French, whose resistance, the *Maquis*, had been incorporated into Allied forces under their own commander, Koenig, the Dutch Queen told Eisenhower that she wished the same status for her fighters. Reluctantly, Eisenhower, who had had mixed results working with other resistance groups, agreed; it was hard, after all, to say no to Queen Wilhelmina. Henceforth captured Dutch resistance fighters would have to be treated by the Germans as prisoners-of-war, rather than *francs tireurs* to be shot on sight. The commander of the new force, Wilhelmina triumphantly announced over Radio Oranje, would be her son-in-law, Prince Bernhard.

False reports from the rapidly shifting battlefront led to self-intoxication. On Tuesday 5 September, the date known in Dutch history as *Dolle Dinsdag*, or Crazy Tuesday, Radio Oranje announced that Allied troops had catapulted across the Dutch–Belgian border and had liberated the town of Breda. Gerbrandy made it official. 'Now that the Allied armies have crossed the Dutch border in their irresistible advance,' he buoyantly declared, 'I wish to give a warm welcome to our Allies on our native soil . . . The hour of liberation has come,' he concluded his electrifying broadcast, after which he made preparations to fly back to his liberated homeland.

These heady proclamations led to mass hysteria. Swarms of excited Dutchmen and women, attired in the best outfits they could assemble from their threadbare wardrobes and including as many orange items as they could find, bore gifts and meagre refreshments to the roads leading to The Hague and other big Dutch cities, and scanned the horizon for their putative liberators. Rumour had it that the advancing troops included the Princess Irene Brigade, as the Free Dutch forces based in London were by then called. Dutch liberating the Dutch. That would certainly be sweet!

The contagion was general. In Leiden, next door, an underground newspaper confidently published a liberation special. In the town of Axel, in the south-west of Holland, German troops surrendered to Dutch policemen. In Naarden, the Nazi mayor handed his pistol to his secretary. People spoke of having seen British tanks in Rotterdam.

'The entire country was in an uproar,' writes Dorrit's old Scheveningen friend and (unbeknownst to either) fellow *onderduiker*, Edith Velmans, then living in Breda, in the south-east of the country, under an assumed name:

> We were sure the end had come. In Breda, what had been a trickle of retreating Germans suddenly turned into a flood. There they came, the enemy, looking beaten and discouraged, in army trucks, civilian cars and even farm tractors. Some were on bicycles, some came on foot, pushing baby carriages loaded with barrels and boxes. Stolen booty, we knew.

> . . . Strengthened by the discouraged air of this rag-tag army, we were
> sure that that this was the moment we had been waiting for so long. We came
> out of our houses and positioned ourselves boldly in the street, staring at the
> Germans, giving them ugly looks of silent accusation.

Thus emboldened, leaders of the Dutch resistance prepared to take
control of the country from the shaken Germans.

Seyss-Inquart demonstrated his nervousness on 4 September, the date
of Antwerp's freedom, by declaring a state of emergency and making
flight from occupied Holland a punishable offence. Before this he had
packed his wife off to Salzburg, together with the Nazi couple's pet dog
and five pieces of luggage.

The NSB hastily organised an automobile caravan to Germany, where
they presumably would be more welcome. Instead of enlisting in the
Wehrmacht, a mortified Mussert looked on as his ten-year-old party and
movement dissolved. Suddenly, the once omnipresent NSB was no more.
It was not missed, either by its countrymen or by the Germans, who had
never considered it much more than a nuisance.

Undeterred by Seyss-Inquart's proclamation, many NSB members fled
to the northern province of Drenthe, where, in an interesting twist of fate,
they were briefly incarcerated at Kamp Westerbork in order to undergo
delousing by the Jewish internees, a job which the latter, many of whom
presumably recognised their former tormentors, performed with élan.

The Franks heard the news of the 'liberation' on the evening of the 5th
from an ecstatic Jeanne, but decided to stay put until they had more concrete
proof. It was well that they did, for as the Dutch soon learned, Radio
Oranje was mistaken. Despite appearances, Breda had *not* been liberated
and Allied troops had *not* crossed the Dutch–Belgian border. Montgomery,
concerned that his fast-moving troops had outrun their supplies, ignored
the pleadings of Prince Bernhard and others and halted at Antwerp.

On Wednesday 6 September, the day after *Dolle Dinsdag* – Crazy
Tuesday – as it was called, reality sank in. It was too early to break out
the *jonge genever* (young gin) and orange dresses. A little more patience
was needed.

Some *onderduikers*, desperate to walk in the daylight of freedom again,
had emerged from their hiding places or otherwise given themselves away
(as Edith Velmans nearly had, in Breda). This did not necessarily please
the Germans, who were preoccupied with other matters, such as saving
their own skins. In most cases, the unfortunate divers were hastily

dispatched to Westerbork, where the commander, Gemmeker, following Eichmann's orders, and likewise interested in saving himself, had begun to wrap up operations.

Thus, on 3 September the 103rd – and, it would turn out, penultimate – trainload of Jewish prisoners to be deported to the East slowly chugged away from Westerbork, thanks to the Dutch State Railways, which had continued to cooperate with the SS and the Germans until the very end.

Amongst the 1,042 passengers on that train were Otto and Edith Frank, and their daughters Margot and Anne. A month earlier, on 4 August, the Franks and their fellow *onderduikers* behind the false bookcase at 263 Prinsengracht, Amsterdam, had been raided by the police. It seemed that their 'secret annexe' had not been so secret after all. Someone, perhaps a neighbour, perhaps an acquaintance of Otto's, had given them up.

Despite the disillusioning aftermath of *Dolle Dinsdag*, many Dutchmen still felt that the end was near.

Wilhelmina and her staff certainly thought so. On the morning of Thursday 17 September, the Dutch Queen looked up and beheld a vast swarm of American and British glider planes and escort fighters headed across the Channel in the direction of Holland. The massive aerial armada, the largest in the short history of airborne operations, was part of Operation Market Garden, Montgomery's bold, if flawed, plan to end the war by laying down a 'carpet' of troops behind German lines in Holland, between Eindhoven and Arnhem, and then speeding on to Berlin.

Eisenhower had approved the controversial plan despite the protests of most of his American commanders, including Bradley and Patton, who preferred the broad-front strategy they had employed up to now with conspicuous success. Ike himself had misgivings about the plan. However, his need for another deep-water port in addition to Antwerp, and his desire to clear the Netherlands of the V-1 missiles the Germans continued to launch from Dutch sites, as well as the unstoppable (and as yet unpublicised) V-2s, led him to agree to Montgomery's daring gamble.

Gerbrandy, the irrepressible Dutch Prime Minister, was once again in high spirits on the morning of the 17th, as he prepared to make another triumphant broadcast over Radio Oranje. This one, he was sure, would not be premature, or misinformed. The Allies would be in Amsterdam within the week, he told his staff. Monty had personally told him so. This, Operation Market Garden, was 'the Sunday punch' that would knock the Germans out and end the war in Europe. Eisenhower also had convinced himself of the soundness of the operation. 'The hour for which you have been waiting has been struck,' he assured the Dutch nation. 'Now your full assistance and obedience to the order of the Supreme Command is necessary.'

CBS London bureau-chief Edward R. Murrow, riding with the airborne troops, broadcast his excited impressions as he flew in a C-47 over the war-weary country:

> Now we are over Holland. We're flying over a country that has been inundated. I can see a railway which still seems to be in operation, but some of the most civilised countryside in Europe now lies under water . . .
>
> We're now passing out of the flooded area, every ship still in perfect formation. The fighters are swirling around below us, going down to have a look at every hedgerow and every small wood that might conceal an ack-ack emplacement . . .
>
> . . . There's one burst of light flak; there's another. More tracers going across us and just ahead of our nose . . . More ships ahead of us are now dropping . . . you can see the men swinging down. In just about forty seconds now our ship will drop the men; the men will walk on Dutch soil. You can probably hear the snap as they check the lashing on the static line. There they go! Three! . . . four! . . . five! . . . six! . . . thirteen! . . . fourteen! . . . fifteen! . . . sixteen! Now every man is out . . .

And so, as the British 1st and American 82nd and 101st Airborne Divisions made their way to their drop zones in eastern Holland, Radio Oranje began its daily broadcast with the first four notes of Beethoven's Fifth Symphony and then issued a startling order: . . . 'On account of a request from Holland and after consultation with the Supreme Command, the [Dutch] Government is of the opinion that the moment has come to give instructions for a railway strike in order to hinder enemy transport and troop concentrations . . .'

The Dutch State Railways, which had efficiently transported over 100,000 Jews, tens of thousands of political prisoners and more than half a million forced labourers from Holland to German extermination camps, and other destinations, were now being asked to strike.

The railway's 30,000-odd employees, who had suffered from Allied fighter attacks and were also having doubts about their compliance with the Germans (doubts enhanced by the actions of the resistance) were, by this juncture of the war, in a mood to strike anyway. So, upon hearing the closest thing to a call for outright insurrection yet broadcast by Radio Oranje, the Dutch railway workers struck and made preparations to become *onderduikers* themselves. If they were successful, shipments of fuel, coal and military supplies would immediately cease, causing chaos for the authorities.

All was in readiness for the Dutch endgame.

The skies over eastern Holland were now covered with a sea of parachutes in red, green and cream – all appearing to spell out VICTORY. Panic gripped many Germans, including members of the SS, who took retributive action against the still captive Dutch population.

At Vught, the Dutch concentration camp, where Corrie ten Boom and other 'political prisoners' were incarcerated, the camp commander, with the full knowledge of Rauter, executed a large group of male prisoners. Ten Boom chillingly recalled: 'Rifle fire split the air . . . Around us women began to weep.'

Listening from her barracks to the volleys ring out, Ten Boom estimated that over 700 prisoners were executed. In fact, the actual figure was closer to 100. Nevertheless, the executions at Vught on 17 September were the greatest mass murder on Dutch soil since the sixteenth century.

Following the mass execution of the male prisoners, Ten Boom and the surviving female prisoners were packed posthaste onto a waiting train which set off for an unknown destination. Then, Ten Boom recalled, it was set upon by attackers, presumably either the BS or Allied troops who had landed near its path. Trapped inside the train with her fellow inmates, Ten Boom could hear the sound of machine-gun bullets bouncing off the side of the car like hail. For an hour the unseen battle – a spin-off of the larger operation under way that day – raged on. But the attack was not a success. The train crawled forward to its final destination, the concentration camp at Ravensbruck, Germany. Ten Boom was fortunate: she was finally released in March 1945.

Operation Market Garden, as readers of Cornelius Ryan's *A Bridge Too Far* will know, was not a success. Doomed by poor weather, inadequate leadership and flawed intelligence – which had failed to detect the presence of two heavily armed German divisions in the area of the drop zone – the assault immediately ran into trouble. Partly because of the poor roads in the area (which Bernhard claimed he warned Montgomery about), and despite the valiant skytroopers' (as paratroops were called in those days) best efforts, it took four days longer than expected to reach the crucial bridge at Arnhem – the bridge too far of Ryan's title – by which time the Germans were prepared for the roadborne relief column. They were captured or turned back. On the evening of 25 September a reluctant Montgomery withdrew his remaining troops across the Rhine under an umbrella of protective artillery fire in one of the outstanding Allied defeats of the Second World War and a crushing blow to Dutch morale.

The south-eastern corner of Holland, where Maastricht is located, had, however, been freed. 'Maastricht is a sea of orange!' Radio Oranje's reporter jubilantly declared on the 15th. But the western provinces, containing Holland's three largest cities, remained under the Nazi yoke. The four and a half million inhabitants of northwestern Holland found themselves penned inside one of Germany's last redoubts.

Half-hearted talk of another grand offensive across the Rhine quickly petered out as the new reality sank in. On 29 September, Eisenhower was forced to swallow his words. 'There are no signs of a collapse in muscle or will to defend Germany,' he conceded.

But bolstered by their unexpected victory in eastern Holland, German morale remained high.

As far as the Allies were concerned, another Arnhem was out of the question. Instead, while the Americans continued their broad offensive against Germany on the southern, 'right' wing, the British and the Canadians turned their attention to clearing the Germans out of the vast, treacherous *Schelde* area south of the Rhine, where they became bogged down in a bitter, costly and all but forgotten battle – the Battle of the Schelde – which would last for months.

Meanwhile, the 120,000 German troops in western Holland who were under the command of their resolute (and soon to be replaced) commander General Christiansen, prepared to make the *Randstad* a fortress for the defence of north-western Germany.

With the coal mines of Limburg, in the liberated southern section of Holland, cut off from western Holland, the prospect of having to suffer winter without fuel or gas, and food supplies already running low, the people of the region braced themselves for the worst.

The Franks' own supplies were also running low, as were their spirits.

'That was the low point, after Arnhem,' Flory said. 'To come so far and to have our hopes shattered again.'

Concurrently, another evil had come into the life of both The Hague and London: the V-2, the world's first medium-range ballistic missile.

The British had begun to counter some of the threats posed by the V-2's predecessor, the V-1, thanks to RAF actions against sites in France. Then in early September the Germans launched their latest *Vergeltungswaffen*, or revenge weapons, across the Channel at London from mobile launchers stationed in The Hague. The first of the missiles, launched on 8 September, completed its 192-mile flight in five minutes and obliterated a row of houses in Staveley Road, killing three and injuring ten.

The V-1, flying horizontal with the ground, could be seen, as well as heard, before it landed, and the sudden silence after the engine cut out presaged a strike. As Edward Murrow told his listeners in a report about the missiles, the V-2 didn't herald its approach:

> [The V-2] arrives without a warning of any kind. The sound of the explosion is not like the crump of an old-fashioned bomb, or the flat crack of a flying bomb; the sound is perhaps heavier and more menacing because it comes without warning. Most people in war have been saved repeatedly by either seeing or hearing; neither sense provides warning or protection against this new weapon.
>
> These are days when a vivid imagination is a definite liability. There is nothing pleasant in contemplating the possibility, however remote, that a ton of high explosive may come through the roof without warning of any kind.

Murrow concluded his alarming report with some acquired British understatement, noting that 'there are good reasons for believing that the Germans are developing a rocket which may contain as much as eight tons of explosives. That would be eight times the size of the present rocket and, in the opinion of most people over here, definitely unpleasant.'

Four years before, after the invasion of the Low Countries, Churchill had warned of a 'long night of [Nazi] barbarism, made longer, darker, and more barbaric by the lights of perverted science'. But like the Messerschmitt jet fighter and most of the 'miracle weapons' that the Third Reich's devoted scientists developed during the final two years of the conflagration, the V-2 came on the scene too late to affect the course of the war. Fortunately, too, Werner von Braun and his fellow rocket engineers could not yet fire the lethal fifty-ton projectile at specific military or civilian targets.

Eisenhower agreed to Operation Market Garden in part to take out V-2s. After that operation failed to liberate the launch sites in The Hague, the only alternative was to remove the sites with strafing and bombing raids, which was not very effective, and disastrous for the people of the beleaguered Dutch city.

The V-2 offensive in the autumn of 1944 horrified the people of London, at least at first, before the London-can-take-it spirit again took hold, but it had no less an effect on the people of The Hague from whose streets and parks the frequently malfunctioning weapon was fired. One out of ten rockets exploded or fell short, obliterating entire blocks or streets. Like the rest of their neighbours, the Franks began the habit of counting after they heard the missiles' otherworldly roar. One Hagenaar remembered:

> Some rockets blew up on their launch stands, killing and injuring crew members; some failed to ignite at all. Others hung in the air for a moment, then crashed to earth and blew up or fell into the sea. Whenever civilians heard the roar of a rocket ignition, everyone would begin to count the seconds. After thirty seconds, they were safe; if the engine stopped after thirty seconds or more had gone by, the rocket would either crash into the North Sea or fall on the other side of the city.
>
> Rockets were seen blasting wildly over the city, out of control; shooting horizontally only to crash a few kilometers from the firing site. Most exploded on impact; if the warhead did not go off, German specialists would try to defuse it. Many of the failed shots fell on the residents of the city.

Sometimes, looking out of the window, the Franks could see the fire-breathing flash of the rockets' engines as they headed across the Channel.

'We were happy when they went away,' Dorrit admitted. 'Even if they were going to England, at least we knew they weren't coming at us!' So engrained was the rocket terror in Dorrit that one evening thirty years later, she was driven to hysterical tears during a showing of the movie *Fail-Safe* on American TV.

With the Allies temporarily at bay, and the Rhine once again an impenetrable barrier, the Germans felt they could act with impunity, unleashing a new reign of terror and setting the stage for a virtual civil war with the population. The time for trying to win over Dutch hearts and minds was long gone. Now there was indeed animosity in German hearts, as German actions in Holland for the duration would prove.

Seyss-Inquart was particularly incensed at the stubbornness of the striking Dutch railway workers. He was also under increasing pressure from Berlin to break the work stoppage, which threatened to interfere with supply shipments, including the shipment of parts and missiles for the high-priority V-2 programme.

Summoning the two top Dutch food officials, Dr H.M. Hirschfeld, Secretary-General for Trade and Agriculture, and Dr S.L. Louwes, head of the Office of Food Supply, he ordered the two hitherto compliant civil servants to call off the strike. Hirschfeld and Louwes refused point-blank. Seyss-Inquart replied that if they continued with their obstinacy, he would have no choice but to impose an embargo on inland shipping, knowing full well that this measure would mean famine for western Holland. Dutch officials still refused.

Seyss-Inquart offered double rations to railwaymen who agreed to return to work. Few did. The frustrated German functionary sent a telex to the leading papers, insisting that they publish editorials warning the strikers that if they didn't return to work a large part of the Dutch population would starve. The newspapers also refused. As punishment for such insolence, on 29 September the *Reichskommissar*, declaring 'biological war' on the Dutch, ordered the destruction of the presses of the *Haagsche Courant*, the city's leading newspaper.

At long last, the Dutch, as a people, were showing some solidarity.

Unfortunately, this came too late for the Jewish population of the Netherlands, most of whom had been killed at Auschwitz or Sobibor or, like Anne, Margot and Edith Frank, were still languishing somewhere within the Germans' murderous extended enterprise.

The final, 104th, trainload of Jews left Westerbork for the East on 5 September. As far as the SS was concerned, the books on the Jews of Holland were now closed. All told, including the last shipment, the Germans had rounded up 107,000 out of the 140,000 Dutch and 'stateless' Jews who had dutifully registered for the original 1941 census. This record was unmatched anywhere inside occupied western Europe.

Dentz, the tobacco merchant who had reported to the government-in-exile his initial findings regarding the deportations, was right: not many would return.

'We failed – we failed as a nation [to stop the killing],' said R. van der Veen, the Amsterdam bystander-turned-resistance-fighter interviewed in 1974 for *The World at War*.

Already the Dutch, contemplating the vacant houses that had once belonged to their deported Jewish neighbours and faced with the mounting evidence of what had truly happened to them, were asking themselves questions such as *Could we have done more? Should we have done more?*

Today, they ask them still.

The occupation authorities were still interested in the whereabouts of Jews. Tips about *onderduikers* continued to be reimbursed. The war against them continued, but in a less orderly, messier way.

Browsing through the possessions that Eva and Alfred Schnell had left behind at 14 Pieter van den Zandestraat, reading their books, the Frank girls sometimes wondered what had happened to them. According to Annie, the Schnells had gone into hiding in Wezep, a small town in central Holland, just outside Zwolle. Annie hadn't heard anything about them for some time, she said when Dorrit and Sybil asked, but that wasn't unusual. After all, they too were in hiding.

Like Anne Frank's family, the Schnells' luck had held until the autumn of 1944. But then they disappeared. Following the liberation, their names appeared neither on the meticulous list that the Germans kept of arrivals at Westerbork, nor on the voluminous and relatively reliable list of murdered deportees compiled by the Red Cross. Nor were they amongst the bedraggled battalion of survivors who actually returned from the camps.

The Schnells' sad fate would not become known until after liberation, when their decomposed bodies were discovered. An article published in June 1945 describes the Schnells' demise, along with four other belatedly discovered Jewish divers from the general vicinity of a park, the *Engelsche Werk* in Zwolle. The murders were traced to a Nazi named Stock.

Entitled WAR CRIMES IN AND AROUND ZWOLLE; THE TRAGEDY AT THE ENGELSCHE WERK, the article reads in part:

> The Dutch Bureau, which is dealing with the tracing of war criminals who committed their crimes in the Netherlands, has . . . been able to solve many murders that were committed in and around Zwolle . . .
>
> First of all there is the tragedy which took place at the Engelsche Werk. On September 30 1944, a Jew, Hans Koopal, who was diving under with the Tensen family in Zwolle, was arrested. Three days later, after a razzia in Wezep, Alfred Schnell and his wife [Eva] were arrested. In addition, three other divers were arrested [with them] . . . J. Koren and C. Bakker, both from the island of Texel, and A. Brouwer from Meppel. They were locked in the building of the Dienststelle SD . . .

Stock, the head of the Polizei Freiwilligen Battalion Niederlande, went to the Engelsche Werk in the evening. There they had to dig their own grave: three graves for six people.

Next, according to the article, Eva told Stock that she had been assured of proper treatment at the prison. The German was unmoved:

> The answer was a shot through the breast. The victim fell backwards into the pit, which was being dug by two of the other divers. Then Stock emptied his rifle at the two diggers, who also fell into the pit. Koopal tried to escape, but was also shot down and killed. The others were also robbed of their lives.

The massacre of the Schnells was one of numerous summary killings of Jews that occurred as the German occupation of Holland entered its final, apocalyptic stage. In *Victims and Survivors*, Bob Moore describes another such atrocity that occurred during the waning months of the war, in which a *razzia* in the north of Holland jointly conducted by German *Schutzpolizei* and Dutch *Landwacht* uncovered another group of 'long-distance' divers, who, like the Schnells, were dispatched on the spot.

Bert Jan Flim, one of the numerous contemporary Dutch scholars who have made the study of the destruction of Dutch Jewry their life's work, estimates that over 500 Jews were murdered on Dutch soil, including those who decided to resist the Germans by joining the fighting resistance and those divers who were discovered during the last nine months of the war.

'We Dutch now have entered a dark tunnel,' a Dutch engineer wrote on 3 October, accurately reflecting the general mood of post-Arnhem Holland. 'We cannot see where we go and we don't see the end.'

That day, reports circulated of an atrocity at Putten, a small town in north-east Holland. The night before, a local resistance group had ambushed a German armoured car, killing three of its occupants and taking the fourth hostage. Upon learning of the incident from Colonel Fritz Fullriede, the colonel in charge of the area, General Christiansen, the local *Wehrmacht* commander – who had recently asked Berlin for permission to shoot any person 'who was not a terrorist [i.e. resistance member] but whose passive attitude endangered fighting troops' – flew into a rage. 'Burn the place down,' he directed his subordinate, 'and line the whole gang against the wall!'

Somewhat taken aback, Fullriede hesitated to comply fully with this bloodthirsty order. Only 87 of the 600 houses in Putten were put to the torch. Following the summary shooting of seven residents of the hermetic, devoutly Calvinist hamlet, Fullriede, with the aid of a special detachment of SS, arrested Putten's entire remaining male population of 660 and shipped them off to Amersfoort, the remaining German concentration camp on Dutch soil. From there 589 of the arrested men were sent to Germany, as Henri A. van der Zee notes in *The Hunger Winter: Occupied Holland 1944–45*:

> The Putteners, used to being guided by their rigidly Calvinist ministers and having lived in almost tribal isolation, were not up to Nazi ruthlessness. Only a few tried to escape and not more than thirteen jumped off the train. Spread over different camps in Germany, their morale soon collapsed. It was God's punishment, they believed, and many worked themselves to death.

Only a few dozen of the men of Putten ever returned from Germany.

On 1 October, five hostages from the town of Wormeveer had been murdered as a reprisal for the killing of a policeman. On the 6th, three innocent Rotterdammers were killed after a successful BS action there. On the 12th, ten hostages from Rijkswijk, a suburb of The Hague, were killed.

And on it went.

The formerly optimistic tone of the Dutch government became desperate as it sought to draw the world's attention to rapidly deteriorating living conditions within northwest Holland. 'The Netherlands is faced with the greatest disaster by flood and famine she has ever known, and the next few weeks will decide whether she will be able to play her part in the world of the future as a modern civilised nation,' Gerbrandy – who just weeks before had been preparing to make his triumphant return to Holland – told a hastily summoned press conference in London on 6 October.

What a difference a mere four weeks had made.

'As a result of the German occupation, the failure of the Allies' attempt to cross the Lek river at Arnhem and the paralysis of her own railroads in obedience to the Allies' request,' *The Times* quoted the palpably alarmed Dutchman, 'her population is now threatened with being starved, frozen, and drowned.'

Radio Oranje broadcast much the same message the following day. 'The curtains have been pulled aside and the whole world has been able to see a tortured and bleeding Holland,' Dutch radio man Den Doolaard told his listeners, including the still captive four and a half million inhabitants of western Holland. Doolaard may have been somewhat melodramatic, Henri van der Zee recalled:

> . . . But the facts were all too true. Apart from the ports of Amsterdam and Rotterdam [which the Nazis had dynamited], the Germans had ravaged those of Schiedam and Vlaardingen. A large part of the islands of Zeeland and Zuid-Holland had been flooded, and the sea had already swallowed a fifth of our arable land. Coastal towns and those along the Rhine around Arnhem had been evacuated. A number of railway workers had been executed, and in Apeldoorn the Germans had killed ten people when they refused to work for them.

Hidden behind the door of 14 Pieter van den Zandestraat, the Franks had difficulty taking in these further depressing developments, as relayed by their friends. They could only apprehend what they could see through their curtains. The woman across the way who washed her pavement every Friday had now stopped coming out. The girl next door seemed to have disappeared as well. So had 'Slimmy' and 'Blond'.

The world, it seemed, had forgotten Pieter van den Zandestraat.

But the *Wehrmacht* hadn't.

On the morning of Saturday 21 November 1944, a German loudspeaker lorry pulled up at the entrance of their short street, and a disembodied voice ordered all able-bodied men between the ages of sixteen and forty to report outside on the pavement.

Having successfully evaded the Germans' 'Jew net', the Franks had fallen into another one, no less lethal, the drive to find slave labour for Germany's undermanned factories. Operation Rosebranch this was called. The previous day, a surprise raid in Rotterdam, employing armed troops and attack dogs, had produced a yield of 30,000 stunned Dutchmen.

However, the men of *Den Haag* would not be such easy game. Forewarned of the raid by Radio Oranje, many went to ground. And so, when the armed German search party arrived, the men of Pieter van den Zandestraat and the surrounding streets were prepared to resist.

So was Myrtil Frank. Unknown to his wife and daughters, he later told his brother Julius, he had obtained a revolver – probably from his friend L. – which he intended to use if the Germans ever came to number 14. Like a latter-day Maccabee, he planned to shoot the first German to come through the door; then he would shoot the rest of the family. There was no way that he was going to let the Germans take them.

Meanwhile, as Flory, Dorrit and Sybil numbly sat around and waited, the armed search proceeded. Gunfire rang out. Someone out of sight down the street was offering resistance. Shortly, the Franks could also hear scuffling above them, as one of the occupants of the upstairs flat put up a fight before being dragged off to the waiting lorry.

Through the curtains, the Franks could see the blurred, hurried silhouettes of the searchers. Time stopped. Myrtil released the safety catch of his revolver, preparing to fire. All four waited for the knock on the door.

But there was no knock.

Eventually, as the Franks sat there, frozen, unable to believe what had just occurred, they heard the lorry drive away.

Somehow the Germans had passed by number 14. They had searched number 12, they had searched number 16. But they had passed by number 14.

Why?

Who knew? Who cared? The Franks could ponder that later. They still do.

First, there was the rest of the Hunger Winter to get through.

Several weeks earlier, Dorrit's best friend, Gerda, who had been sent to Westerbork the previous year after her Jewish Council exemption had been revoked, was murdered with her mother at Auschwitz. At first, according to the account of one of the inmates standing in the queue behind them, the white-gowned German 'doctor' who inspected arrivals and decreed who was healthy enough to work as a slave labourer and who should be sent to the crematoria motioned that the relatively fit Gerda be put to work. Her older, less fit mother was told to join the line for the 'showers'. Seeing this, Gerda instead took her mother's hand, and mother and daughter walked together to their deaths.

Holland SOS

It seems that something wholly outside the present experience may face SHAEF in Holland.

Desmond Morton, secretary to
Winston Churchill, October 1944

The expression 'starved to death' has been used so often in a figurative sense that it is difficult to realise that people are dying in the streets from exhaustion and privation. I do not mean that these people are 'deadly' tired, but quite definitely that their corpses can be carried away. And when the question arises: 'But how can you people stand it?' my answer is: 'Those people cannot stand it; they are really going completely to pieces' – HOLLAND SOS.

Message from occupied Holland received in
London, March 1945

To the general misery, caused by hunger and sickness, was now added a feeling of abandonment and of resentment of the dilatoriness of the allies.

Dutch historian Robert Fruin, in an essay about
the siege and relief of Leiden, 1874

After they moved to Holland in the 1930s, one of the first stories that Dorrit and Sybil learned in their Dutch history classes was the siege and relief of Leiden. This was a pivotal event in Holland's long and ultimately successful war of independence against Philip II and the Kingdom of Spain, a campaign only dimly recalled by most people today. However, in the early part of the twentieth century, before the Second World War obscured everything that occurred before it, the savage siege and miraculous Relief (usually capitalised) still bulked large in the imagination of the Western world for the heroism the sixteenth-century Leideners displayed and the suffering they endured. It was an event of huge significance for Dutch and European history. Thomas Macaulay wrote in his foreword to Robert Fruin's 1874 essay about the event, 'the Relief of Leiden claims, indeed, an equal place with the Defeat of the Armada as having given the decisive check to the conquest of Europe by the Spanish Monarchy and the Spanish Armada'.

On 31 October 1573, the Spanish army surrounded Leiden, then one of the largest and most prosperous cities in the restive Dutch provinces, where a rebellion against Spanish rule had just begun. The populace, then numbering 50,000, was able to withstand without too many casualties the first siege, which ended on 21 March 1574, when the besiegers, under the Spanish general, Valdez, suddenly departed. However, the second siege, which began on the night of 25 May, when Valdez returned, catching the citadel city completely unprepared, was calamitous. Starvation and disease ravaged the citizenry, causing more than 6,000 deaths. The frantic inhabitants ate cats, dogs, rats, and worse.

Nevertheless, Leiden, stalwart in the face of tyranny, refused to succumb, all the while waiting and wondering whether their allies had forsaken them. In the end, relief came by water after the Dutch cut their dykes and opened the sluices in the area surrounding Leiden, allowing the liberating forces literally to sail to the dying city's rescue in October 1574 and bringing to an end one of the most inspiring and catastrophic chapters in Dutch history.

Following the siege and successful Relief of Leiden, the Dutch crown gave the gallant inhabitants a choice of reward: exemption from taxes, or their own university. They chose the latter, and the State University of Leiden soon became one of the foremost institutions of learning in Europe. The many dead were given a proper burial, the physical damage remaining from the siege was repaired. With its great university as its centrepiece, the city recovered its poise and its prosperity and was celebrated in the works of Rembrandt, Jan Steen, and other Dutch artists who called the beguiling canal city their home. By the time the Franks arrived in Holland, Leiden had become a popular destination, a pleasant place to while away an afternoon in the quiet, picturesque streets, with a cone of *frites* and perhaps a piece of fish from the daily canalside market, before hopping back on the train.

Then came the war, the invasion and the occupation. Like those of its sister cities in the area today known as the *Randstad* – Amsterdam,

Rotterdam, Haarlem, Utrecht, Hilversum, Delft and The Hague – Leiden's population of 100,000 suffered greatly under the Nazi repression. Its small Jewish minority was persecuted and deported. The university joined its faculty in making a stand against the Germans and had closed in November, 1940. Three years later in 1943, Leiden's equally stubborn students refused to sign the compulsory loyalty oath that the German authorities insisted on that spring and dived under, many of them in the city itself, putting pressure on the still inchoate local resistance to house and feed them, while others were shipped off to work as slave labourers. By 1944 this historic site was a mere shadow of its pre-war, prosperous self.

Nevertheless, neither the people of Leiden nor those of her neighbouring cities expected to witness a reprise of the horrific conditions their ancestors had suffered during the siege of 1574.

But this is what now occurred. Starvation and disease returned to the banks of the Rapenburg and throughout north-western Holland. Once again, malnourished Leideners shuffled through the old cobblestoned streets in search of food. Once again, people ate their pets, and worse.

Would Anne Frank and her family have survived this *hongerwinter*, as the Dutch know it, even if they had not been betrayed the summer before? Their namesakes in The Hague almost didn't. And neither did the four and a half million people of western Holland who also lived through that season in hell.

The besieged Third Reich was the setting for some odd functions at Christmas 1944, but none was stranger than that given by Seyss-Inquart for his staff at *Clingendael*. This former royal estate in the Haagse dunes had been seized from the exiled Dutch Queen, and Seyss-Inquart had lived and entertained there for four and a half years. Despite the conspicuous absence of his wife, who had returned in haste to their native Salzburg, the bespectacled, music-loving Nazi proconsul was, by all accounts, the consummate host as he welcomed his carefully screened guests to his home that holiday evening.

The *Reichskommissar*'s dinner parties had never, in fact, been particularly popular with his subordinates in Holland because of the prudish and puritanical sobriety which prevailed, a trait Seyss-Inquart shared with his idol, Adolf Hitler.

The cavalcade of by now somewhat pockmarked Mercedes Benz and BMW staff cars descended upon the great house in the dunes to celebrate Christmas 1944, Nazi-style, while a mile up the beach, at

Scheveningen Prison, dozens of *Todeskandidaten*, or death candidates – resistance fighters who had been selected for future reprisal executions – languished in their cells, awaiting the moment when the door would open and they would be marched out to the firing squad. Elsewhere amidst the deserted streets of the once grand royal city (its pre-war population of half a million shrunk as a result of both the Atlantic and Jewish evacuations to less than 440,000), the remaining inhabitants – including some 1,500 to 2,000 local Jews – huddled over scrawny rations in dark, cold houses and hiding places.

But at Seyss-Inquart's well-lit, well-heated, well-stocked manse, all was warmth and light, as the *Reichskommissar* – whom Hitler had once described as 'clever as a snake and as charming as an eel' – read aloud the *Führer*'s Christmas message to the 150,000 resolute German soldiers and civil servants stationed in the Netherlands, wishing them 'strength and good health'. Swastika-embossed menus offered a choice of three different meats, five vegetables, and two types of ice.

The guest list for that memorable Christmas Eve dinner at *Clingendael* no longer survives. However, the rest of Seyss-Inquart's 'Austrian Mafia', including Herr Rauter, Herr Aus der Fünten and Herr Fischer, were presumably in attendance; Mussert and the homegrown Nazis whom Seyss-Inquart despised probably were not. And if there was music that evening, it was probably provided by German musicians.

While Seyss-Inquart was disseminating the *Führer*'s blessings at *Clingendael*, the Dutch population which had access to radios capable of receiving BBC tuned in to Radio Oranje's allotted fifteen minutes to hear their distressed Queen, Wilhelmina, broadcast another version of the message she had so often broadcast before, of hope to her subjects for a better and peaceful future 'in the sure expectation of speedy and complete liberation'.

Wilhelmina closed her poignant broadcast by reminding the people of both the liberated and occupied Netherlands that 'the message of Christmas enables us to call a courageous and convincing "no" to the dark powers that threaten us with destruction'.

These dark forces, incarnated in the current house guests at *Clingendael*, were not concerned. On New Year's Eve, according to the report of an exuberant German press, the *Reichskommissar*, still radiating Yuletide cheer, paid a visit to a group of German troops during which his *Kameraden* listened over a field radio to the *Führer*'s New Year speech, the experience of which reinforced 'their indestructible loyalty to their Leader'. Afterwards, the men, including Seyss-Inquart, reportedly 'sang and made jokes'.

The singing may have been propaganda; Seyss-Inquart was not the sort to burst into song. But there had indeed been a miraculous upturn in their fortunes.

On 16 December, the Ardennes counter-offensive had been launched: three entire German armies, led by General Rundstedt and forty other generals, suddenly poured across the German–Belgian border, creating havoc amongst the US troops facing them and disquiet at SHAEF head-quarters in London. The well-armed and trained German divisions broke out of the snow-covered forests in the Ardennes and raced headlong for Antwerp, creating a massive bulge (hence the name the battle acquired) in the Allies' overstretched lines.

The offensive, Hitler's idea, was intended to drive a wedge through the British and American troops in Belgium, sever their supply lines and force them to ask for an armistice.

Widely distributed newsreels of thousands of glum American prisoners-of-war marching into captivity must have been a tonic to Seyss-Inquart and his fellow bitter-enders. That Christmas Eve, the outlook from the German point of view appeared promising; although Eisenhower and his generals had already moved to contain the sixty-mile-deep bulge, and Patton and his 3rd Army were speeding up from the south, the Nazi tide was still swift-flowing to the west, and a number of US units, including the 101st Airborne Division at Bastogne, were surrounded.

The *Führer*'s Christmas surprise must have been the prime topic of conversation at *Clingendael*. Who said that the war was over? one imag-ines the guests reassuring each other. How could a country that was capable of mounting such a bold and complex operation be *kaput*? Who *says* that the *Führer* doesn't know what he is doing?

And could you pass the ice, please!

The Ardennes offensive filled the people of the liberated provinces of Limburg and Noord-Brabant with very real fears that they might be reconquered, and further damaged the morale of the four and a half million people living in western Holland – including the Franks and their fellow Jewish *onderduikers*.

'Oh, that was the nadir,' said Dorrit. 'Just when we thought the news couldn't get any worse, it did.'

Neither Dorrit nor Sybil recalls what they had for dinner that black Christmas Eve. 'Most likely we had sugar beets,' said Sybil. 'That's one of the main things I remember about that winter. They were just awful. They would just kill your throat.' Or perhaps they made do with a bowl of the thin pea soup that Flory, already suffering from malnutrition, made. 'There was a bag of pea meal that Myrtil managed to buy,' she remembered thirty-five years later, 'and so we made do with that. Not every day, but every few days perhaps. That was the mainstay that kept us going through that winter.'

Everything is relative: that evening the Franks were comparatively fortunate. All around western Holland people had begun to starve.

In early December, at the specific request of the *Wehrmacht*, which feared that this obstinacy might lead to a full insurrection, Seyss-Inquart lifted his embargo on inland shipping. He also agreed to allow the churches to assist with food distribution in the hardest-hit areas. But this didn't help. The transportation system was too disrupted to make a difference in the crisis. There was little cooperation between Nazi civil and military offices, and Dutch skippers didn't trust the Germans not to confiscate their boats. Weekly food rations, already at a minimum, continued to be cut, from a daily allotment of 1,300 calories per person in October – already only half of what a normal person needs – to a mere 900 in November. Soon, as supplies further dwindled, even that number would be a luxury.

Gerbrandy's prediction that the western provinces, now bypassed by the Allies in their drive for Berlin, would starve to death if they were not liberated by December now began to come true. London received the first alarmed reports of deaths from malnutrition in metropolitan Holland on 20 November. The casualty reports continued to mount throughout December as food stocks, already depleted by German thefts, all but vanished.

Then, just as the frantic efforts of Dutch food officials to organise a relief expedition of several hundred barges bound from the eastern farmland to the famished west were about to bear fruit, a 'severe frost' struck, as Van der Zee writes: 'The canals and the IJsselmeer froze over and on 23 December one of the coldest winters in memory began, lasting until 31 January.'

Technically, the winter of 1944–45 was not exceptionally cold. With average temperatures of 36 and 24 degrees Fahrenheit respectively, December 1944 and January 1945 were very cold, but a look at the temperature charts for the two previous decades shows that several winters, notably that of 1941–42, were in fact much colder.

But during that horrific winter of 1944, the Dutch lacked gas, heat and light. The frozen winter landscape, straight out of the sixteenth century of Hendrik Avercamp, lacked the cheer of the famed landscapist. The ill-dressed, ill-fed, ill-spirited Dutchmen of the twentieth century weren't in the mood to go skating. They were simply trying to survive.

There was a great rush for wood or anything that burned. 'Early in the morning or after sunset,' one observer wrote, 'you can see respectable gentlemen creeping through parks and public gardens, past lanes and canals, judging everything on its burning qualities.' Inevitably, this led to deforestation. Amsterdam's largest and leafiest park, *Vondelpark*, was forced to close because of wood theft, although hunger-winter entrepreneurs continued to auction off its trees at a high price.

Houses were also at risk: 'In the all but empty Jewish district [of Amsterdam] no less than 1,500 houses were robbed of every bit of wood, joists, beams, staircases, door and window frames . . . most [houses] collapsed in ruins, often killing their wreckers.'

As the bitter cold continued, every conceivable source of fuel was exploited by the inhabitants of the famished region. Canal bottoms were dredged. Even tram-lines weren't safe, as desperate people prised loose the wood blocks between the tracks.

The locusts had come to Holland.

Like many other Dutchmen, the Franks relied for heating and cooking on a new contraption called the 'miracle stove'. The stove – a little grid in a small tin, inside an even larger tin – was supposed to provide maximum heat with minimum fuel. Obtaining fuel for it was evidently not a problem; Annie and Jeanne were able to keep the Franks supplied with firewood, and there was plenty of extra furniture in the storage room that could be cannibalised, with Annie's permission. The oven actually provided a minimal amount of heat in exchange for a copious amount of fuel, and the greater challenge was to keep it lit.

'Oh, the trouble we had making splinters to keep that damn thing going,' Sybil said. 'And then it created so little heat it almost didn't seem worth the trouble. On the other hand, it did give us something to do.'

'One of my chief concerns during that last winter was whether that little stove would catch fire so we could have a little warmth,' Flory agreed.

By now, the routine that Flory had originally instituted when the Franks dived under had broken down. The family had too little energy to exercise any more; moreover, it was simply too cold. Often they would go to bed to keep warm and to conserve their strength.

They still did their best to clean the tiny flat, a chore which became even more difficult as a result of the daily invasion of white mites from under the floor, driven out by the cold. Once content to spend their lives hiding in the warm woodwork, the tiny insects were as desperate for warmth as the humans who dwelled above them.

'*That's* what I remember about that winter,' said Dorrit. 'The white mites. Every morning we would get down on our knees and scrub the floor to get rid of them. They were *horrible!*'

Hunger. Darkness. Cold. These dominated the Franks' lives as they commenced the final and arguably the most horrific part of their thousand-day journey. 'They were terrible,' said another *onderduiker* in The Hague, referring to the wintry triumvirate, an engineer who had dived under in order to escape the labour draft, 'and the worst is that they intensify each other.'

In 1946, C. Banning, the chief inspector of the Dutch public health service, recalled the events of that winter for a special number of *The Annals of the American Academy of Political and Social Science*, analysing one of the first and perhaps the best-documented instances of famine to occur in an industrialised nation. 'The situation became more and more unbearable for the population and, from the point of view of public health, a catastrophe,' Banning wrote.

> Throughout the winter of 1945 the population sat without light, without gas, without heat; laundries ceased operating; soap for personal use was unobtainable; shoes, textiles and adequate clothing were lacking in innumerable families. In hospitals and in sanatoriums, many of which had been evacuated by the Germans to be confiscated for their own use or pulled down for military reasons, there was serious overcrowding as well as a lack of medicines. Hunger dominated all . . .

Banning notes that the food shortage was particularly acute in The Hague:

> The Hague is disadvantageously located in relation to the domestic food production and supply area. Therefore, it was more difficult than in other places to bring in the official food supplies, and also it was more difficult for the people themselves to procure food from the farmers than it was, for instance, for the people of Amsterdam.

The worsening food situation is reflected in the weekly reported deaths for the capital. During the first week of January 1945, the records show a total of 168 deaths reported in The Hague – a 40 per cent increase on the previous year. The next week, the total reported deaths in the city jumped to 183, the next to 239, then to 245, then, during the first two weeks of February, to 288 and 324. And on it went.

These were only reported deaths. With the onset of the famine, many family members didn't report the deaths of their loved ones so that they might be able to hold on to their ration cards. Much the same thing had occurred during the siege of Leiden, as Robert Fruin noted in 1874: 'For every mouth two pounds to last four days – half a pound of meat and bones as the only nourishment for twenty-four hours. No wonder that in many households a death was partly concealed, so that the ration could be fetched.'

The death of an *onderduiker* posed an even greater disposal problem. Morgues wouldn't accept bodies without proper identification, and neither would the few remaining undertakers. The ground was too cold to dig. And even if one were able to bury an *onderduiker* on one's own, there remained the attendant problem of what to bury them *in*. With wood scarce, wooden coffins became a luxury. Often, just as in 1574, the solution was to dump the bodies of the dead into rivers and canals. When morning came, corpses could be found floating in the internal waterways of The Hague, Amsterdam, Leiden and other cities.

As the citizens of The Hague and its sister cities starved and froze to death, the Germans stepped up missile production. The approaching Soviet army had forced the German rocket detachments of the *Sonderkommando* to abandon their eastern launch sites and shift the bulk of the V-1/V-2 campaign to Holland. The increasingly experienced Dutch-based crews were managing to catapult four or five V-2s per day at the British capital, with frightful results.

On 25 November 1944, in one of the deadliest attacks, 168 Londoners were killed when a Dutch-based V-2 fell, obliterating a Woolworth shop in Deptford. American bomber crews, en route to their targets in Germany, would sometimes see the fast-moving rockets' contrails against the blackness of the upper stratosphere. There was nothing they could do.

One of the *Wehrmacht*'s favourite launching sites was the woods behind the Peace Palace, the ornate castle donated by Andrew Carnegie which had formerly housed the International Court of Justice. The German launch commanders found the palace woods a convenient place to conceal the lethal projectiles and their launchers from Allied reconnaissance. After the war, visitors to the battered Peace Palace grounds found seared places in the foliage caused by the flames from the monsters. The building itself was intact but all its windows were shattered, the result of a mid-air misfire.

There were many such misfires. On New Year's Day 1945, the Franks and other residents of Pieter van den Zandestraat whose windows faced north heard the by now familiar dragonish V-2 roar and looked out to see the vapour trail of another of the fire-breathing behemoths that had been launched near Ockenberg. Then, as it reached 3,600 metres, the missile suddenly swerved 160 degrees before disappearing out of sight. A second later there was an explosion – the sound of a row of houses being vaporised along with at least five of their occupants.

On 4 February, the *Sonderkommando* launched a record sixteen V-2s at London – about one every hour and a half.

Concerned by the increasing number of Dutch casualties, German civil officials in The Hague, who were as endangered by the rockets as the rest of the population, suggested to their military counterparts that they might find a less inhabited area to launch from. If there were casualties near the missile sites, the cynical rocket commander reportedly replied, they were the fault of the Dutch themselves, because only Dutch sabotage could make them fail.

The resistance could only wish that were true. In fact, their mobility made the missiles virtually impervious to sabotage.

Though still plagued by infighting amongst its various units, Dutch resistance fighters were now theoretically operating under the command of Prince Bernhard and his fighting adjutant, Colonel Koot, and were clearly more competent than before. They also were more brazen. On 8 December 1944, in one of the BS's more spectacular operations, a group of raiders disguised as Dutch police broke into the jail at Leeuwarden, in Friesland, and freed fifty-one resistance workers. The Gestapo retaliated by shooting a number of hostages.

Sometimes hostages were disposed of in the already blood-drenched dunes at Scheveningen or at Overween, outside Haarlem, where, it was later calculated, 422 Dutchmen and Dutchwomen were shot during the war.

During these last bitter months of the German occupation, the newly assigned SD chief for Holland, Dr Karl Schoengarth, a particularly beastly specimen who would later be hanged, executed hostages and *Todeskandidaten* in public, leaving their bodies in city squares and streets as a warning. When it was possible to do so, the bodies would be covered with a Dutch flag. One of the most memorable images from the winter of 1944–45 shows one Amsterdammer briefly posing for an underground photographer while he covers the body of a hostage by a desolate city canal. On the other side of the canal, apathetic people look listlessly on.

On 2 January 1945 the Dutch government-in-exile broadcast an order to civil servants in the occupied areas not to assist the Germans with their latest *Liese-Aktion*, or slave-labour drive, for which all remaining Dutchmen between sixteen and forty were supposed to register. A few of the clerks, including the local fascists drafted by the Germans, refused to heed the order. The resistance now sprang into action: three days later, on the 5th, armed members of the Dutch Forces of the Interior invaded the Amsterdam *Liese-Aktion* offices and shot ten of the collaborationist officials dead, while other offices around the country were put to the torch. The Germans retaliated by shooting dozens of hostages.

In the darkened, terror-ridden cities of western Holland all semblance of normal life had stopped. Economic life came to a halt. Public services of all kinds – transportation, education, sanitation – ceased. 'Those who are hungry shout, but those who are starving keep still,' one Dutch journalist wrote at the end of January. 'The traffic has stopped, all enterprises are paralysed. Footsteps are smothered by the thick snow and this immense silence is penetrated by one single thought, that of the daily bread that is lacking.'

Now the faces that the Franks saw on the other side of their frost-covered window were as grey and haggard as their own.

In the Ardennes, the bulge that the Germans had punched into the Allied lines was gradually eliminated. In late January, *Nordwind*, another offensive aimed at Allied lines in the Saar, also collapsed. Hitler had shot his bolt. While the Allied armies resumed their broad-front assault on Germany from the west, the Soviets continued their drive from the east, smashing into Poland.

On 17 January 1945, the Red Army entered Warsaw. As Soviet troops approached, the SS began the evacuation of Auschwitz, forcing about 66,000 surviving prisoners – including several hundred Dutch Jews, a tiny fraction of the 60,000 who had been shipped there – on a death march.

Ten days later, the Soviets liberated the camp, finding 2,800 invalid survivors. One of these was Otto Frank. Several weeks earlier, his wife Edith had perished of starvation. He knew this. However, at that point he still held out hope for his daughters, Anne and Margot, from whom he had been separated in October, when they were sent to Bergen-Belsen.

Their troops were disgusted and outraged by what they discovered at Auschwitz, but the Soviet authorities kept the news to themselves. The Dutch people, preoccupied with their own struggle for survival, knew no more about the camps than they had before. The Dutch government continued to believe that the majority of the 107,000 Dutch deportees would eventually return.

The war progressed. By 1 February, the Red Army was within a hundred miles of Berlin. Goebbels, in his newly granted capacity as Minister of Total War, prepared the German capital for a last stand. It would take another three months for Berlin to succumb.

On 4 February, the Big Three, Churchill, Roosevelt and Stalin, met at Yalta to confer and to divide up the postwar world.

Ten days later, Budapest was liberated. The fight in Europe was not over, but the end was in sight.

The Dutch situation, however, remained desperate. Near frantic with dread about the deteriorating situation in the besieged famine provinces, Gerbrandy made repeated but unsuccessful appeals to Allied leaders through January and February of 1945. On 6 January he visited Eisenhower and urged the SHAEF commander once again to expedite the liberation of western Holland. Eisenhower received Gerbrandy graciously and noted his request, but insisted that he would not order a diversion from the main offensive against Germany.

Six weeks later, the stricken Dutch official renewed his plea during an audience with Ike's chief of staff, General Walter Bedell Smith. Once again, Gerbrandy was rebuffed. Impossible, the bewildered Dutchman was told by the blunt-spoken US officer. The requisite divisions and equipment were simply not available. At the rate the war was going, the best he could promise might be for the Allies to liberate western Holland by mid-May, a prediction that proved accurate. Gerbrandy replied that that would be too late. Hundreds of thousands might be dead by then. 'The fate of our nation is in the balance,' he said.

Gerbrandy was hardly exaggerating. The lowest figures of food supply available to Dutch officials was reached on 28 January. The bread ration, formerly 1,000 grams a week – two slices of bread – was now reduced to 500 grams.

Seyss-Inquart, who fancied himself compassionate, was not totally oblivious to the situation. In late January, a group of Dutch doctors sent an appeal for emergency assistance to the *Reichskommissar* in which they cited the help which the then considerably better-off Dutch, who had remained neutral during the First World War, had generously extended to German and Austrian schoolchildren. 'We cannot resist asking you,' the doctors wrote, 'if you have forgotten that, at the time when German and Austrian children were suffering, they received hospitality, food, and clothing in this same country that is now looted by your compatriots and driven to starvation.'

To a degree this appeal worked. Previously, Hirschfeld, the hard-pressed Dutch food official, whose shipping operations were still paralysed because of the frost, had asked Seyss-Inquart to allow through trains manned by German personnel.* Now, however, Seyss-Inquart relented, and on 26 January, three trains arrived in Amsterdam, Rotterdam and The Hague, carrying just enough potatoes to keep the central kitchens in those cities running. Seeing an opportunity to break the railway strike, Seyss-Inquart offered to let even more food through. But he insisted that they carry Dutch personnel. The Dutch government refused, maintaining the strike had now become a matter of Dutch prestige. The crisis continued.

At 14 Pieter van den Zandestraat, the Franks tried to make do with their own declining stores. As Flory put it, 'Everything was less and less.' Occasionally, their now nearly exhausted bag of pea meal would be supplemented by the gift of a few potatoes or sugar beets from Annie and Jeanne during the latter's increasingly rare visits. Never safe to begin with, their friends' sorties were much more dangerous now. By walking the deserted streets they risked being robbed by the gangs of street urchins who prowled the city, or being stopped and searched by a suspicious member of the *Landwacht*, which often carried out policing after the regular police had gone underground.

---

* Hirschfeld was half-Jewish; however, Seyss-Inquart did not seem to mind. After the war, he, like many Dutch officials who stayed at their jobs, was criticised for cooperating with the Germans at all. He replied that he did so in order to prevent famine. His actions seem more defensible than most.

Across the Channel, Gerbrandy continued to do his best to get the message out, buttonholing this general, collaring that official. Meanwhile, the Resistance sent an urgent telegram to SHAEF depicting the situation and beseeching the Allies for assistance.

'The people of the Netherlands have fought, for four, nearly five years among the United Nations,' began this searingly eloquent telegram, received in January.

Hundreds and thousands have sacrificed their lives. Tens of thousands have been sent to German concentration camps. A still greater number have lost their possessions.

Many of our towns are ruined, but we shall build them again, many of our factories have been destroyed, but we will build better ones. Water has flooded our fields, we shall drain them again. The German tyrants are trying to make us submit by starvation, but we will overcome this trial, too, thinking of those fighting on the fronts and the grief endured by other nations.

We know what we are fighting for [but] we call out to the free world: an old civilised nation is threatened with destruction by the German barbarians. Let the free world raise their voices. We shall hold on.

Staunch words. But how long *could* Holland hold on?

Churchill himself, originally sceptical of reports about the Dutch famine, had now been concerned for several months, and had indeed tried to get SHAEF to act. 'I am trying to have Holland cleared up behind us,' he wrote to his friend Jan Smuts, the South African Prime Minister, on 3 December. 'But,' he lamented, referring to his waning influence on the other two Great Powers, 'it is not as easy as it used to be to get things done.'

What was true in December was doubly true in February. Ike was the man in charge now in the West. Churchill could not have arranged a diversionary attack on the Nazi redoubt in north-western Holland even if he had wished it. As before, Berlin continued to be the main target, and the road to Berlin lay through the Rhineland, not through Holland. SHAEF sympathised, but as Smith had informed Gerbrandy, the Dutch would have to hold on.

By now, Holland's distress was well known in the greater world.

On 15 February, Richard Law, the British Minister of State, rose in the Commons to report on the economic and supply position of the liberated countries of north-western Europe. In France, he reported, the situation was good: 'France is producing as much foodstuffs as she did during the enemy occupation.' In newly freed Belgium, food production was also good, Law stated, although distribution was less than satisfactory. In the liberated areas of Holland, he continued:

> . . . our difficulties have inevitably increased by the fact that [the liberated areas] are still the scene of active military operations. However I am glad to say that increased supplies are coming in.

'But,' he continued,

> I would be misleading the House if I did not point out that, so far as Holland is concerned, the most formidable problem will arise only when the areas at present in the occupation of the enemy have been liberated.

Four days later, *The Times*, noting on its leader page the formation of a Help Holland Council, put the formidable plight of the Dutch in historic, indeed lofty terms. 'In the past, the peoples of Britain and Holland were often rivals,' the editors noted:

> . . . but it was a chivalrous conflict between nations of similar qualities and aspirations honourably competing for pre-eminence in those specific spheres of national and individual enterprise in which the genius of both of them is traditionally expressed, and it did not expunge the memory of an earlier and prophetic partnership in the defence of common ideals of civic liberty and cultural independence. In recent times Holland has often seemed to Englishmen to embody much that is most enduring in the civilisation of Europe in a form specially attractive to the English mind.
>
> The plight of the people of occupied Holland, all the harder to endure because it followed hard on the bright prospect, suddenly withdrawn at Arnhem, of freedom and the beginning of restoration, has made a profound impression on British opinion.

This was duly noted. However, the four and half million Dutchmen 'at present in the areas under the occupation of the enemy', as Law put it, were not able to consume British public opinion. And so, by the hundreds and thousands, they continued to starve.

February did bring a kind of relief. The bitter cold, which had held the country in its vice, gave way to a period of relatively mild weather, including intermittent sunshine. This welcome development also accelerated the so-called 'hunger trippers'. Since the beginning of the winter, residents in the western, 'hungry' provinces had been making expeditions to the rural provinces to obtain additional food from the farmers there – potatoes, vegetables, whatever was available. 'Hunger trips', these sorties were called.

With the break in the cold, the voyagers, once a trickle, became a flood. Each day, as dawn broke over occupied western Holland and the still assiduously enforced curfew ended, a new procession of the desperate and the malnourished would set out from The Hague and her sister cities for the farmland to the north and east. Some 'trippers' rode their bicycles – usually with wooden wheels now, the original rubber tyres having worn out or been traded for other goods. Others walked, pushed baby carriages in front of them, or dragged sleds behind. The better-off bartered for food with generally sympathetic if hard-pressed farmers. Others simply begged, and some in their voraciousness consumed whatever vegetation they found along the way. Tulips were a popular form of desperation food and flower beds were particularly at risk. VERBOD VELLEN VAN BOOMEN! warned a government sign at the time – CUTTING DOWN TREES FORBIDDEN! Other less selective food prospectors fell on their hands and knees and foraged on grass, like cattle.

Finding food and supplies was only the first challenge for the hunger trippers; bringing them back was another. Dutch food distribution officials saw the scavengers as a threat to the rationing system they were desperately struggling to maintain, and so stationed agents at the approaches to the main cities with instructions to seize illegal foodstuffs. It was not easy to find men willing to act as food police, but the *Landwacht* was only too happy to step into the breach. That long winter, miserable trekkers just returned from a ten- or thirty- or fifty-mile expedition could often be seen being stripped of their small bounty of potatoes or sugar beets.

Meanwhile, the Germans continued to squeeze Holland to a pulp. A special 'plunder commando' made up of Ruhr Valley miners was sent through the country to steal anything of value. Cars, bicycles, farm equipment, anything that wasn't tied down – even entire factories – were seized and shipped back to the Fatherland. Food, too, if they wished. The same German soldiers who seized food parcels from the hunger trippers were themselves free to send as many parcels of Dutch produce back to Germany as they liked. As one Dutch engineer described the final pillage, 'stolen horses were harnessed to stolen carriages in which stolen food and furniture were loaded, escorted by guards mounted on stolen bicycles'.

The Germans were not the only looters: in the absence of public order, Dutchmen, especially teenagers, also helped themselves. One such looter was caught in the midst of robbing a store in The Hague, not far from Pieter van den Zandestraat. A crude sign was fashioned and hung around the brigand's neck. 'I am a thief', it said. Then, as horrified bystanders looked on, the unfortunate youth was shot.

Just as during the siege of Leiden, the famine and misery led to the spread of infectious diseases; diphtheria, scarlet fever, typhoid fever, all scourged the cities of both Leiden and her neighbouring sister cities. Hospitals, robbed of supplies by the Germans, struggled to cope with the onslaught of casualties in impossible conditions and with dwindling staff as the diseases took hold. This health catastrophe was exacerbated by a lack of soap, water and normal sanitation as the Germans sabotaged many sewage facilities. In Amsterdam, the sewers overflowed, compounding the misery of the inhabitants.

More than 20,000 people ultimately died of disease or starvation during the *hongerwinter*, including nearly 3,000 in The Hague alone. Flory came close to being one of them. For over thirty months she had kept her family going, husbanding supplies, bolstering spirits, warding off chaos. That the Franks had all survived while others nearby, both above ground and underground, were expiring was due in no small part to her diligence and example.

However, her strength eventually deserted her, and one day in February or March she collapsed on the floor. Tine's physician husband, Willem, was quickly summoned. Sadly he looked at the semi-comatose forty-seven-year-old woman slumped on the chair, her frame now shrunk to less than one hundred pounds, her once beautiful brown hair long gone white. The physician, who was suffering from malnutrition himself, shook his head. There was nothing he could do, he said. 'She needs food.'

She was given whatever was available and somehow she survived.

On 5 March, Patton's surging Third Army conquered Cologne. Two days later, at Remagen, American troops crossed the Rhine, the last major natural border separating them from Berlin, after finding the bridge there still miraculously intact.

But Anne and Margot Frank continued to waste away at Bergen-Belsen, where the famine and pestilence were many times worse than in western

Holland. Ernst Schnabel, author of *Anne Frank: A Portrait in Courage*, the first biography of Anne Frank, described the two sisters' last days:

> In the last weeks at Bergen-Belsen, as Germany was strangled between the Russians and the western Allies, there was almost no food at all. The roads were blocked, the railroads had been bombed and the SS commander of the camp drove around trying unsuccessfully to requisition supplies. Still, the crematoriums worked night and day and in the midst of the starvation and the murder there was a great epidemic of typhus.
>
> Both Anne and Margot Frank contracted the disease in late February or early March of 1945. Margot lay in a coma for several days. Then, while unconscious, she somehow rolled from her bed and died, as did Mrs Van Daan [their fellow diver – actually Mrs Pels – who also had been shipped to Belsen from Auschwitz the year before].
>
> The death of Anne Frank passed almost without notice. One woman said, 'I feel certain she died because of her sister's death. Dying is easy for anyone left alone in a concentration camp.' Mrs B., who had shared the pitiful Christmastide feast with Anne, knows a little more: 'Anne, who was very sick at the time, was not informed of her sister's death. But a few days later she sensed it and soon afterward she died.'

As American troops were crossing the Rhine, the Nazis' reign of terror in Holland reached its apex after the 'accidental' ambush by resistance forces on the evening of 6 March of a car carrying Rauter, the Dutch SS chief. The local resistance group had no idea that Rauter was one of the four occupants of the BMW. If they had, they might have let it pass rather than provoke the reprisals which they knew would surely come after an attack on such a high official – as they had after the assassination of Reinhard Heydrich. In the event, three of the four Germans in the car were killed. Though gravely wounded, Rauter was discovered unconscious several hours later and survived the ambush.

Himmler's revenge was swift. The next day, as his subordinate recovered, he ordered the execution of 500 people. Seyss-Inquart thought the number excessive, and told Himmler so, as he would later state at Nuremberg. He may have reduced the number. As a result of the incident, between 250 and 400 were executed.

On the morning of Thursday 8 March, near the site of the assault, 117 death candidates from the prisons at Arnhem and Apeldoorn were driven by motor coach and forced to line up along the road. Learning of the impending executions, the Apeldoorn resistance group, which had been responsible for the original attack, drove full speed to the spot, hoping to stop the bloodbath, but by the time they arrived, the green-uniformed Order Police were arranging the bodies for exhibition along the roadside.

It was, as *The Times* later noted, 'merely a new example of the unparalleled terror to which the people in Occupied Holland are now subjected'.

Four days later, the people of Amsterdam witnessed another such example when thirty-six men, picked at random from the passing crowd, were lined up and shot on an Amsterdam street.

Just as the hunger continued until the end, so did the terror.

The people of The Hague – including the Franks – had suffered an earlier terror on 3 March, this time at the hands of the Royal Air Force. That morning, in the deadliest, most inaccurate air attack in the capital's history, a large group of bombers, intent on attacking German V-2 sites in The Hague, appeared in the skies over the city. At first the fifty-six B-24 Mitchell bombers seemed to be headed in the direction of the *Haagse Bos*, a V-2 site where the Franks had gone for Sunday walks before the war. However, the briefing officer had confused vertical and horizontal coordinates on the maps distributed for the raid, and suddenly the bombers turned and dropped their payload over *Bezuidenhout*, the residential district south of the park where Annie lived. The Korte Voorhout, a street not far from the Franks, was also bombed.

The result of the botched raid was a firestorm that killed over 500 people and razed large sections of the already devastated city. An aerial reconnaissance photograph of The Hague shot by one of the bombers' crews shows large portions of the stricken city swathed in smoke. One of the smoke columns, from the Korte Voorhout, could clearly be seen by the residents of Pieter van den Zandestraat.

Fearing for Annie's safety, a panic-stricken Myrtil ignored his wife's and daughters' plea and ran headlong out of the door into the smoke and confusion. 'It doesn't matter any more,' he said in response to Dorrit's plea for him to stay put. 'The Germans won't be looking for Jews now.'

Several hours later, Myrtil returned and wearily delivered his report. The fireball had indeed reached Annie's street, but had stopped just in front of the wooden fence surrounding her house. Annie, thank God, was all right, and so was the small sum of money she had been keeping for the Franks.

In addition to the hundreds killed and wounded in The Hague that day, over 3,000 houses had been destroyed and 12,000 Hagenaars made homeless.

Churchill was outraged at the mistake and the briefing officer responsible was court-martialled.

'FAMINE IN HOLLAND', shouted a leader in *The Times* on 5 March, two days after the accidental bombing attack on The Hague, 'A COUNTRY DYING UNDER AGGRESSION'.

A representative of the International Red Cross was dispatched to investigate the situation. 'At the beginning of March,' the alarmed official wired his superiors in Geneva, 'Dutch estimates placed the proportion of flooded arable land at between twenty and thirty per cent . . . The sewage systems in the cities no longer work since the pumps cannot be used. In rainy weather the water level rises in the lavatories – and in the Netherlands it is often wet . . .'

Thousands of people were suffering from hunger diseases, the report continued. If something was not done soon, '*the three western provinces will no longer be able to exist* [author's italics]'. A report to the Swedish Red Cross from its representative, Count Hakon Morner, told much the same story.

Meanwhile, cries for help continued to come from Holland itself. 'The expression "starved to death" has been used so often in a figurative sense,' read a dispatch to London from an anomynous resister, on 17 March, 'that it is difficult to realise that people are dying in the streets from exhaustion and privation. I do not mean that these people are "deadly" tired, but quite definitely that their corpses can be carried away. And when the question arises: "But how can you people stand it?" my answer is: "Those people cannot stand it; they are really going completely to pieces" – HOLLAND SOS.'

Two hundred miles to the east, the Russians closed in on the Germans, and from the west the Americans continued to push, moving through the *Rheinland-Pfalz*, the Frank family's former home, where they still faced stiff if unorganised resistance from *Wehrmacht* remnants based there.

On 12 March, the 36th US Army Division entered Meisenheim, where Myrtil Frank and his brother Julius had once attended *Shul*. Three days later, they occupied Breitenheim, where, according to divisional records, they liberated an anti-aircraft gun.

Meanwhile, in Holland, impatience with the Allies continued. When would public concern be translated into action? Who *cared* about the Rhineland? *What about us?* the beleaguered people of western Holland cried. *When are the Allies going to come for us?*

On 23 March 1945, the first week of spring, Holland's turn finally came. At 2.30 p.m., after a thundercloud of artillery from Allied guns, the great Rhine offensive between the Dutch border and the Ruhr began, as American, British and Canadian troops finally crossed the northern stretch of the river in four places.

On the 14th, the Allied top command, impelled to action in part by the dire reports issuing from western Holland, had ordered Eisenhower to 'clean up' the beset region. The night before the attack, Montgomery sent the following message to his soldiers: '21 Army Group will now cross the Rhine – having crossed the river we crack about the plains of Northern Germany, chasing the enemy from pillar to post.'

Four weeks of hard fighting lay ahead for the liberating Allied troops. The 120,000 German troops remaining in Holland were now under the command of one General Johannes Blaskowitz, who had relieved his predecessor, Christiansen. Four years before, Blaskowitz, no admirer of the Nazis, had ordered the court-martial of a group of SS troops for their cruelty to Jews in Poland, a brave and unusual move that put him in disfavour.

But now the dutiful Blaskowitz made preparations for his own bitter end. Holland's inner offensive perimeter, the Grebbe Line, which had originally been intended to stave off the Germans, was now flooded by them. Explosive charges were placed in dykes all across the western part of the country – charges which, if set off, would ruin Holland's entire inland waterway system for years to come; sluices were closed so that the water in the IJsselmeer rose to an alarming level; the guns of *Festung Scheveningen* and the other coastal forts, originally intended to fend off an invasion from the sea, were now turned around to point inland.

Blaskowitz told Berlin that he was ready to fight 'to the last man and the last bullet'.

Two weeks earlier, Adolf Hitler, surveying the remains of his vaunted Thousand-Year Reich from his bomb-cratered *Führerbunker* in Berlin, had issued his infamous 'scorched earth' directive – enjoining the destruction of all industrial installations and anything else that might be of use to the Allies within the Reich's remaining territories, including Holland. Albert Speer, who was by then conducting his own one-man resistance movement against Hitler in a belated effort to salvage what was left of Germany – and, no doubt, to save his own neck – decided to ignore it.

Although some inundations did take place in April – most notably the blowing of the dykes guarding the great *Wieringermeer* polder, flooding 20,000 hectares and making the food situation in the west even more parlous – Hitler's orders for wholesale demolitions and flooding were ignored, thanks to Seyss-Inquart's qualified and calculated disobedience.

Blaskowitz knew nothing of Seyss-Inquart's 'disobedience' and neither did the residents of western Holland. As the long guns of *Festung Scheveningen* swung around over their heads to point at Allied troops, now advancing towards them, many wondered whether their homeland might still be turned into scorched earth as Blaskowitz's men fought to 'the last man and the last bullet'.

Spring had now come to western Holland, but only officially. In The Hague, Amsterdam, Leiden and the other cities of western Holland it was still very much winter.

With the Germans focusing on defence, some of those who had gone underground dared to venture outside. They could hardly believe their eyes when they saw what had become of their cities. 'In streets half ripped up, people kneel down to look for coal, the parks are completely uprooted, many houses have broken windows,' one non-Jewish *onderduiker* in Rotterdam recorded in his diary. 'Here and there in a doorway, a half-dazed and emaciated old man or woman is sitting with closed eyes.'

At 14 Pieter van den Zandestraat, Flory and Myrtil, half dazed and emaciated themselves, also sat with closed eyes, waiting, fighting their hunger pangs, holding on. Flory, in particular, continued to suffer.

April 1945, the fourth month of the *hongerwinter*, was the deadliest of all.

'It's going well,' a Dutch physician confided to his diary, 'except,' he said, meaning the millions still trapped within the walls of *Festung Holland*, 'for us. Death, particularly from oedema, is increasing alarmingly even in the better-off circles [i.e., those Dutchmen who still had some monetary resources], chiefly because of lack of protein.'

'Hunger, hunger . . . it's getting worse,' another Rotterdammer wrote on 22 April, after the official ration had dropped again to a less than meagre 290 calories. 'We don't even get our one slice a day. We don't know where to turn. We just stare at each other with hollow eyes.' Of course, the Franks, like most *onderduikers*, had to make do with even less.

On 10 April Churchill wrote to Franklin Delano Roosevelt about the terrible plight of the Dutch, telling him that if something was not done soon, the Allies faced a major human catastrophe in western Holland. The British Prime Minister suggested asking the Germans to allow additional supplies from neutral Sweden into the country. He even thought that the Germans might be willing to accept further supplies 'by sea or direct from areas under military control of the Allies'. Roosevelt, of Dutch descent himself, was already aware of the dire situation in western Holland. It is likely that he would have approved Churchill's request, but several days later he suffered a cerebral haemorrhage and died.

In any case, unknown to either Allied leader, Seyss-Inquart had opened secret negotiations with lower Allied officials and had agreed to something along the lines Churchill had suggested. However, it would take several weeks more for the tortuous discussions to bear fruit.

As Blaskowitz had vowed, most of the *Wehrmacht* troops facing the Allied armies in Holland indeed fought to the last man and the last bullet. Canadian troops faced one of their toughest fights on 6 April, when they sought to recover the old Dutch fortress at Zutphen, which was held by 1,500 determined paratroops between the ages of fifteen and twenty. Fighting as fanatically as their equally diehard Japanese allies in the Pacific, the young berserkers were only overcome after the Canadians used flamethrowers to burn them out one by one.

As elsewhere, Zutphen's suffering under the Nazi reign of terror persisted to the end. When Allied troops entered the scarred, newly freed city they encountered the bodies of ten Dutchmen who had been murdered by the SS at the last minute. Following a routine that would soon become familiar, the enraged liberators forcibly escorted some of the captured soldiers to the corpses, which had also been mutilated, in order for them to acquire a proper appreciation of their countrymen's ghoulish handiwork.

Canadian Broadcasting Corporation reporter Matthew Halton, accompanying the troops, recorded the scene as follows:

> As the frightened paratroopers looked on, Sergeant-Major Austin, cold with hate, bent over the dead men and showed me things too horrible to describe. Some of the men had been tortured and then shot. Their hands were still tied behind them, but some of them hadn't even been shot. They had been tortured to death in an unspeakable way. The worst things you've ever read about in any account of Nazi atrocity were there.

Western Holland was now finally drawing attention in the American press too. 'For five long years the Netherlands lay in the shadow of death,' opined an editorial in *The New York Times* on 3 April. 'Now it is lifting.'

> Long lines of German troops clog the roads, struggling to get out of the land they tortured and despoiled. Bursting bombs from Allied planes tear great gaps in the moving ranks . . . The liberating Allied tide that swept through France and Belgium last fall cleared only three provinces in the Netherlands. The rest of the country remained in slavery and passed into famine . . . The German soldiers redoubled their cruelties.

'What they did when discipline broke down,' the editorial continued, referring to atrocities such as those recorded above, 'will be whispered tales of horror in Holland for generations.'

On 7 April 1945, the Franks passed their thousandth day underground. The Germans might not be searching for Jews as before, but it still wasn't safe to go outside.

As always, as in 1942, and 1943, and 1944, the fundamental challenge remained the same: how do we get through *this* day? Somehow they got through it. Flory had been right to insist on the family staying together. It is difficult to imagine Dorrit and Sybil or their older parents surviving the ordeal alone, but together, this once not especially close family managed it. Somehow – with considerable help from their Dutch friends – they got through February and March and April. Somehow the Franks got through the last winter. No small feat.

The war progressed, as did the unfolding tale of Nazi genocide.

On 10 April Buchenwald, where thousands of German prisoners had died – and from whence Flory's brother Fred had had a lucky escape when he had been incarcerated there seven years before – was liberated. In his famous broadcast five days later, Edward R. Murrow struggled to put into words what he saw and experienced there:

> Buchenwald . . . is on a small hill about four miles outside Weimar, and it was one of the largest concentration camps in Germany, and it was built to last . . .
>
> We reached the main gate. The prisoners crowded up behind the wire. We entered. And now there surged around me an evil-smelling horde. Men and

boys reached out to touch me; they were in rags and the remnants of uniform. Death had already marked many of them. I asked to see one of the barracks. It happened to be occupied by Czechoslovakians. When I entered, men crowded around, tried to lift me to their shoulders. They were too weak to talk. I was told that this building had once stabled eighty horses. There were twelve hundred men in it, five to a bunk . . .

When I reached the centre of the barracks, a man came up and said, 'You remember me. I'm Peter Zenkl, the one-time mayor of Prague.' I remembered him, but I did not recognise him . . .

We proceeded to the small courtyard. The wall was about eight feet high; it adjoined what had been a stable or garage. We entered. It was floored with concrete. There were two rows of bodies stacked up like cordwood. They were thin and very white . . . I tried to count them as best I could and arrived at the conclusion that all that was mortal of more than five hundred men and boys lay there in two neat piles.

'It appeared that most of the men and boys had died of starvation,' Murrow informed his harrowed listeners, 'but the manner of death seemed unimportant. Murder had been done at Buchenwald.'

Several days later British troops liberated Bergen-Belsen. Amongst the 40,000 corpses they discovered there (unbeknownst to them) were those of Anne and Margot Frank. In her journal Anne Frank had written that despite everything people were fundamentally good. Murrow might have disagreed.

In Holland the liberation progressed town by town, village by village. The Germans continued to cede the Allies no quarter. On 14 April, the Canadians entered Leeuwarden, the capital of Friesland. Two days later, after a fierce battle with the hardened defenders, Groningen was freed. On the 17th, Canadian troops entered Apeldoorn, where Rauter had been ambushed. By the 18th, all of eastern and northern Holland except for the remote Frisian islands had also been freed.

Finally, the northwest's turn had come.

But on 22 April, to the dismay of western Hollanders, Montgomery, mindful of Blaskowitz's promise to blow Holland's remaining dykes to smithereens, ordered the British and Canadian troops under his command to halt at the Grebbe Line. The famine provinces of north Holland, south Holland and Utrecht were left under German control.

Secret negotiations between the Allies and the Germans to permit some form of emergency food relief into the famine provinces had continued. On the 23rd, the Allied Combined Chiefs of Staff specifically authorised Eisenhower to seek a truce with Seyss-Inquart for this purpose. In the meantime, planning for an emergency airlift continued in London. Called Operation Manna it sought to supply starving Holland with food from the skies.

On the 26th, Seyss-Inquart and Blaskowitz agreed a number of sites outside the major cities, including The Hague, for emergency food drops. In England, RAF and US Air Force crew eagerly loaded their life-giving payload, consisting of 5,000 tons of bread, margarine and other essential foodstuffs, on to waiting B-17 and B-24 bombers. On the 30th, the first group of the food-bomb-carrying planes finally received permission to take off. It was the first such wartime humanitarian mission in history and a trial run for the 1949 Berlin airlift.

On that glorious day – 30 April 1945 – Amsterdammers, Hagenaars and Rotterdammers heard the all-too-familiar sound of bombers flying overhead. But these were different from the ones they had heard and seen before. 'It was much louder than usual,' Dorrit recalled, 'because they were flying so low.'

And then people saw what these warplanes were dropping: not bombs – but boxes of food!

Still confined to their hiding place, the Franks couldn't see the blessed planes, but they could feel the explosion of joy along Pieter van den Zandestraat, as everyone who could ran out to cheer or wave at their airborne saviours.

'We knew it was nearly over when we heard those bombers,' Dorrit said.

That same day, as the RAF was bombing western Holland with bread and margarine and as Russian troops converged on the battered remains of the Reich Chancellery in Berlin, Adolf Hitler took a quiet lunch with his mistress, Eva Braun, and his private secretary. Then they swallowed cyanide capsules. Several blocks away, in the ruins of the Propaganda Ministry, Joseph Goebbels also took his life, as did his wife Magda, after forcing their five children to swallow cyanide capsules as well.

PART FIVE

SAFE HARBOUR
HOLLAND, USA, 1945–49

CHAPTER 12

To See the Sky

It is not possible to put on paper the expressions on the faces of the people –
faces that in many cases were pinched and drawn. It is not possible to put on
paper the desperation with which one youngster in a ragged coat clung to my
hand as we rode along and the enthusiasm with which each time we slowed
down, he yelled, 'This one speaks Dutch . . .'

William F. Boni, Dutch-speaking correspondent of
The New York Times, 5 March 1945

The Netherlands News Agency said yesterday that several Netherlanders had
been killed and more than thirty had been seriously wounded on Monday when
drunken German marines opened fire with hidden machine guns upon thousands
of joyful Netherlanders jammed in the public square in Amsterdam . . .

The New York Times, 10 May 1945

Death sentences were demanded today at the start of the first trials of persons
accused of collaborating with the Germans in the Netherlands. One defendant
is accused of betraying Jews as well as persons who sheltered them and of testi-
fying against ten members of the resistance movement . . .

Associated Press, 22 August 1945

It is the afternoon of 6 May 1945, the first day of Holland's and the Frank
family's freedom. Dorrit and Sybil are wandering around The Hague 'in
a daze', as Dorrit later recalled.

The day before, 5 May, at exactly eight a.m., following their agreement, all enemy forces in the Netherlands, north-west Germany and
Denmark, including Helgoland and the Frisian islands, had surrendered
to Montgomery's 21st Army Group. Elsewhere around the Reich, in

eastern Germany, where pockets of German troops continued to put up fierce resistance, in Czechoslovakia, where Nazi diehards battled Soviet troops, in Norway, where Admiral Dönitz, now titular head of Germany in the fallen *Führer*'s place, had yet to surrender German forces, the war in Europe continued.

But in Holland it was over.

The preceding week, the Franks' 147th underground, had been a nerve-racking one for them as they waited for official word of their individual and collective deliverance.

The food drop, of course, had been a good sign.

So was the news, breathlessly passed on by Annie several days later, that the hated Seyss-Inquart had at last fled the country.[*]

On 30 April, while the glorious Allied planes were still bombing the delirious Dutch with food parcels, the *Reichskommissar* had refused a demand from Eisenhower's chief of staff, Bedell Smith, that he capitulate. At first, Smith had tried to reason with the obdurate German official. After all, Hitler was dead. Seyss-Inquart refused. 'What would future generations of Germans say about me – what would history say about my conduct?' he answered.

Now Bedell Smith decided to get tough. 'Now look here, Reichs-Marshal,' the irate American said to the Austrian, mangling (deliberately or not) Seyss-Inquart's title, 'General Eisenhower has instructed me to say that he will hold you directly responsible for any further useless bloodshed. You have lost the war and you know it. And if, through pig-headedness, you cause more loss of life to Allied troops or Dutch civilians, you will have to pay the penalty. And you know what that means – the wall and the firing squad.'

Seyss-Inquart still refused. 'You know you will probably be shot?' Smith asked again. 'That leaves me cold,' said the *Reichskommissar*. 'It usually does,' Smith retorted.

Seyss-Inquart returned to his offices in The Hague, where he issued a statement in German about Hitler's death: 'German men and women, German youth in Fortress Holland, I call you, listen and understand with a strong heart: our leader has fallen in battle, his visible work has ended . . .'

Then the proconsul, his own visible work in Holland also concluded,

---

[*] Seyss-Inquart was captured and arrested by British forces in Germany shortly after the German capitulation.

hopped aboard a speedboat and departed for Germany to join Dönitz as Foreign Minister of the moribund Reich, as the *Führer*'s last will and testament had ordered.

Behind him, in Fortress Holland, Blaskowitz, the German commander, also refused to surrender German forces. The inundations, the raids, the terror, the useless bloodshed would continue until the last minute. In The Hague, in Amsterdam, in Rotterdam, the sound of shooting still reverberated at night.

As Bedell Smith predicted, Seyss-Inquart would pay dearly for his intransigence. He would not be shot. He would be hanged.

At number 14, the Franks continued to wait. The bag of pea meal which had supported them through the winter was gone. So were the few additional morsels Annie and Jeanne had diverted to them from the food drops. Flory, suffering from severe oedema, sat with her eyes closed, while Myrtil, Dorrit and Sybil took turns at the window, waiting.

On the morning of 5 May word came officially. In London, broadcaster (and future Dutch foreign minister) Henk van den Broek made the dramatic announcement over Radio Oranje: 'The Germans have capitulated,' said the emotional announcer. 'Five years of waiting and longing are rewarded . . . the country of the Netherlands is free again.'

In the distance, church bells rang. Dimly at first the Franks could hear them, then louder and louder with each peal. They gazed at each other as they realised the bells' significance. At last, at long last, one thousand and thirty-two days – nearly three years – since they had first walked into number 14 Pieter van den Zandestraat and shut the door behind them, it was over. The Frank family was free.

Yes, Annie and Jeanne joyously confirmed when they paid their first post-liberation visit that afternoon: it was, indeed, over. And so the next day, the 6th, Dorrit and Sybil hesitantly ventured outside their former hiding place for the first time.

The two Jewish women walked down the Noordeinde, feeling as if they were on another planet. The Lange Voorhout, the long avenue where The Hague's most famous hotel, the Hotel des Indes (under whose roof several Jewish *onderduikers* allegedly spent the war), and the capital's former Embassy Row, and other nearby streets, once so familiar, were now unutterably strange. The ravages of the *hongerwinter*, the empty shop windows, the missing trees, the army of gaunt faces were only too visible. Yet these things barely registered.

'We felt like zombies,' Dorrit said.

Then, as the two pale-faced girls continued to stroll, a sight shocked them out of their dazed state: a detachment of *Wehrmacht*, still in uniform, still armed, was marching down the street, heading straight for them.

Looking around, the girls saw other Germans, also in uniform, also armed.

What was going on? Had they been mistaken? Was this a reprise of *Dolle Dinsdag*? Were the Germans still in power?

'It was so strange,' Dorrit remembered. 'We were trying to figure out who was real, them – the troops – or us. But something was definitely wrong with that picture.' Trying not to draw attention to themselves, Dorrit and Sybil ran back to Pieter van den Zandestraat and resubmerged.

The Germans *had* capitulated, but Allied troops had not yet arrived to disarm them and take authority. As Van der Zee writes in *The Hunger Winter*: 'It was a strange time. The SS and the SD were still roaming around, capable of anything.' Another Dutchman said, 'We were sitting between coercion and freedom.'

The next day, on 7 May, freedom finally came as the liberators arrived to take up the reins of power. That afternoon, motorcycle units of the 1st Canadian Army, the unit assigned to The Hague, entered the Dutch capital to encounter bedlam.

'The joyous reception was greater than any could have imagined,' the divisional history records. 'Everywhere [in The Hague] people were literally jumping with joy. The advent of a military vehicle was a signal for a bombardment of flowers. Crowds closed in everywhere. People jumped on jeeps, trucks, tanks . . .'

Two of those delirious people were Dorrit and Sybil. Earlier that day, the two sisters, now full-grown (if half-starved) women of twenty-four and twenty, had re-emerged from their hiding place along with their parents – this time for good.

'Hi, soldier!' Dorrit greeted the first Canadian she saw, sitting behind the wheel of his jeep, using her once fluent English for the first time in years. 'What's your name?'

'Hi,' the grinning soldier answered. 'I'm Charlie Martin from Toronto.'

'Hi, Charlie Martin from Toronto!' Dorrit and Sybil replied in unison, as the Canadian soldier filled their arms with parcels of chocolate and Spam. 'That's all we ate for days,' Sybil recalled. 'Chocolate and Spam from Charlie Martin!'

The elder Franks were too tired to join the throngs, electing to stay at number 14 while their more ambulatory countrymen celebrated. Flory, little more than a walking skeleton, could barely stand. Neither could Myrtil. But they were happy. The Frank family's long flight from the Nazis which had begun at the central Berlin railway station on a grey morning in March 1933 was over. As Flory said later, 'For us the idea of walking around and not having to look over our shoulder was the most wonderful thing you can imagine.'

Perhaps the most moving description of the liberation was written by William F. Boni, a Dutch-speaking correspondent for *The New York Times*, who accompanied troops into Utrecht. His words apply as accurately to The Hague. 'It was not like France or Belgium last summer when the Allies were pelted with fruit and flowers,' Boni reported. 'It was too early for flowers and the last fruits as well as other food were eaten long ago.'*

> But they waved bits of orange ribbon, Dutch flags, large and small, and one woman proudly the Stars and Stripes . . . We moved into the city in low gear, our driver barely able to see where he was going over the shoulders of the kids sitting on the hood. My shoulder grew lame from the pounding by men and women, who yelled themselves hoarse . . .
>
> It is not possible to put on paper the desperation with which one youngster in a ragged coat clung to my hand as we rode along and the enthusiasm with which each time we slowed down he yelled, 'This one speaks Dutch!'
>
> It is not possible to give the emphasis with which time and again we heard the same words – 'We waited so long for your coming.'

Some German troops refused to recognise the surrender. In the worst incident, in Amsterdam, in a replay of what had taken place in Paris and other liberated cities, a group of drunken *Wehrmacht* soldiers opened fire on a mob of celebrants, killing nine and wounding many more before they were suppressed by Dutch forces. Elsewhere, other soldiers took hostages. After five years of lording it over the Dutch, it was difficult for some to accept the reality of defeat. The last German troops in Holland, including units assigned to the Frisian islands, did not tender their surrender for another full month.

By 10 May, most German troops were headed home, by foot. First, however, in an aptly Dutch form of payback, the vanquished troops were

---

* Evidently, to compare Boni's account with that of the First Canadian Army (p. 234), the Hagenaars had done a better job of hoarding their flowers than the citizens of Utrecht – or perhaps the Canadians just remembered it that way.

forced to hand over their helmets, thousands of which were used to make bedpans.

'Let this be known,' wrote Dutch poet Johan Fabricius, 'you marched into Holland against our will. Today your soldiers march into captivity, taking with them the curse of the Dutch people.'

As in France and other liberated countries, much of the unshackled people's bitterness was visited upon those who had collaborated or fraternised with the enemy. Women who had openly consorted with the occupier were vilified. A horrific image from those feverish days of the liberation shows one such woman in The Hague, her head tarred and shaved as a group of youths laugh nearby.

But Dorrit had little time or inclination for bitterness or recrimination. She was more interested in seeing who had survived.

One of the first things she and Sybil did once the cheering stopped was to go to the Red Cross station set up on the Lange Voorhout, where, they had been informed, the first lists of the dead were coming in from the extermination camps. Like many of those who would file into that and other stations over the next few weeks, she *knew*. She knew what had happened to Edgar, she knew he was probably dead. But still she hoped.

And there, sure enough, on the first list she looked at was the name of Edgar Reich, murdered at Auschwitz. And there, a little further down from that, was the name of Leontine, murdered at Sobibor. And there was 'Gerda Buchsbaum . . . Auschwitz' and 'Ed Weinreb . . . Mauthausen'. There, too, were the names of some of the other members of the old Hilversum group. Many familiar names met her eye, those of neighbours, school friends, acquaintances. All gone.

A Red Cross aide saw that Dorrit was in shock. The aide wished to be sympathetic, but at the same time she needed help: people were beginning to pour into the station. Soon the staff would be overwhelmed. Would Dorrit, she asked, mind staying to help answer questions?

Of course, Dorrit said, of course.

And so she got to work. It helped.

A few days later, while Dorrit was still absorbing Edgar's loss, Myrtil's florist friend came to number 14 and asked Dorrit and Sybil to come to a dance that was being held on the Noordeinde for the men of the 1st Canadian and the other British troops. 'We need to show our gratitude,' he explained. English-speaking girls were needed. Would Sybil and Dorrit mind coming?

Of course, the girls said, anything for the boys. Well – almost anything.

Myrtil insisted on coming along as chaperone. Very well.

The affair was a success. The men who came got to dance, and sometimes a little more. Gratitude was shown. Dorrit immediately hit it off with a Welsh sergeant-major by the name of Fred S., 'the most gorgeous man I ever saw', she recalled.

'Fancy meeting Little Dorrit in the middle of Holland,' the strapping sergeant said, after they were introduced. The regimental band struck up 'I'll Be Loving You Always'. They danced. And for a moment, as Dorrit fell into the arms of the first man she had held in years and the couple whirled around, she thought she was in love again.

There was only one problem: her gorgeous Welshman was married.

Ten days later, on 21 May, the Franks watched the Canadians stage their formal victory parade down the Vijverberg, the long, tree-lined boulevard parallel to the Binnenhof and the *Ridderzal*, where Seyss-Inquart (who had just been captured and imprisoned) had given his 'magnanimous' inaugural speech as *Reichskommissar* five years before.

As Dorrit continued to help out at the Red Cross station, the scale and enormity of the Nazi genocide, as well as Holland's disproportionately large loss, began to sink in.

Only 5,200 Jews returned from the camps. All told, nearly 110,000 Dutch Jews – an estimated 77 per cent of the pre-war Jewish population – were dead, the highest proportion of any country the Germans had occupied apart from Poland. Approximately 15,000 Jews who had dived under, like the Franks – perhaps two thirds of the total who had become *onderduikers* – had also survived.

One day in May, Dorrit and Flory went to an Allied information centre on the Lange Voorhout near the still shuttered US embassy to catch up on what was happening in the rest of the world. There they read the 7 May 1945 issue of *Life* Magazine, which contained a comprehensive illustrated report on the liberation of Buchenwald and some of the other extermination camps, with grisly detailed images. The surviving Franks confronted for the first time the actuality of the terrible fate that had consumed six million fellow European Jews and had somehow missed them.

Why did *we* survive? the Franks asked themselves as they scanned the lists of the dead. Why did they get through? they wondered, as their emotions oscillated from joy to despair during those first few weeks following the liberation.

In May, the Franks attended the service at the old synagogue on

Molenstraat, just a few blocks away from where they had been hiding. The rabbi of the Princess Irene Brigade, the repatriated Free Dutch troops who had led the victory celebrations, presided over the emotional service. As the Franks looked around the reopened synagogue, swelling with the sound of prayer, mourning as well as thanksgiving, they were struck by the number of the missing.

Then, to their surprise and joy, they saw two familiar faces, those of Myrtil's cousin, Gabi Rose, daughter of Myrtil's cousin Betty, and her husband, Sol, who had been amongst the few Jews who survived the war as 'protected' Jews because of Sol's Gentile background.

'You can't imagine how it felt when we found each other,' Dorrit said.

Unfortunately, there were too few such reunions.

In addition to thanking God, the Franks also thanked their friends Jeanne, Annie, Ans and Tine for their life-saving support. But how in particular to thank them? Where could the Franks begin?

It wasn't necessary. Their Dutch helpers could see and feel the family's gratitude every time they looked into their eyes.

Years later, after Israel created the Garden of the Righteous of Nations, a section of *Yad Vashem*, the Holocaust memorial, as a tribute to the many Gentiles of all the occupied countries who assisted Jews during the Nazi genocide, Jeanne specifically asked the Franks not to nominate her.

'I did nothing special,' she said, speaking for herself, as well as for Annie and her sisters. 'I did what I had to do.'

And what about their neighbours on Pieter van den Zandestraat?

The Franks felt grateful to them too, of course. What had they known? What had they thought? Surely some of them must have suspected there was something odd about the occupants of number 14. As the former *onderduikers* met their neighbours for the first time over the next few weeks, they learned that some of them had. The woman who lived at number 18, for example, said she had suspected that the residents of number 14 were Jewish, as had a number of others.

There were also a number who had believed the original rumour that Myrtil had planted while he was preparing to take the family under – that he was a Swiss-German doctor with a demented wife – and were surprised to learn that the doctor they had long thought was living in their midst was actually a German-Jewish émigré with a quite sane wife.

Others, who had only seen Myrtil leave and enter, were flabbergasted to learn that there was an entire family at number 14. 'They couldn't *believe* that a family could be living there all these years,' Dorrit said.

Their astonishment was mirrored by that of other Hagenaars around the city as they found out about the hundreds of Jewish *onderduikers* who had secreted themselves in hotel roofs and water closets and other odd places, as well as those who, like the Franks, had essentially been hiding in plain sight.

There were sufficient survivors in The Hague to form a social club, which Dorrit attended several times. One of the clubbers took a liking to her and invited her out, but she wasn't interested.

The majority of those who survived in The Hague were Jewish children who had either been placed with Gentile protectors before the war, or, more rarely, had dived under with their parents, like the Frank girls. In the Jewish Museum in Amsterdam there is an especially moving photograph taken of a special service for the youngest of these survivors that was held that summer at one of the three reopened synagogues in The Hague. In the centre of the photo, on the synagogue stage, a number of the reasonably healthy-looking children, wearing costumes and happy faces, are acting out an entertainment, perhaps a Purim play; to judge from their expressions, these young survivors have either forgotten or sublimated their dreadful experiences. They seem very happy to be there, on stage, performing. The superficially festive feeling of the event is belied, however, when one pans to the left and beholds a man, possibly one of the children's parents, sitting with his head in his hands. It is difficult to tell whether he is overcome with gratitude for the children who did survive, or sorrow at the many more who didn't.

There were many such emotional scenes around Holland that summer, as the Jews who had survived the war, together with the Gentiles who had resisted the Nazis and also suffered for it, returned to their places in Dutch society. In August, the *Concertgebouworkest*, the leading Dutch symphony orchestra, gave its first post-liberation performance in Amsterdam. As the orchestra took its seats, the audience was pleased to see that an astonishing number, fifteen, of the eighteen Jewish musicians who had been sent to the camps by the Nazis, were back in their chairs. Conspicuous by his absence was the orchestra's conductor, Willem Mengelberg, who had joined the official *Kulturkammer*, whose imprimatur was required for Dutch musicians to perform during the occupation, and had conducted in Berlin. Mengelberg's place at the conductor's stand was taken by associate conductor Eduard van Beinum, an outspoken anti-Nazi. Five other musicians whom the Honour Council for Music (the body charged with purging collaborationists) had banned were also excluded.

As van Beinum walked out on to the stage under a frieze on which the names of Jewish composers Felix Mendelssohn and Gustav Mahler had been painted out on German orders, the audience spontaneously stood and sang the Wilhelmus, the once-banned national anthem. Many, including the returning Jewish musicians, wept.

While some survivors were being lauded, many others – including the Franks – were given a rough time by the overwhelmed and underprepared Dutch authorities. Reclassified as stateless refugees, the same status they had held before the war, the Franks were issued humiliating new passports with the huge word STATENLOOS stamped on them, like a brand, and were told to report regularly to their local police station.

Their treatment paralleled the insensitive handling given their fellow Jewish survivors, particularly the 5,200-odd exhausted and disorientated souls who came back from the concentration camps and were granted no special status or facilities by the government. Rightly or wrongly, the government saw the Jewish camp survivors as no different from the 400,000 political prisoners and forced labourers who returned from the vanquished Reich and who also were, more often than not, in quite bad shape.[*] 'There was no one to meet us when we returned,' one such survivor lamented. 'People shrugged their shoulders in response to our story.'

A number of returning Jewish camp survivors were even interned with a group of ex-German SS, to the former's consternation and the latter's amusement before this grotesque mistake was discovered and rectified.

During the summer of 1945, the Franks were so distressed at this and other assorted indignities they had endured that Myrtil got the somewhat far-fetched notion of approaching Yehudi Menuhin, the virtuoso violinist, who was scheduled to perform in The Hague, in the hope that the American-Jewish musician might do something to help them, perhaps expedite the American visas they had applied for years before. In the event, Dorrit was assigned the duty of petitioning the touring wonder.

Menuhin shrugged his shoulders at the Franks' story. 'Why don't you go back to Germany?' he told a stricken Dorrit when she approached him backstage at his concert.

But the Franks' disillusionment with liberated Holland was short-lived. 'It was just at the beginning that we were upset, especially with those

---

[*] Dienke Hondius, of the Anne Frank House, is one of several Dutch historians who feel very strongly that Jewish camp survivors should have been accorded special status.

horrid passports,' said Dorrit, looking back a half-century later. 'It was so difficult, after what we had been through, to be treated . . . as strangers. But that feeling passed. I *loved* Holland. I still do.'

Dorrit's romance with her Welsh sergeant continued. Neither Flory nor Myrtil was exactly thrilled with the notion of their daughter going out with a married man. At the same time, the fact that Sergeant-Major S. was looking forward to eventually returning to his wife meant that they didn't have to worry about Dorrit getting too serious about him.

She didn't. Instead, she had fun.

Flory, who only weeks before had looked set for the grave, started to look outward again. One day, when Fred came to 14 Pieter van den Zandestraat in his jeep to take Dorrit to a football match in Rotterdam, Flory accepted his invitation to join them. She had one caveat: she wanted to go to the *Museum Booimans*. It was time to see some art again.

Rotterdam itself, still bearing the scars of the *Luftwaffe*'s 1940 terror bombing, seemed not much more than a cloud of dust at first. Flory, Dorrit and her Welsh sergeant-major gazed speechless at the giant hole that the *Luftwaffe* had left in the middle of Holland's second largest city.

The once thriving port was not the only part of Holland that still looked considerably the worse for wear, according to David Anderson, correspondent for *The New York Times*, in July 1945. 'The physical deterioration of what was once the richest corner of Europe must be seen to be understood,' Anderson wrote in his report on the still-inundated and palpably shell-shocked country. 'Altogether 6 per cent of the total land area has been inundated – that is half a million acres, 200,000 under salt water and a quarter of a million acres flooded by fresh water. From one to six years will be needed to repair the salted areas.'

Although the Germans did most of the physical damage, Anderson pointed out, the Allies were responsible too: 'By far the most spectacular of all the flooding has been that of the island of Zeeland, where British bombers cut the dykes last October in the battle for Antwerp. It has been learned that there is little hope of repairing the damage before winter.'

'The Hague,' the US writer noted, 'bears fresh scars. Dust from the tragic bombing mistake of March flies wildly around "the most beautiful village in Europe".'

The correspondent also noted the devastation at Scheveningen, the once beautiful resort where the Franks had lived before the invasion and which the Germans had perverted into *Festung Scheveningen*: 'Years of work lie ahead in clearing away the evidence of war, particularly on the waterfront, where the concrete emplacements of Hitler's *Westwall* lie heavily across the resort at Scheveningen.'

Then there was Rotterdam.

To Flory, the sight of the vast weed field which had replaced the destroyed city centre brought back memories of the German *Blitzkrieg* of May 1940, when the Franks had been uprooted – again – and Rotterdam had became a byword, like Guernica or Coventry, for terror. Five years, she thought to herself; it might as well have been fifty.

But that was then, and this was now, and now it was time to have a spot of fun and culture. As she took in all of the wonderful paintings again, Flory was the same wide-eyed teenager who had strolled through the Städel in Frankfurt with her mother years before, communing with artistic spirits past, or had conquered the Louvre on her own.

There was one minor *contretemps*, however, after Flory spotted a soldier wearing a New Zealand uniform strolling the gallery grounds. Did they have museums in New Zealand as well? the reawakening *grande dame* asked.

'Madame, do you think we are all *savages* there?' the aggrieved Kiwi retorted.

Myrtil translated his own not inconsiderable knowledge of art, acquired from Flory and augmented by his friend L., into a new career as an art dealer. According to Dorrit, Myrtil fell into a conversation with a gallery owner. Pleasant conversation turned to business: the gallery owner had a frame that needed a painting. Perhaps Mr Frank would know where to find the right one?

If ever there was a good time to dive into the European art market, the period immediately following the war was it, as collectors both in the Netherlands and elsewhere who had been hoarding their art during the war decided to sell. Within a few months, Myrtil was doing well enough in his new career to enable him to move the family out of 14 Pieter van den Zandestraat into a larger flat in the undamaged part of *Bezuidenhout*.

He also hired a photographer to take an 'official' post-liberation portrait of the Franks to distribute to their friends and family worldwide. In the photo, the first of the Franks *en famille* in many years, the former *onder-duikers*, particularly the elder Franks, still look considerably the worse for wear. Myrtil has lost weight, as has Flory, whose still beautiful hair is now white; however, his incandescent pre-war smile is back.

'You see,' said the radiant image, which Myrtil was pleased to send to Julius in England, to Lisbeth and Ernst and Johanna in Palestine, to Ferdi in Morocco, to Fred in New York – and to all the Franks' other relations around the world, many if not most of whom had long since given them up for dead: 'you see . . . we *did* survive.'

The Red Cross continued to update its lists from the camps. One by one, the dwindling hopes of the relatives of those inmates who were as yet unaccounted for were quashed, as the names of the tens of thousands of Dutch Jewish dead filtered in.

'Sorry,' Dorrit, who continued to assist at the Red Cross station on Lange Voorhout, would say again and again. 'Sorry.' Or, occasionally – gently – 'Yes, we may have something for you.'

One of the disappointed was Otto Frank. On 24 October 1945, Otto, the lone survivor of the group of eight *onderduikers* at 263 Prinsengracht, received a letter informing him that his daughters Anne and Margot had died at Bergen-Belsen.

On a return visit to the Franks' violated hiding place, Miep Gies, his former secretary and one of the Franks' principal helpers during the twenty-five months they had managed to evade the Nazis before their betrayal, gave Otto the diary that Anne had diligently kept during their ordeal. Astonished, Otto began to turn the pages . . .

As in France and Norway, a spirit of vengeance and embitterment characterised the Dutch reckoning at first. It all seemed very straightforward: just arrest anyone who had anything to do with *Reich-Holland*. Under these nebulous guidelines, Dutch forces arrested close to half a million suspects – approximately 5 per cent of the country's population – between September 1944, when the southern part of Holland was liberated, and the end of 1945, by far the highest such number and proportion in any part of the former Reich. Of these, a little over 200,000 had their files forwarded for prosecution.

It was no surprise when, on 4 September, the tribunal handed out its first death sentence to one J. Breedvelt, of Delft, after finding him guilty of having been a paid betrayer of Jews. There would be more death sentences to come.

If anything, the desire for vengeance grew harsher as winter came on, reminding many Dutchmen of the rigours and atrocities of the previous *hongerwinter*, and memorials and services for the dead and the martyred continued. On 27 November, thousands gathered in Haarlem to pay homage to the hundreds of resistance members who had been shot in the dunes outside the city at Overween, amongst them one woman, Hannie Schaft, whose remains were reburied in a field of honour at Bloemendaal; Schaft had belonged to an anti-collaborationist liquidation squad before she was tracked down in the final weeks of the war and was liquidated herself.

The following month, the Amsterdam Opera staged *Tosca*. The Honour Council for Music, the same body that had banned collaborationist musicians from appearing on a Dutch stage, had given the members of the cast, many of whom had played the same opera during the war, a clean bill of health. However, the audience did not think the Council had done its job thoroughly enough. The post-liberation *Tosca*'s last act was interrupted by shouts and catcalls. A full-fledged riot, with crowds of enraged Amsterdammers shouting '*Sieg Heil!*' ensued.

'In the prevailing mood of embitterment,' wrote Daniel Schorr in *The New York Times* in February 1946, 'the hostility to pro-Nazis does not draw any fine distinctions. Anyone who performed publicly during the occupation must have had German permission, and is automatically branded as suspect.' That month the first death sentence was carried out against a German stormtrooper, named Heineman, who had been found guilty of forty murders, including those of two British officers captured at Arnhem. The Queen rejected Heineman's plea for mercy, as she would reject most such pleas.

Wilhelmina was in no mood to forgive, and neither was Holland.

The Dutch eventually found, however, that, unlike in France, where the tumbril continued to roll, vengeance did not become them. Although the war crimes tribunal continued to hand down death sentences, few were carried out. Additionally, the country was ill-equipped to house the large numbers of prisoners awaiting trial. In June a deadly riot broke out at the Duindorp internment camp near Scheveningen, where some of the 70,000 accused had been pent up.

David Anderson noted the Dutch reluctance in his report in *The New York Times*. 'The whole procedure of concentration camp military courts and the death sentence is distasteful to the Netherlanders,' he wrote, 'who, nevertheless, admit that Netherland Nazis must be punished.'

'The time has come to exercise compassion,' said Louis Beel, the new Prime Minister, in a speech before the *Staten-General* in June, in which he promised to cut down the number detained to 25,000 by October. Successive Catholic ministers of justice, following Beel's call, continued to pursue this policy of 'compassion', for a combination of moral and practical, as well as politically expedient reasons: many of the accused collaborators, it seems, were Catholic.

In the end, Holland's reckoning was relatively mild compared with the rest of the Reich. Fourteen thousand, five hundred and sixty-two Germans or Dutch collaborators were convicted and sentenced in Holland. One hundred and nine death sentences were passed down; thirty-nine were carried out. By contrast, in neighbouring Belgium, which did not suffer as much in loss of either life or property, but where the process was more 'businesslike' (in the words of Anderson), nearly three times as many executions were carried out.

It is safe to assume, however, that there were few tears shed when Anton Mussert was marched out to the Scheveningen dunes, where so many Dutch patriots had been shot, to meet his fate. 'Diminutive Anton Mussert, Führer of the Netherland Nazis, died before a firing squad today after bidding farewell to his followers, who clicked their heels, stood at attention and addressed him solemnly as leader,' reported *The New York Times* on 7 May 1946. 'Mussert's whole career was that of a little man pretending to be big,' the paper opined. 'The only big thing he accomplished was the crime of treason to his country.'

Eager themselves to move on, the Franks were also of two minds about the Dutch war crimes tribunals, which they followed with mixed interest, their anger at the many Dutch who had collaborated overridden by their respect and awe for the brave few, like Jeanne and Annie and the others, who had gone against the herd instinct to collaborate or accommodate, and to whom they owed their lives.*

They could afford to be magnanimous: they had survived.

In November 1945 the Nuremberg trials began. The following June, ex-*Reichskommissar* Arthur Seyss-Inquart sat in the dock together with twenty-one of his former Nazi comrades, accused of taking part in crimes against peace, crimes against humanity – i.e. exterminations, deportations and genocide – and war crimes, or conspiracy to commit the above. Seyss-Inquart, the seventeenth of the accused war criminals scheduled to present his defence, was charged with crimes against peace in connection with his role in the *Anschluss*, and crimes against humanity in connection with his position in Holland and his leading role in the

---

* Amongst those who were put on trial were Asscher and Cohen, the former heads of the Jewish Council; however, though disgraced, the two were found innocent of committing any crimes and released. They were enjoined from holding any further office in the Jewish community.

murder of a quarter of a million Dutchmen, including the majority of the Dutch Jewish population.

The tribunal contained no Dutch judges – only American, British, French and Russian ones – but the Dutch people trusted that justice would be served. Regarding the *Anschluss*, Seyss-Inquart testified that his role in Hitler's *coup d'état* had been exaggerated. 'I told Hitler I would not offer myself as a Trojan-horse leader,' he said, supplying records of his meetings with the *Führer*. Speaking out against his former leader for the first time, the one-time Austrian Minister of the Interior said evenly that Hitler had 'double-crossed' him by breaking his promise that Austrian ideals would be maintained as a requisite for a peaceful union with Germany.

But the Franks, like their countrymen keenly following the proceedings in the reborn Dutch press (which included a number of underground papers that had 'surfaced' and become legitimate), were not interested in Seyss-Inquart's role in the *Anschluss*. They were more interested in what he had to say about what he did in Holland.

Seyss-Inquart did not disappoint, launching into a spirited if spurious self-defence. He was 'proud' of his record in Holland, he said with apparent sincerity. He was 'constantly' at odds with the Gestapo over the shooting of Dutchmen without trial, he claimed, citing his 'success' at cutting down the number of hostages shot after the March 1945 assassination attempt on Rauter from 500 to 'only 117'.

Anyway, the defendant continued, the stories of the shootings of hostages were exaggerated:

> Leaders of the resistance were arrested and examined by the Elite Guard and police and were subject to be shot under the Führer's orders. For example, there was the case of a plot to blow up a bridge, and instead of taking hostages, these men were shot. That is the opposite of shooting hostages – at least it was supposed to be.

He said that he was aware of 'excesses' committed against Dutchmen, 'but that in wartime is almost unavoidable'. Anyway, compared to the other occupied countries, 'things were not so bad'.

And what about the extermination camps? Several months later, when the so-called 'atrocity film' was shown before the tribunal, with footage of the liberated extermination camps, Seyss-Inquart's reaction to the grisly scenes was a stoical one, in contrast to the apoplectic reactions of several of his co-defendants. 'It gets you,' he said afterwards, enigmatically, 'but I can take it.' In court he feigned surprise. He had done his best to ameliorate conditions in the camps in the East, as far as he was able, he indignantly insisted. Anyway, 'a representative of the Netherlands Red Cross was allowed to visit these camps and never directed any complaints to me. I considered that remarkable, because the Netherlanders complain about everything.'

Gustave Steinbauer, the Austrian lawyer hired to defend Seyss-Inquart, picked up where his client left off. Did you know what my client did to save Dutch agriculture? he enquired. Or to safeguard Holland's art treasures?

In November, when the trial came to an end, Seyss-Inquart was one of the dozen top Nazis to be sentenced to death and one of the two German proconsuls to receive the maximum sentence; the other was his former boss and mentor, Hans Frank, who had overseen the ruthless occupation of Poland and the extirpation of Polish Jewry.[*]

In late May, just as Seyss-Inquart was about to begin his defence, Winston Churchill, the former British Prime Minister, appeared in The Hague to give a speech before the reactivated Dutch legislature. Hagenaars cheered to see the man attached to the voice that had promised them deliverance when they were occupied and had – in concert with the United States army – made good on that promise.

Contemplating the terrible conflict just ended, Churchill had no qualms about telling the Dutch, I told you so:

> After the end of the great conflict from 1914–18 we hoped that the wars were over. Yet we have just witnessed an even more destructive world-wide struggle. Need we have done so? I have no doubt whatever that firm guidance and united action on the part of the victorious powers could have prevented this last catastrophe.

If only the United States Senate had ratified the Treaty of Versailles and joined the League of Nations, the war would not have taken place, Churchill said. He made no mention of the other articles in the flawed treaty, including the war guilt clause and the extortionist Allied food blockade, which had helped pave the way for Hitler. Now he advocated

---

[*] It is likely that Seyss-Inquart's fellow Reichcommissioner, Josef Terboven, the ruthless ruler of occupied Norway, would also have received the death sentence; however, he had already cheated the gallows by sitting on a box of explosives and blowing himself up on 6 May 1945.

an updated league, a United States of Europe parallel to the just-formed United Nations, a precursor to the European Union, as the best means of staving off another such catastrophe.

Churchill was not loath to remind his audience of the British contribution to their freedom. 'Upon Britain fell the proud but awful responsibility of keeping the flag of freedom flying in the Old World till the forces of the New World could arrive. But now the oppressors are cast out and broken.

'We may be wounded and impoverished,' the Great Man continued, referring to conditions on both the English and Dutch sides of the Channel, 'but we are still alive and free. The future stands before us to make or mar.'

Wounded and impoverished – fitting words to describe Holland in the summer of 1946, one year after its liberation from the Nazis.

The ambitious programme of *Herstel en Vernieuwing* – Rebuilding and Renewal – announced the previous July was well under way by now. But the evidence of war was still everywhere – in the missing rows of houses in the *Bezuidenhout*, in the dragon's teeth and bunkers in the dunes at Scheveningen, in the woods adjoining the Peace Palace where the V-2s used to be launched.

Flory was deeply conscious of the most important absence: the people, especially all the young people who had died. 'It was so empty,' she recalled. 'There was nothing left.' Myrtil and Flory didn't mind so much for themselves, but they feared for their daughters' mental health. They wondered if they would ever really be able to move on while they remained in Holland.

CHAPTER 13

Wonderful Town

When Frank Sinatra joins Your Hit Parade *[a popular American radio show]*
this fall the minimum age for studio audiences will be raised from 14 to 18. It's
part of a campaign to present Sinatra as less an idol of screaming bobby-soxers,
more of a dignified singer.

Newsweek, 18 August 1947

> *Shimmering clouds*
> *In canyons of steel*
> *They're making me feel*
> *I'm home*
> *It's autumn in New York*
>
> *That brings a promise of new love*
> *Autumn in New York . . .*

Lyrics to 'Autumn in New York', the 1947
Frank Sinatra hit song

> *Shining towers, in the sky.*
> *The Torch of Liberty, lifted high,*
> *Blazing lights, of the Great White Way*
> *Spelling glamour – bright as day!*
> *Sights and sounds where dreams come true,*
> *Her magic skyline welcomes you!*

From a postcard sold in Manhattan in the 1940s

In the autumn of 1946, Dorrit received a strangely familiar call from her
Uncle Julius in Manchester: would she like to come over for a few months
and help him around the studio?

249

Would she? Of course!

Flory and Myrtil were all for it. They were still worried about their daughters' future and their psychological health. Dorrit had complained of not being able to concentrate; Sybil had trouble sleeping. They had begun to wonder how wise it was, after all, for the family, at least the girls, to stay in Holland. There seemed to be too many ghosts. As much as the family loved the Netherlands, and especially *Den Haag*, they wondered – had to wonder – what sort of future they could have in their still wounded, impoverished and haunted city.

And so, on a sunny day in October 1946, Little Dorrit, not so little now, once again took the train from The Hague to catch the ferry from the Hook to England.

There were tears when uncle met niece again in Manchester. There was no talk about the war: Julius could find out about that in time. He was just happy – stunned indeed – to see his niece alive.

Dorrit had a productive time with Julius again, as she had had seven years before. She even learned to put up with his temper tantrums.

Churchill was right: Britain *was* wounded and impoverished as well – especially the latter. The scars of the war were still very much in evidence on the English side of the Channel, particularly in London. Pockmarked with bomb sites and piles of rubble, the combined vestiges of the blitz and the V-1/V-2 campaign, the city looked considerably older than when Dorrit had seen it last, and much the worse for wear.

So this is where they hit, said the Dutchwoman – for that was what she considered herself now. This is what those monstrous things she had heard at number 14 did, when they hit. For a moment there would be a brief, searing imagined flashback to what had transpired at the death site. Then she would walk on.

The faces of civilians she passed, like those of the Dutch, looked older too. The English had been through their own ordeal: nearly 300,000 British servicemen were dead, as well as 50,000 civilians. Just as in Holland, the sense of loss and emptiness was everywhere apparent. The joy of VE-Day, the cries of the crowds at that delirious celebration, were long gone. England, still, was wounded.

How poor everything seemed! As in Holland, there were shortages of everything. Rationing was still in place, the glamour of pre-war London was gone. There was little sense of triumph.

'I couldn't believe it,' she recalled. 'The English were in worse shape than we were! And yet I rejoiced in the thought that I was in a country that had won the war. I loved England. I still do.'

Dorrit enjoyed selling her uncle's wallpaper designs. But however much she loved working for Julius and loved England, her destiny did not lie there, and somehow she knew it.

In April 1947, her father called with electrifying news: the family's US visas, the same ones he had applied for in Rotterdam in 1938, the one he had been told he would have to wait for indefinitely, had, somehow, come through. US immigration was still highly selective, but with the aid of Fred (still living in New York), who had continued to push the family's case, they had made it past the velvet rope: the Franks had been admitted into Club America. At least Dorrit and Sybil had. Flory and Myrtil would be staying in Holland, it was quickly decided. After all, Myrtil was now a successful art dealer in his adopted country.

Over the past half-year, Holland's recovery had gathered pace. The scars of the war were disappearing. Money was coming into the country again. The centre of Rotterdam had been cleared for new construction. Holland was moving again. The cornerstone of recovery was the massive US aid plan for postwar Europe, announced by George Marshall, the visionary US Secretary of State and former army chief of staff in a speech at Harvard University that spring as the Marshall Plan.

That was very well for the Dutch, but now the Frank girls were actually moving to the source of this largesse, America. Passage was booked from Antwerp to New York on 21 August on a Liberty ship, a veteran of the Atlantic lifeline with the apt name of SS *Shooting Star*.

And so Dorrit said her goodbyes to her latest boyfriend, a vice-consul of the British embassy, and she and Sybil began working on their American slang.

First, however, Myrtil had other pressing family business to attend to. Lisbeth, his sister in Palestine, called to say that their mother, Johanna, who had been living with her, her husband Ernst and their two daughters in the northern city of Nahariyah, was dying. Aged eighty-four and suffering from cancer, she only had one last request: to see her sons before she died. She would hold on until she did.

Myrtil and Julius made preparations to sail to Palestine. The talk of Nahariyah that spring was of old Mrs Frank, hanging on to see her sons. At the end of April, Johanna saw Julius and Myrtil. Two days afterwards she died.

Johanna Frank's odyssey, which had begun in the Hunsrück at the beginning of the age of Bismarck, the Iron Chancellor, whose reforms paved the way for the Golden Age of German Jewry, had come to a close.

The funeral in the town cemetery was a moving one. Later Julius, still a talented artist, made a drawing of the wagon that had carried his mother through the orchards to her final resting place.

On 21 August 1947, Flory and Myrtil took the train to Antwerp to see Dorrit and Sybil off to America. Flory had gone to the trouble and expense to dress her daughters for the big departure scene on the SS *Shooting Star*, but they were taken aback to find that the huge ship of their imagination was a mere freighter, with capacity for a dozen or so passengers.

The requisite goodbyes were said, and the girls were off.

The Atlantic passage was a pleasant one. The *Shooting Star* may not have been the SS *Rotterdam*, but she was a game lady nonetheless, and her diminutive size allowed the crew to lavish attention and supplies on the passengers. Sybil recalled that they were served sherbet, her most vivid memory of the crossing. Quite an improvement on biscuits and Spam. 'It was *wonderful*.'

Shortly before they had embarked, the Franks were belatedly confronted with another wartime ghost: that of Anne Frank, whose underground journal had just appeared for the first time in Dutch as *Het Achterhuis* (*The Secret Annexe*). The first edition, published after her father's strenuous exertions to bring his gifted daughter's work to life, was only 1,500 copies. The Franks, not especially eager to look back, read excerpts in the newspapers. What they did read sent shivers up their spine.

The coincidences between their movements and experiences and those of their *doppelgänger* family in Amsterdam seemed too numerous to be true. Here, they read with amazement, was another Jewish family named Frank that had fled Germany in late 1933, just about the same time that they had. The author's family had also lived in the River Quarter, where *their* family had lived for those dreadful few months in the spring of 1942, after they had been forced to move there from Hilversum.

More coincidences: the Franks – the other *Franks* – had dived under on 9 July 1942, a mere five days before they did.

Both families had been careful. Indeed, if anything – if one considers

Myrtil's seemingly reckless sorties outside their hiding place – the other Frank family had been even more careful than theirs. The author's 'secret annexe' had been completely concealed, whereas theirs, behind the door of a ground-floor flat, had not really been concealed at all. And yet the author's family, the *other* Franks, along with the four other hapless *onderduikers* who were sequestered with them up until their betrayal in August 1944, were the ones who had been given away and had died, with the exception of the father, Otto.

Why?

Later, the Franks would differ about this. Flory, the most religious of the family, would say it was the hand of God that had saved them. Dorrit, the romantic, would attribute the miracle of their survival to something called Destiny. Sybil, the aspiring chemist and the most hard-headed of the foursome, held no truck with such cloudiness. They had merely been lucky, she said.

Such perspectives influenced what the three Frank women would recall of their underground experiences. But in the short term, the publication of *The Diary of a Young Girl* (as Anne Frank's diary would be called in its English edition) only seemed to make the Holland they were leaving all the more haunted, and to reinforce the wisdom of their decision to move to America.

Later, when they had more distance from the events described, the Franks bought the book and marvelled at the precocity of Anne Frank's style, and her insight into her predicament and the human condition; and they, too, wept, like millions of her posthumous readers.

But in 1947 she was just another ghost. Now they simply wanted to move on, to forget about the war. If Anne Frank had survived, would she not have felt the same?

Moved as they were by Anne Frank's diary, they differed from her on at least one point. 'In spite of everything,' Anne had written, 'I still believe that people are really good at heart.'

Contemplating the unprecedented murder and destruction that Hitler had wrought, the Franks didn't think so.

The crossing on the *Shooting Star* took eight long, sherbety days.

Dorrit knew they were approaching their destination when she heard piped over the PA system the syncopated sounds of *The Make Believe Ballroom*, a jazz show on radio station WNEW that had been a New York radio staple for many years. It drenched the delighted passengers and crew with the serenading tunes of Glenn Miller, Benny Goodman and other ballroom maestros.

The next thing the girls found themselves drenched in was their own sweat: they had timed their arrival to coincide with the dog days of August, and the worst heatwave in years. The thermometer hit 97° on the molten, semi-tropical day that the *Shooting Star* docked. In addition, there was a dock strike, delaying the girls leaving the ship. It was hours before the young émigrées got through US customs.

A middle-aged gentleman in a boater and white suit was waiting for Dorrit and Sybil. He identified himself as a representative of HIAS, the Hebrew Immigrant Aid Society, the noted Jewish relief association for victims of the Holocaust. Evidently the society had been contacted about the girls' arrival ahead of time, perhaps by Myrtil or by their uncle, Fred.

The man from HIAS was surprised: he had been under the impression that Dorrit and Sybil were elderly, at least in their sixties, probably older.

'He kept looking at us as if we were impostors,' Dorrit recalled.

Welcome to New York.

Then Fred found them. The Buchenwald survivor, now a bona fide American, was waiting to give his nieces a proper introduction to New York. One of the first things he did, Sybil recalled, was to take them to a genuine New York cafeteria.

'Oh, that was the best cafeteria,' Sybil recalled. 'And all that food! It was good! It was *swell*!'

The heat passed, as August melded into September. Now it was time for Dorrit and Sybil to find jobs. After all, they had rent to pay.

That could wait, Fred said. Enjoy yourselves. See the town. And what an amazing town mid-1947 New York City was. The awestruck refugees walked up and down Manhattan's rectangular grid, amazed at the dimensions of their new home, its energy, its variety, its wealth; through the Sheep Meadow in Central Park, filled with well-dressed families, lovers, friends, picnicking, relaxing, cavorting, playing; along Fifth Avenue, lined with department stores filled with happy shoppers, arms filled with goods, toting shopping bags; up and down the towering 102-storey Empire State Building, with its 'Longest Uninterrupted Elevator Above the Earth's Surface'; up and down canopy-lined Park Avenue; and Madison Avenue and Third Avenue too; through the concrete canyons filled with life, movement, power, promise. Nothing in their wildest dreams could have prepared them for such a spectacle.

America too had suffered and sacrificed; over 300,000 GIs had died during World War II. But whatever psychological wounds remained from the conflict had healed. Only the occasional sight of a wounded war veteran in the street reminded them that there had even been a war.

Implicit in the contentment, the self-assuredness, the power they felt rising from the city pavements and bouncing off the skyscrapers was the satisfaction that America had triumphed – that these same New Yorkers they passed on the street, whom they glimpsed confidently slipping in and out of hotels, hobnobbing at restaurants, hailing taxis, zooming by in limousines, were the people who had won the war. This was the bouncy, blaring city represented by the electrified grid of Dutch painter Piet Mondrian's celebrated painting, *Victory Boogie-Woogie*. In 1947 New York was still very much doing the victory boogie-woogie. What a contrast to the pallid faces and shabby, broken-down, blitzed buildings of London, The Hague and Amsterdam. Here was the new *Großstadt*, the great city, as Berlin had once described itself *après le déluge*.

Here was the city Jan Morris depicted in *New York 1945*.

This was the Wonder City, the Last Word on almost anything.

Were not the Rockefeller Center roof gardens four times the size of the Hanging Gardens of Babylon? Had not one Manhattan building after another gained the title of the highest building on Earth – after the Singer, the Metropolitan, Life after the Woolworth Building, to Wall Street, the Cities Service Building, the Chrysler and the matchless Empire State?

And the museums! There were so many museums – the Met, and the Frick, and the Museum of Modern Art. Mother would have such a wonderful time when she came over. And the movies! One of the first things Dorrit wanted to do was to catch *Gone With the Wind*, the 1939 blockbuster with Vivien Leigh and Clark Gable, based on the book she had read and reread in hiding. As luck would have it, there was a revival of the film playing at a theatre in Times Square. One afternoon in early September, after another walkabout, Dorrit and Sybil went to see it. For three hours they gasped and wept (at least Dorrit did; Sybil was not the crying type) as Atlanta burned and Scarlett and Rhett performed their *pas de deux*.

'It was *so* fantastic,' Dorrit said, her eyes still bright with the memory.

'And then to come out of the theatre in Times Square and to see the smoke coming out of the Camel [the Times Square advertisement for Camel cigarettes]. It was like a dream.'

The girls quickly found jobs, Dorrit as a secretary for a temporary agency in Rockefeller Center, Sybil as a lab assistant with the US Vitamin Corporation. The fact that both of them spoke fluent English certainly helped.

Immediately, both of them were in the grip of the mania that was sweeping New York: World Series fever. The New York Yankees were playing the Brooklyn Dodgers – also known as The Bums. Of course, neither of the girls knew the first thing about baseball. 'Are they winning? Are they winning?' Dorrit anxiously asked her office colleagues, even though she had no idea who was winning what.

And so, just as Dorrit and Sybil had become enthusiastic Dutchwomen in 1933, now, in 1947, they became enthusiastic Americans. Or, rather, New Yorkers.

The following spring, Flory came over to visit. She was pleased with Dorrit's new boyfriend, Kurt Sander. A naturalised German Jew who had fled Germany in 1933 but had decided to come to the United States, after a two-year interregnum in Denmark, Sander had enlisted in the United States army in 1942, one of a number of Germans who put their knowledge of the language and psychology of their former homeland to use as interrogators of captured prisoners of war. Joining the 83rd Division, which fought in France and Germany, Captain Sander had played a pivotal role in negotiating the surrender of the German bastion of St Malo. He was there when the 83rd Division became the first US unit to cross the Elbe river, en route to liberate Berlin – or so it thought, until the order came down from Eisenhower for the men to hold their ground. Berlin, it had been decided, was the Russians' party.

Winning a Bronze Star for his services as an army interrogator, Sander had, following the end of the war, been asked to serve as an interrogator at Nuremberg. He was designated to interrogate Hjalmar Schacht, the man who had helped save the mark in 1923 and later had become Hitler's economics minister.

Dorrit was drawn to Captain Sander's story. She was also drawn to Captain Sander. 'We dated twelve times,' she recalled.

Dorrit and Kurt Sander were married at the Hotel Madison on 11 September 1949. 'It was an elegant affair,' said Sybil.

That winter, Flory and Myrtil took an apartment on Riverside Drive, on Manhattan's West Side, from where they could see the sun set over the Hudson River and their new adopted homeland. The Franks had found safe harbour at last.

Epilogue

Unlike Holland, whose asylum had proved a cruel mirage, America, where the Frank family's odyssey terminated in the late 1940s, was a bona fide safe harbour. If the Franks didn't live happily ever after, they certainly came very close to it over the next twenty years.

Shortly after her sister's wedding, Sybil found romance in the person of Carl Ehrlich, another naturalised German Jew and US army veteran. Like his future brother-in-law, Kurt Sander, Ehrlich, another pre-war refugee, had seen action in the Battle of the Bulge. At one point, during the scare over American-speaking infiltrators whom the Germans had planted behind American lines, Sergeant Ehrlich's accent nearly got him killed.

Sybil and Carl were married in October 1950 at the Hotel Pierre in a small, but elegant affair. This time both Myrtil and Flory, who had now also moved to New York while maintaining a second residence in The Hague, were on hand to witness the happy occasion.

Dorrit and Kurt moved to Long Island, where I was born in 1951, the first of the next generation of Franks. My brother Lee followed in 1956. Kurt, who had returned to civilian life rather than remain in the Regular Army (a decision he would later rue), continued to work as a merchandising executive, his pre-war profession. However, his true love continued to be the army. He remained in the Active Reserve, retiring as a lieutenant colonel in 1964; it was his proudest accomplishment.

Sybil's first child, Gerald, was born in 1953. His sister, Vicki, followed four years later. And now the American Franks were ten.

In the meantime, Myrtil, with Flory's help, prospered as an art dealer specialising in twentieth-century art. The Franks' Riverside Drive apartment, where Myrtil conducted his business, was a veritable gallery itself, where the Frank grandchildren played in the shadow of Kandinsky, Signac and the like. Predictably, Flory revelled in her role as one of the *grandes dames* of the New York art scene. Nothing pleased her more than to attend a new *vernissage*, or for the smiling Myrtil to accompany her.

And this time, unlike in Berlin, Myrtil's smile was genuine. Although it would probably be an exaggeration to say that the Franks fell in love again, I certainly recall their taking great and genuine joy in each other's company, as the photos of them from the 1950s and 1960s show. Summering in The Hague, which they used as their base to explore the rest of Europe, wintering in New York, travelling back and forth on the SS *Rotterdam* and other luxury ships, they truly seemed to enjoy the best of both worlds. I don't recall them discussing the war very much: they were having too much fun.

The Franks never forgot their debt to Holland, and the Dutch people, for helping to save their lives. In gratitude, in the 1960s, Myrtil donated a work of art to the Gemeentemuseum in The Hague.

During a visit to Venice in 1947, Myrtil was startled to encounter an old friend, the Rubens – *his* Rubens, the one he had sold on the black market in 1942 before the family dived under – in an art gallery there. However, he lacked the means to repurchase it. As far as I can ascertain, it now hangs in the Prado in Madrid.

Myrtil never lost the impish sense of humour which had proved such a lifesaver while the Franks were underground. I still remember his whooping, slightly maniacal laugh. He died in 1968, aged seventy-four. Though shaken, Flory recovered from her husband's death and continued to cross the Atlantic every summer, travelling widely in Europe and even managing to handle a few art deals of her own.

She died in 1981 at the age of eighty-five. If, as the saying goes, living well is the best revenge, Flory and Myrtil were proof positive.

In 1965 Dorrit made her first, emotional visit to her former adopted country, and number 14 Pieter van den Zandestraat. It was then that the seed for this book was born (as described in the Afterword, following). In the event, the current occupants of the flat were not at home.

In 1982, the year following Flory's death, the surviving *onderduiker* returned to Holland once again, this time with Sybil in tow. The occupants, a family of three, including one boy, were happy to receive their guests. During that trip, the two sisters also visited their former saviour,

Annie, who by then was ailing and living in Zeeland; she died two years later, followed shortly by her sister Tine, who died in 1986.

Jeanne Gutschmidt, née Houtepen, their other helper, currently lives in Enkhuizen, a picturesque Dutch village on the *IJsselmeer*. She remains one of Dorrit's best friends. The two reunite every year or so in The Hague, where they spend most of their visit in touring the local museums, including the Mauritshuis, and making small talk. They rarely discuss the war.

The Franks were, of course, not the only Jews who survived the war in hiding. According to an estimate by Bert Jan Flim, approximately a thousand other Jews survived the war in The Hague by diving under, including one other diver just around the corner from the Franks, as well as half a dozen on the Noordeinde.

The aftermath of the war in Holland, and particularly the destruction of Dutch Jewry, continued to trouble Dutch life for many years.

In 1949 Hans Albin Rauter, the former head of the SS in Holland and the man, after Seyss-Inquart, most directly responsible for the decimation of the Dutch Jewish population, was tried and executed by the Dutch, the last of the so-called 'Austrian Mafia' that ruled Holland during the war to be put to death.* Franz Fischer, the last German war criminal incarcerated on Dutch soil and the SS official who oversaw the deportations from The Hague, was released amidst widespread protest in 1989.

The war, and the question of whether more could or should have been done to save the over 102,000 Dutch Jews who died in the extermination camps or the small number – like the Schnells – who were murdered on Dutch soil, continues to be a topic of controversy.

Dutch 'war guilt' was a major factor in Dutch foreign policy in the immediate postwar period. For many years, the Netherlands was Israel's best friend in Europe, for which the Dutch were duly punished in 1974 when Holland became the only European nation to be targeted by OPEC for an oil boycott.

Since its original publication in Dutch in 1947 as *Het Achterhuis*, the diary of Anne Frank, issued in 1952 in English as *The Diary of a Young Girl*, has become the most widely read document to emerge from the

---

* One German-born Nazi who played a prominent role in the ruthlessness of the final year of the occupation—August L.H. Albrecht – was put to death later. As head of the Einsatzkommando of the security police in the town of Leeuwarden in 1944–45, Albrecht was held personally responsible for numerous murders by a special court of justice and executed in 1952.

Holocaust. It has also been adapted for the stage and performed throughout the world. In 1956, the first dramatisation of the diary received its European première in Gothenburg, Sweden; the following year it caused a sensation when it was first shown in Germany. However, as Melissa Muller, one of the biographers of Anne Frank, notes, 'while the dramatisation made the book a worldwide best-seller, it contributed greatly to the romanticising and sentimentalising of Anne Frank's story.'

In 1960, as a result of the efforts of Otto Frank and a group of other concerned Dutch citizens, the Anne Frank House opened as a museum at 263 Prinsengracht, where the Franks had hidden out from the Germans, before being discovered as a result of a tip from an informant whose exact identity remains a source of mystery to the present day. In 2002, the writer Carol Ann Lee made front-page news in Holland when she claimed that the Franks were betrayed by a former business associate of Otto's and, more controversially, that Otto was blackmailed by the same man following the war. However, the Netherlands Institute for War Documentation announced that it could find no proof to back up Lee's claim.

The Anne Frank House continues to be one of Holland's most popular tourist attractions, receiving more than 800,000 visitors every year.

In 1987 the site of the former Westerbork transit camp was also made into a remarkable museum. The hideous original camp structures, including the barracks that housed the inmates, have been torn down, except for an eerie guardhouse. Nearby in the town cemetery are the graves of Eva and Alfred Schnell, who were murdered in Zwolle in November, 1944, after their hiding place was discovered. As one of her last *mitzvahs* Annie had their bodies reburied there.

In April, 2003, I made my own pilgrimage to Westerbork, following the path that my mother had taken to visit Edgar sixty-one years before. The train from Amsterdam takes about the same time as it did in 1942.

The staff kindly stayed open later for me, so I could tour the museum, as well as the distant campground. Even though the barracks where Edgar and his parents were incarcerated, and where Dorrit visited them in May, 1942, no longer exists it is not difficult to conjure it up. In my mind's eye, I could see my mother and her doomed fiancé take their final walk together to the edge of the field, where the heather had once again begun to blossom.

More difficult to imagine was the hellish scene that transpired on the evening of 15 July, 1942, when Edgar and eleven other frightened souls were marched to the Hooghalen station six miles away to board the first transport from the Netherlands to the East.

According to Martin Gilbert, author of *The Righteous*, at the last count, over 4,000 Dutch have been nominated as Righteous Persons – Gentiles who risked their lives to save their Jewish brethren – and commemorated in Yed Vashem, the Holocaust memorial in Israel. Only Poland has more.

Although a vestige of its lively, pre-war self, the Dutch-Jewish community has managed at least in part to re-create itself. Today there are approximately 30,000 Jews living in Holland. Although Jewish life there can hardly be described as flourishing, it is certainly alive and well.

Thanks to a wave of Jewish immigrants from the former Soviet Union, Jewish life in Germany has recently experienced something of a renaissance. The total Jewish population in Germany numbers over 100,000, about a fifth of its size in 1933, when the Nazis took power and the German-Jewish diaspora began.

The Franks were the last Jewish family to live in Breitenheim.

Afterword

Since the Frank family story is also my story, it is difficult to state exactly when the odyssey of this book actually began. In a sense, it started when I was very young, when I first heard my mother's horrific but miraculous wartime tale. Although I was not consciously brought up as a 'child of the Holocaust' (a term I am personally uncomfortable with, with its connotations of victimisation) my mother has long maintained she believes that the reason why she survived the war, the reason she got through it all, was because she was destined to give birth to me and my younger brother, Lee.

I was never quite sure what she meant by that, although it no doubt helps explain a certain hubris on my brother's part and mine. From a very early age we were conscious of being different. Being Jewish was part of it, but this meant very little in our heavily Jewish neighbourhood of New York City. But the war and the Holocaust had a lot to do with it.

My mother did not give me a detailed account of her experiences in hiding when I was a child. If anything she tried to shield us from them and from the earlier time when she was growing up in Germany. How could she possibly convey what she and her family had experienced, felt, suffered, and seen during their three-year-long ordeal? It was much easier for our father, a naturalised German Jew who served as a decorated intelligence officer on the front lines with the US army in Europe, to regale us with straight-forward stories about *his* war than for my mother to harrow us with her darker and more complex tale. And so, after sketching in the outlines of her story, she kept closed the curtains in front of our star-crossed past. Finally, one day in July 1965, as part of a commemorative tour of Europe, my mother took me to Pieter van den Zandestraat for the first time since her departure for the US in 1947 and knocked on the door of number 14, the flat where the Franks had hidden years before. The current occupant of the flat was at home and he welcomed my mother inside.

Rather than join her, novice documentary-maker that I was, I ran across the street to the stairwell opposite and took a melodramatic photo of the flat, framed by a broken window, looking very much as it might have to the four fugitives' neighbours twenty years before. The curtains were closed, just like the curtains behind which the Franks had waited for the knock on the door that fortunately never came:

I also took several street-level shots of Pieter van den Zandestraat, including the vacant corner shop where my grandfather planted the rumour that he was a Swiss-German doctor with a mad wife.

The visit to The Hague and the site of the Frank family's calvary had a huge impact on me. Indeed, one could say that it was on that memorable day close to forty years ago, when I was fourteen, that I conceived this book, at least subliminally.

Throughout my teens and my early post-collegiate years as a freelance journalist, my mother's experiences did not play a significant role in my life. The doorway to number 14, and the Pandora's box – or, should I say, the *Rasho Mon* – that lay behind those curtains remained sealed to me.

There were occasions when the war, and the emotional damage it had caused to my mother, suddenly jutted into view. One such took place in the early 1970s during a familial viewing of the Cold War thriller *Fail-Safe*. The film, a cautionary tale of nuclear Armageddon, ends with a harrowing filmic 'countdown' consisting of a montage of New Yorkers, their city having been secretly slated for obliteration by mutual agreement between the United States and the Soviet Union to compensate for the former's accidental incineration of Moscow – innocently awaiting their imminent demise at ground zero. In the middle of the 'countdown', which evidently triggered memories of the misfiring V-2 missiles and mis-targeted Allied bombs that nearly incinerated the Franks when they were in hiding, my mother burst into hysterics, as if that cinematic bomb was actually headed for our Queens, New York, home. I recall my father comforting her in the kitchen, while sheepishly trying to explain to us what had happened.

However, in the main my mother's war remained as opaque as the muslin curtains in front of the window at number 14. Like some Holocaust survivors, she did not feel especially impelled to bear witness. It was sufficient that we had seen the site of the Franks' wartime ordeal, and that we knew the basic story, especially the tale of the house-to-house search that the Germans conducted on their street on 11 November 1944, and how, for some inexplicable reason, they passed by their door; so that we could pass this on, at least in outline, to the next generation. That was also the attitude of my grandparents, Flory and Myrtil, as I recall it, when my brother and I were growing up. The future was more important than the past. Indeed, we *were* the future!

At some point, inevitably, I also became aware of the parallels between my mother's family story and that of her namesake, Anne Frank, including the uncanny symmetry of both Frank families' movements between 1933, when Otto Frank and his wife and his two daughters and Myrtil Frank and *his* two daughters fled Nazi Germany for Dutch exile; and 1942, when, during the first raids against Amsterdam's ghettoised Jewish community, the two hounded Jewish families, then living a few blocks from each other in Amsterdam South, went into hiding within days of each other, Otto Frank's family in Amsterdam, and Myrtil's in The Hague. And yet I didn't feel especially moved to write about it.

One legacy from the past which my mother *did* hand down to me was an interest in Holland and the Dutch people, who, she felt, had played an instrumental role in saving her and her family. After all, if not for the brave band of four Dutchwomen, led by Annie van der Sluijs, the woman who leased number 14 and conspired with my grandfather to take the Franks 'under' and protect them there, the Franks truly would *not* have survived. Later, when I delved deeper into this still sensitive subject and tried to square the heroism of Annie and her sisters, Tine and Ans, as well as the bravery of their friend Jeanne Guthschmidt, with the Nazis' 'success' in eradicating over three quarters of Holland's prewar Jewish population, I discovered that things were not quite as black-and-white as I had once believed. I also discovered that the relationship between Tine and my grandfather was more complicated than I had thought.

But that was not until much later. When I was young, all Dutchmen were heroes. I *loved* Holland. I certainly was the only boy in my elementary school who could hum the Wilhelmus, the Dutch national anthem.

Today I still love Holland. And I can still hum the tune to the Wilhelmus. I just don't think that all Dutchmen are heroes. But Annie and her sisters and Jeanne certainly were, and so were the thousands of other Dutchmen and Dutchwomen who risked their lives in order to save their Jewish friends and neighbours. There just weren't enough of them.

My grandfather, a driven, charismatic lovable bear of a man with an impish sense of humour who was happy to be *alive* and not afraid to show it, was also my hero when I was growing up. He still is, if not more so, especially now that I know the ingenuity and cunning he used to keep his family alive. Maybe I understand him a little better. But I am getting slightly ahead of myself.

My inherited love for Holland and the Dutch, and for Dutch history, led me to travel to *Nederland* on my own for the first time in the autumn of 1974, where I wrote a profile of that country, putting the sudden bout of social and economic difficulties the Dutch were then experiencing into proper historical context for *The New York Times Magazine*. 'Innocence Lost' I entitled my piece. Its thesis was that after a quarter of a century of prosperous and trouble-free existence, the Dutch – suddenly buffeted with a combination of a royal scandal, as well as an unprecedented racial problem (thanks to the influx of a flood of refugees from the former Dutch colony of Surinam) – had finally and irrevocably lost their innocence about the world, completing a process that had begun on 10 May 1940, the day of the shock Nazi invasion.

And yet, although I wrote about the war in my piece, I still avoided writing or thinking about my mother's war. I am not sure whether I even visited number 14.

I returned three years later to The Hague, and stayed with my grandmother, who was spending the summer there. I remember going to a lot of art shows with my imperious, still beautiful, somewhat maddening grandmother. I also recall doing a lot of talking. Flory liked a good dinner table conversation. Indeed, she required it. But I don't recall – nor do my reasonably meticulous diaries mention – our discussing the war. I didn't even visit the Anne Frank House. I wanted to, but the lines were too long.

Of course, it was difficult to spend any significant time in the Netherlands at that time and not be aware of the war. Walking along the pleasant, dune-enclosed beach at Scheveningen, near where the Franks spent the first part of their Dutch exile and from where they watched as the skies filled with German parachutes on that infamous day in May 1940, I sometimes found myself re-enacting the events of that day, which has been called the Dutch Pearl Harbor. The long line of bunkers that the Germans built along the beach as part of the Atlantic Wall, still looking every bit as formidable as thirty years before, were also quite a jog to the memory. But after a few such strolls, I didn't see them any more.

My diaries record at least one war-related fit of pique that took place during my first sojourn in The Hague in 1974, when America was still mired in Vietnam and Americans abroad sometimes found themselves the target of angry remarks. Not long before, I myself had been a vehement protester of the war in Vietnam; nevertheless, when a cranky Dutchman sitting at the next table of my favourite local café suddenly started badmouthing the United States, I fired back, surprising myself: 'If it wasn't for the United States, Seyss-Inquart,' I exclaimed, 'would still be living in the Palace *Noordeinde*!' Located in the centre of The Hague, only a few blocks away from Pieter van den Zandestraat, the Palace Noordeinde remains the traditional residence of the Dutch sovereign, Queen Wilhelmina, who lived and grew up there.

In the event, my history was a little off: Seyss-Inquart actually never lived in the Palace Noordeinde. He *did* confiscate another one of Wilhelmina's residences for his own use, her duneside house in *Clingendael*. Close enough; I didn't claim to be an authority on the war. Also, technically speaking, it was the *Canadian* army, not the US army, which liberated The Hague and the rest of western Holland in May 1945, and my mother's family to boot.

In any event, the righteous anger behind my patriotic salvo derived more from my father's war, and *his* righteous anger at the arrogant Nazi officers he interrogated in his POW cage as his division, the famed 83rd 'Thunderbolt', blazed through France and Germany, and not from my mother's soul-bending, subterranean war, which still remained distant.

It was not until 1979, when I was twenty-eight, a decade and a half after my first visit to number 14, that I finally decided to write something about my mother's war. Essentially, it was my idea to publish a version of her story on what would have been the diarist's fiftieth birthday, which used the parallels between the two star-crossed family stories – Anne Frank's tragic one, and my mother's more fortunate one – as a kind of miraculous appendix to *The Diary of a Young Girl*. I wanted to do a *mitzvah*. And yes, perhaps to make my mother happy as well.

Instead, I wound up re-enacting my own version of *Rashomon*.

Rashomon was the 1951 film by the great Japanese director Akira Kurosawa. Based on two short stories by Ryunosoke Akutagawa, the work is overtly a thriller about the rape of a woman, Masago, and the murder of her husband, Takehiro, in a forest, but it is also about the nature and knowability of objective truth itself.

Set in the eleventh century, the film opens with a conversation between three men, a woodcutter, a priest and a commoner, who have taken refuge from a rainstorm under the ruins of Rasho Mon Gate. The priest recounts the details of a rape-cum-murder trial that he has just witnessed.

As he talks, the audience sees the four principal defendants: Masago; the bandit Tanjomaru; the spirit of Takehiro, which is conjured up by a medium; and the woodcutter who admits that he witnessed the murder. Each viewpoint of the event is depicted, leaving the audience with the challenge and the task of trying to reconcile the conflicting perspectives.

A film buff, I was deeply moved by *Rashomon* when I first saw it at the Museum of Modern Art back in 1970, when I was on involuntary leave from Cornell (a fancy term for suspension) and was spending my days inspecting microfilm in the rear of the second floor of the New York Public Library, and my evenings catching up on the foreign classics – *were* there any American classics? – at MoMA. I am sure that I saw *Rashomon* at least twice.*

Little, however, did I expect to re-enact the film myself. And yet that is what occurred as, now confident of my skills, I interviewed the three then survivors of the tale, my mother, my aunt and my grandmother. Alas, I had missed my grandfather, nor, much as I would have liked, could he be conjured up by a medium. But I felt that between the three witnesses I had enough to piece together the original story.

Immediately, there were serious problems. First, although I was familiar with the dramatic events in the tale and thought I had an idea of the impact those experiences had had on my mother, I soon realised that I had no idea whatsoever what really took place behind the door of number 14 Pieter van den Zandestraat between 14 July 1942, when the Franks first dived through that door into the unknown, and 8 May 1945, when they finally emerged into freedom.

Now, as my mother recounted for me the endless days and nights of waiting and praying while the bombs and missiles fell and the Germans searched the streets for Jews and slave labour, I realised why she had run away during the broadcast of *Fail-Safe* years before. Also, once I began

---

* My supervisor at the library was Herbert Boucher, the same Herbert Boucher whose story and memoir, *Miracle of Survival*, is referenced earlier in this book. The Sanders and the Bouchers became friendly in the 1950s.

to comprehend just how slim the chances were of her surviving all of that – the bombs, the missiles, the Germans, as well as the perfidious Dutch of the sort who betrayed her Amsterdam namesake family, and finally the Hunger Winter of '44–'45, when thousands starved to death – not to mention an entire family of four surviving all of that, *my* family – I began to understand what my mother had meant when she had said that she was destined to get through.

As I got my first good peek behind the drawn curtains at number 14 I understood from where my unaccountable store of hubris derived. Now I understood where I *really* came from.

More troublingly, and perhaps not so surprisingly, my mother's inter-pretation of the 'miracle of 14 Pieter van den Zandestraat' differed from that of my grandmother and my aunt. Why had the Franks got through those endless (1022 to be exact) days? Why had the search party in November 1944 inexplicably passed by their door? Why did they go upstairs but not beneath?

My grandmother, the most religious of the three surviving *onderduikers*, felt sure that it was His inscrutable will. My Aunt Sybil, the least senti-mental of the three, was convinced that the Franks' survival had just been pure luck, nothing inscrutable about it.

And they differed on other things, as well. Very rapidly – too rapidly – I had lost my former innocence about the story of 'The Frank Family That Survived', as I entitled my projected, and increasingly thorny, project.

The absence of a diary or journal, such as Anne Frank had kept, made it difficult, if not impossible, to reconcile these contrasting images: *Rasho Mon* redux. What had started as a *mitzvah* had turned into an autobio-graphical quagmire.

Then, too, hovering above the project was the ghost of Anne Frank, author of the most widely read document to emerge from the Holocaust. Was my mother's story *really* different enough from hers to merit telling? Did it really add something to the public record? And who was I to think that I could write even an appendix to her miraculous journal?

A friend of mine, David Harris, who was my confidant at the time and is now executive director of the American Jewish Committee, saw my dilemma and, wisely, advised me to put the kaleidoscopic story aside for ten or fifteen years, until I had a little more perspective on it.

And so that is what I did. My editor at the *Times Magazine* was disap-pointed, but she understood. I needed to get some more distance first before I walked through the door of number 14. I also needed to read and

learn more about the Dutch experience during World War II, and especially the destruction of Dutch Jewry, before I could make any worth-while
generalisations about the plight of the Frank family and how it related to
the plight of their fellow Jews, no less that of Anne Frank and her family.
Most important, I needed to have a life. I was only twenty-eight.

I actually waited longer, over two decades in fact, until one day in 2000,
while I was having a drink at the Oxford and Cambridge Club with
Richard Bannerman, a sympathetic producer at BBC Radio 4, I happened
to mention the long-buried story of our Frank family. 'I'd like to do something with that,' Richard replied.

And so we did. The two-part radio documentary, *The Frank Family
That Survived*, which was broadcast on successive Sunday evenings in
September 2001, was the gratifying result.

Evidently the twenty-two years that had elapsed since I had first opened
the figurative door to number 14, during which time I had continued to
read up on Dutch history, and to visit and report on Holland itself, had
been sufficient for me to acquire the additional maturity and perspective,
as well as background knowledge, to finally go through that troublesome
door of memory and do justice to my mother's family story, as well as
put it into its proper historical context.

Both Dorrit and Sybil allowed me to reinterview them for the broadcast. Flory, of course, had long since left us. Thankfully, I still had the
handwritten notes from our original interviews, so my grandmother was
able to participate from beyond the grave, so to speak.

A return visit to number 14, which I had photographed with my Fujica
35-SE forty years before when my mother first took me there, was also
helpful (although I found, somewhat to my surprise, that I lacked the
courage to actually knock on the door). So were the good offices of the
remarkable Dutch war archive, the Netherlands Institute for War
Documentation, where, one unforgettable morning in July 2001, after
spinning back and forth at the microfilm machine, I found the entry for
the Franks in the census of Dutch Jews which the Germans conducted
– or, rather, had the pliable Dutch authorities conduct for them – in early
1941, before they dived under; and, later, on another reel, the documents
that indicated when and where my great-grandmother, Leontine, who
had baulked at diving under with the Franks and was later seized at her
Amsterdam pension in one of the last great *razzias*, and my mother's
fiancé, Edgar Reich, who was amongst the first Jews sent to Westerbork,

had been deported from Westerbork to Sobibor and Auschwitz, respectively, and killed.

A visit to the stirring and informative Resistance Museum in Amsterdam, where one can 'walk through' an imaginative and haunting exhibit about the five-year-long German occupation, and the varying (and still debated) Dutch responses to the same, from active collaboration to violent resistance, provided me with further inspiration.

Did the nightmares I had the first time I had tried to write something about this story come back? Of course. Eventually they went away. So, too, at least to some degree, did the aforementioned *Rashomon* effect, as I encountered the same gnawing contradictions in my interview notes I had years before.

But they were less of a problem, partly because the essential and overarching truth of the Franks' incredible tale stood out so much more clearly this time, which was that they *had* survived. According to the numerous authorities on the Dutch Holocaust whom I consulted, the chances of a family of four surviving the last three years of the draconian German occupation, a) *intact*, i.e., as opposed to splitting up, as most Jewish *onderduikers* did, b) in *one* place, as opposed to a succession of places, as most divers did, and c) in *The Hague*, where the German administration, including the zealous Seyss-Inquart and his especially enthusiastic SS colleague, Franz Fischer, who was responsible for the deportations from the capital, were based, were virtually nil. 'There couldn't have been more than a handful of families, if that, who survived this way,' Dienke Hondius, the historian at the Anne Frank House, told me.

Sixty years after the fact, and after all the hundreds of hours of interviews I conducted with my late grandmother, and my mother and her sister, how the Franks managed to get through all they had to 'sit through all that,' as Sybil refered to her ordeal, is still astonishing to me. But I have more insight into how they managed to accomplish the feat.

Certainly one of the reasons why they survived was (as Flory suggested earlier) because they *did* remain intact and did not 'split their forces' by sending their children away. 'I was against breaking us up,' Flory said during our (already quoted) original interview. 'I am sure this is one of the reasons why we made it.' I wasn't sure what my grandmother meant when she said that back in 1979, but I am now, particularly after learning more about the final, agonising *hongerwinter*, when many isolated *onderduikers* gave up the long fight and succumbed to the hunger and cold.

My grandfather's courage in running the risks he did, including leaving the hiding place to augment the family's food supply – even if, in retro-spect, some of the risks he took seem a little foolhardy – was also clearly a major factor in the Franks' survival.

As for the rest – destiny? God? Luck? Who knew?

In any event, *this time* I was able to go all the way through that door and finish the job. I shall never forget the sense of satisfaction, and of closure, I felt after I had finished recording *The Frank Family That Survived* at the rooftop studios of Broadcasting House, from where Edward R. Murrow, one of my journalistic heroes, had reported to America about the blitz sixty years before.

I received many e-mails and messages from those who listened to the September 2001 broadcast, the first instalment of which was aired during the black days following the terrorist attacks of 11 September, when it appeared that humanity might be headed for the abyss again. 'This is the sort of thing that gives me hope,' one listener said.

And then *The Frank Family That Survived*, the radio series, became *The Frank Family That Survived*, the book, and this long-gestating, partly realised project entered its final form.

In a sense, I began from scratch with this book partly because I knew I *could* start from scratch. Granted the expanded space, and two more years of research, I have been able to do considerably more than I did with the radio version two years before.

This book is the first place where I have been able to tell the Frank family saga properly. The radio programmes focused almost entirely on the Franks' Dutch years, and on the years they spent in hiding in The Hague.

Here I have been able to draw the camera back and begin the family saga in the nineteenth-century Rhineland, where it originated, taking Myrtil and Flory from their youth as assimilated young German Jews, through the Great War to their move to the revolutionary Berlin of the early 1920s, when they lived in a large flat in the fashionable *Hansa Viertel*; through the short-lived happy days of the mid-to-late 1920s, when the Franks joined the upper ranks of the cosmopolitan Jewish elite which was so responsible for that much romanticised moment known as Weimar Berlin.

A full third of this book – and three quarters of its total historical arc of eighty years – takes place in Germany, from the birth of Max Frank, Myrtil's vintner father, in 1866, the same year that Bismarck came to power, through 1933, when the Franks fled Germany for the long mirage of Dutch exile.

Showing the Franks in their original context and depicting the life they led and including the decisions they made – particularly Myrtil's decisions – during that time, one can better understand their behaviour later on. The tensions that racked the Frank household in Berlin in the 1920s, particularly those between Myrtil and Flory, presaged the tensions they would experience and overcome when they submerged a decade and several eras later at number 14. By the same token Myrtil's decision to send Flory and Dorrit out of Germany during the dangerous hyperinflation of 1923 presages his decision in March 1933 to leave Germany within weeks of Hitler's assumption of power, as well as the even more difficult decision twelve years later to take the family into hiding.

Casting my net further, interviewing all the family members I had wanted to interview for the radio series, but could not – including Myrtil's niece, Celia, and his ex-sister-in-law Louise, as well as his Israeli niece Lotte (who also happens to be the family historian) – I learned volumes about the first, German part of the Frank family saga, as well as a fair number things about Myrtil and Flory that I didn't know.

At the same time I have tried to use the Frank family as a prism through which to view their tumultuous times, particularly the third, fourth and fifth decades of the last century, as experienced by a not atypical, well-to-do family of Berlin Jews. This is exactly how they saw themselves: as Germans, and Berliners, first, and Jews after that; until, of course, the rise of the Nazis made them think otherwise.

In a way, the German section of this book was more difficult than the Dutch. Between all of my various visits to Holland over the past thirty years, I have spent something approaching a year in Holland; at one time, after my back-to-back visits in the 1970s, I even spoke and read the language in a rudimentary way; I am still proud of my 'Scheveningen.' By contrary, before I began the German section, I had only a rough, college-level understanding of German history and had visited the country once, and then only briefly – partly because of the block about things German that I inherited from my (understandably) Germanophobic parents.

So, the first order of business was to immerse myself in Germany and German-Jewish history, with the aid of such seminal texts as Amos Elon's *The Pity of It All*. A copy of a book about the village of Breitenheim, published on its 700th anniversary – sent me by Nina Senger, the Berlin art historian, whom I met over the Internet and who became my enthusiastic German correspondent – was also very helpful.

Moving on to Holland, I have tried to seize a number of historiographical opportunities: with the help of other historians, particularly Bob Moore, author of *Victims and Survivors* the authoritative study of the destruction of Dutch Jewry published in 1997, I have assayed to show the deceptively halcyon Holland of the 1930s, as well as the beaten-down and devastated occupied Holland of 1940–45; and to provide a new overview of the tragedy within a tragedy that was the Dutch Holocaust.

There have been many fine monographs, as well as general histories about various aspects of the latter episode. In addition to Moore's opus, these include the less exact but still fascinating predecessor volume, *The Destruction of Dutch Jewry* by J. Presser; *The Hunger Winter*, Henri van der Zee's illuminating personal-cum-general history of the desperate winter of '44–'45 and the liberation; and the entire outstanding catalogue of the Resistance Museum written by its curator, Liesbeth der Horst, to name but a few. Nevertheless no reliable overview exists of the war in Holland – including the Nazi drive to extirpate its venerable Jewish community.

Most readers of the diary of Anne Frank assume that her entire group of eight *onderduikers* would have survived the war – and not just the one who did, Otto Frank – if only they had not been betrayed to the Nazis in August 1944, a heartbreaking twenty-six months after they had first sequestered themselves in Otto's elaborately constructed, concealed *achterhuis*.

And yet they would still have had to survive nearly another full year before liberation. As this account makes clear, there is no guarantee that the Amsterdam Franks would have withstood the cold, hunger and disease that claimed so many more lives, Jewish and non-Jewish, below and above ground, during the even more hellish months to come.

And if Anne Frank had lived, what then might have happened to her? Like their counterparts in The Hague, Otto Frank might have decided to send her and her sister, Margot, to America just as Myrtil and Flory decided to do with their daughters after the liberation. The ill or indifferent treatment accorded the more 5,000 Jews who returned from the extermination camps as well as to the estimated 15,000 to 18,000 *onderduikers* including Myrtil's more fortunate group suggests that Otto Frank might also have taken the same steps, had Anne and Margot survived.

In any event, although Anne Frank and her family are only peripherally present in these pages, this historical memoir is intended at least in part to put her story, as well as that of my own Frank family, into wider historical focus.

Indeed, instead of being put off by the reputation of Anne Frank, as I was a quarter of a century ago, when I first tried to tell this story, I like to believe now (as we observe what would have been her 75th birthday), that the martyred diarist, who speculated in her journal about Jews in other circumstances, would have wished it to be known that sixty miles away there was another Jewish family who shared a similar journey, and who ultimately survived.

References

Prologue

'*Killing nine strikers and sympathisers*' Liesbeth van der Horst, *Dutch Resistance Museum*, Amsterdam, 2000, 42

'*Aus der Fünten had done already*' Bob Moore, *Victims and Survivors: The Nazi Persecution of the Jews in the Netherlands, 1940–1945*, London, 1996, 92

'*Something had to be done*' ibid.

'*had agreed to allow the Dutch*' ibid.

1 Breitenheim

'*We Jews*' *Israelit* (Ger.), August, 1914

'*If we are not German*' ibid., 177

'*My Germanness and Jewishness*' ibid., 347

'*Banned from farming*' ibid., 107–8

'*Only the Papal States*' ibid., 25

'*The Jew brings*' ibid., 25

'*No less than twelve thousand*' ibid., 203

'*The truth is that*' Paul Johnson, *A History of the Jews*, London, 1993, 404

'*If there is a region*' Elon, op. cit., 21

'*Most of the vineyards listed in the town records*' *Breitenheim: einst und heute*, Breitenheim, 1992, 35

'*Presumably the latter proviso*' ibid., 38

'*No country in the world*' Karl Baedeker, *Baedeker's Rhine*, Leipzig, 1878, 17

'*money-making frenzy*' Elon, op. cit., 26

'*The whole appearance of the city*' Karl Baedeker, *Baedeker's Rhine*, 1911, 282

'*The lamps are going out*' Barbara Tuchman, *The Guns of August*, New York, 1962, 146

'*Die Juden sind unser Unglück*' Elon, op. cit., 217

'*I am convinced that*' Elon, op. cit.

'*We Jews are Germans*' ibid.

'*necessary for the defence*' David Clay Large, *The Perils of Prominence: Jews in Weimar Berlin*, New York, 2002, 10

'*I am a German of the Jewish faith*' ibid., 11

'*Virtually alone*' ibid., 18–19

'*According to the original*' Tuchman, op. cit., 43–5

'*Holland prepared for the worst*' Kees van Hoek, 'Wilhelmina Regina', *Atlantic Monthly*, October 1938, 478

'*The Dutch Army*' ibid.

2 Ultra-Dada Days

'*A terrorist revolution*' *The New York Times*, 5 December 1918.

'*There comes a moment*' 'The Street', commercial film, Germany (UFA 1923)

'*A poor provincial town*' Otto Friedrich, *Before the Deluge*, New York, 1972, 5

'*almost every part*' Karl Baedeker, *Baedeker's Berlin*, Leipzig, 1905, 25

'*It is a new city*' Friedrich, op. cit., 5

'*Only parts*' ibid.

'*the civil strife in Lichtenburg*' *The New York Times*, March 11, 1919

'*not now brightly lighted*' ibid.

'*hate crawled in*' Herbert Hoover, *The Memoirs of Herbert Hoover*, New York, 1951, 463–7

'*what hand*' Friedrich, *Encyclopedia Americana*, viii, New York, 2002, 118

'*75,000 food retailers*' *The New York Times*, 4 September, 1919

'*food situation*', *The New York Times*, 8 January, 1921

'*should Germany continue to*' ibid., January 1921

'*they were buying up*' Friedrich, op. cit., 61

'*Day by day*' Emile Coué, *Self Mastery Through Conscious Autosuggestion*, New York, 1924, 3

'*or besieging an artificial*' Friedrich, op. cit, 63

'*the failure of the Kapp Putsch*' ibid., 63–4

'*I was on a train*' Conrad Rosenstein, *Memories of Weimar Germany*, Leo Baeck Institute, No. 328 (1954), 50–60,

'*linking up with the world*' Friedrich, op. cit., 82

'*dear friend*' ibid, 98–9

'*this atrocious crime*' ibid., 115

'*Jews and Gentiles*' Large, op. cit., 14

'*the mark stood at*' ibid., 15

'*then he went home*' ibid.

'*in addition to finding*' ibid., 16

'*a pogrom-like riot*' ibid., 17

'*now we expected*' Sebastian Haffner, *Defying Hitler* (tr. O. Pretzel), London, 2002, 51

'*the American painter*' Townsend Ludington, *Marsden Hartley*, Ithaca, 1992, 163

3 Once You Had Berlin, You Had the World

'*Once you had Berlin*' Large, op. cit., 25

'*So long as your panties*' Friedrich, op. cit., 12

'*mad dreams*' Haffner, op. cit., 42

'*during the Stresemann era*' ibid., 62

'*As long as Stresemann*' ibid., 66

'*In Berlin, one had it better*' Large, op. cit., 10

'*I wouldn't say the Jews*' Rosenstein, op. cit., 52

'*The man has everything*' ibid., 67

'*The foreign minister's death*' Haffner, op. cit., 68

'*an article*' 'Renascent Germany', *National Geographic*, October 1928, 655

'*The Nazis polled*' Friedrich, op. cit., 301

'*It's all over with Germany*' ibid.

'*The savage swooping arrow*' John Gunther, *Inside Europe*, London, 1936, 46

Tomorrow Belongs To Me, 'Cabaret', commercial film, US, (MGM, 1972), lyrics by John Kander and Fred Ebber (VHS)

'*In general, today more than*' Saul Friedlander, *Nazi Germany and the Jews: The Years of Persecution 1933–1939*, London, 1997, 15

'*There I saw*' Rosenstein, op. cit., 54

4 The Long Mirage

'*Quaint is no more appropriate*', R.T. Fuller, 'Bicycling Through Holland', *Travel*, April 1933, 16

'*Holland's proximity*', H. De Leuw, 'Holland Strikes the Modern Note' *Travel*, March 1939, 37

'*Mr Colijn*' Winston Churchill, *Their Finest Hour*, Boston, 1949, 34–37

'*The government soon*' E.N. van Kleffens, *The Rape of the Netherlands*, London, 1940

'*The Low Countries*' Oliver Grambling, *Free Men are Fighting*, New York, 1942, 93

'*Like thousands of other German Jews*' *Literary Digest*, 27 April 1935, 12

'*In the next major*' ibid., 5 June 1937

'*I'd like to see*' 'Wilhelmina Regina', op. cit., 479

'*This is the marriage*' ibid., 482

'*The former storm trooper*' *Newsweek*, 16 January, 1937, 15

'*Goering denounced*' ibid., 482

'*Hold the sea!*' *Literary Digest*, 19 September 1936, 16

'*Between 1935 and 1937*' *Literary Digest*, 5 June 1937, 24

'*He explained to me*' Churchill, op. cit., 34

'*According to the photo*' Breitenheim, op. cit., 123

'*The US proved*' Saul Fredlander, op. cit., 299–300

'*More than 30,000 German Jews*' Bob Moore, 'Jewish Refugees in the Netherlands', Leo Baeck Institute Yearbook XXIV (1984), 73–5

'*I advise all not to be anxious*' *Time*, 24 April 1940, 40

'*This is what most*' Van Kleffens, op. cit., 52

'*In November, the Führer*' William Shirer, *The Rise and Fall of the Third Reich*, New York, 1960, 721

'*Rotund Dutchmen*' Bernard Lansing, 'Letter from Amsterdam,' *The New Yorker*, 9 March 1940, 40

'*There are British military*' ibid., 42

'*As the 25,000*' Moore, 'Jewish Refugees in the Netherlands', op. cit., 74

'*The power of a state*' Churchill, op. cit., 34

5 Shadowland

'*Although 5,000 Wehrmacht*' 'The World at War: Occupation: Holland 1940–1944 (BBC, 1974), Volume 6, Episode 18, (VHS)

'*Many Dutchmen have been*' D. Bess, 'Occupied Holland', *Saturday Evening Post*, February 1941

'*The power of the resistance*' Shirer, op. cit., 722

'*Over eight hundred*' ibid.

'*Goering denied*' Shirer, ibid.

'*Nowhere was the Jewish*' Gerald Reitlinger, *The Final Solution*, New York, 1953, 329

'*We will not persecute*' W. N. Posthumus, ed., '*The Netherlands Under German Occupation*', *Annals of the American Academy of Political Science*, February 1946. 1–180

'*Dutchmen sported white carnations*' Dutch Resistance Museum, op. cit., 31.

'*He was fired*' Bart van der Boom, *Den Haag in de Tweede Wereldoorlog*, The Hague, 1995, 290

'*As Christopher Browning*', Christopher Browning, *The Origins of the Final Solution*, London, 2004, 202–5

'*By contrast*' Marion Schreiber (tr. S. Whiteside), *The 20th Train*, New York, 2002, 42

'*Then in September 1940*' J. Presser (tr. A. Pomerans), *The Destruction of Dutch Jewry*, London, 1969, 15

'*It happened step by step*' Telford Taylor, *The Anatomy of the Nuremberg Trials: A Personal Memoir*, Boston, 1992, 634

'*There was no need*' Moore, Victims and Survivors op. cit., 56

'*The Februaristaking*'' ibid., 72–3

'*By May 1941*' Presser, op. cit., 111

'*the Belgian authorities referred*' Schreiber, op. cit., 42

'*the Germans continued*' Moore, op. cit., 262–3

Peter Romijn, 'The Experience of Jews in the Netherlands during the German Occupation', *Dutch Jewry: Its History and Secular Culture 1500–2000*, Jonathan Israel and Reiner Salverda, ed., 312

'*recently Lobstein had appealed*', ibid., 307

'*when the Reich's*' Moore, op. cit., 264

'*there was also an abominable*' Jacob Boas, *Boulevard des Misères*, New York, 1985

'*in six weeks*' *Encyclopedia of the Holocaust*, op. cit., 432

John Garland, ed., *The Holocaust: Deportation of Jews to the East*, New York, 1982, 1

6 The Decision

'*to the decree*' Garland, op. cit., 8

'*there were other preconditions*' Moore, *Victims and Survivors*, op. cit., 150.

'*the real tragedy*' ibid., 154

'*the logistics of going into hiding*' Interview with Leo Ullman, September 2003

'*this helps explain why*' Moore, op. cit., 150

'*people were not aware*' Ullman interview

'*by this point*' Moore, op. cit., 196

'*the end of the war the total number of*' Dutch Resistance Museum, op. cit., 86

'*they, along with several hundred*' Moore, op. cit., 264

'*as the Franks later learned*' Carol Ann Lee, *The Biography of Anne Frank*, London, 1999, 103

'*thus on 29 April 1942*' Moore, op. cit., 89–90

'*the Jewish Council protested*', op. cit., 314

'*that is a fantastically*' George Kennan, *Sketches From a Life*, New York, 1989, 75

'*because of this*' ibid.

'*measure against the Dutch Jews*' *The Times*, 10 May 1942

'*a few Gentiles*' ibid.

'*The awareness that the Jews*' Dienke Hondius, 'Survivors in the Netherlands and their Return', *Patterns of Prejudice*, Number One, 1994, 51

'*The Dutch are*' A. J. Barnouw, *The New York Times*, 10 May 1942

'*they are firmly convinced*' ibid.

'*A growing number of Dutchmen*' Dutch Resistance Museum, op. cit., 67

'*On 11 May, the Germans*' Walter Laqueur, ed. *The Holocaust Encyclopedia*, New Haven, 2001, 438

'*Adolf Hitler*' *The New York Times*, 21 May 1942

'*So help me God*' Rene Kok and Erik Somers, *Het 40–45 Boek*, The Netherlands Institute for War Documentation, Zwolle, 145

'*He has more corpses*' *The New York Times*, 21 May 1942

'*the only Jews*' Moore, op. cit., 96

'*After 1940*' Anne Frank, *The Diary of a Young Girl*, New York, 1995

'*Our freedom*' ibid.

'*and there to the East*' Moore, op. cit.

'*two days later*' Reitlinger, op. cit., 332

'*This was new*' ibid., 334

'*nine days later*' ibid.

'*At three o'clock*' Frank, op. cit., 19

'*Jews who lived in Rivierenbuurt*' L. Ullman interview

'*The call up was not*' ibid., 20

'*all hell broke loose*' Geert Mak, *Amsterdam*, Cambridge, 2000, 274

'*Once the notices*' L. Ullman interview

'*There stood a girl*' Mak, op. cit., 267

'*Failure to report*' Moore, op. cit., 151

7 Submerging

'*The Germans*' *The Times*, 7 July 1942

'*Rauter and his lieutenant*' Moore, op. cit., 93

'*Based on our experience*' Mak, op. cit., 258

'*severe and well-publicised*' Moore, op. cit.

'*According to*' Mak, op. cit., 266

'*the razzia was succeeded*' Moore, op. cit., 93

'*but Erich Deppner*' *Encyclopedia of the Holocaust*, op. cit.

'*thus, as early as December 1941*' Martin Gilbert, *The Holocaust*, London, 1989, 237

'*Rauter and the SS chief*' Reitlinger, op. cit., 333

'*My biggest headache is*' ibid.

'*A group of Swedish Jews*' Martin Gilbert, *The Atlas of the Holocaust*, London, 1988

'*The deportation of the Dutch*' *Encyclopedia of the Holocaust*, op. cit.

'*the trains from Holland*' Dienke Hondius, op. cit., 51

'*the German's satanic plan*' *The New York Times*, 26 July 1942

'*All Jews that do not come forward*' Herbert Boucher, *Miracle of Survival: A Holocaust Memoir*, Berkeley, 1997, 124

'*The situation [regarding the Jews]*' *Encyclopedia of the Holocaust*, op. cit.

'*After the Jews*' ibid

'*Thanks to some funny*' Mak, op. cit., 264

'*We have stopped*' ibid.

'*The British radio*' Frank, op. cit., 59

'*Rauter instructed his colleagues*' Reitlinger, op. cit., 335

'*both a brute and a bureaucrat*' Van der Boom, op. cit., 291

'*only 1,200 of the 4,000*' ibid.

'*It is estimated*' ibid.

'*The figures scheduled*' ibid.

'*there was now a financial*' Moore, op. cit., 207

'*the Dutch police behave*' Mak, op. cit., 260

'*Christopher Browning*', Browning, op. cit, 204

'*the Dutch police behaved outstandingly*' Van der Boom, op. cit., 270

'*the Dutch part*' Reitlinger, op. cit., 339–40

'*a number of factors*' Renee Tallantype, 'Holland on the Eve of the Invasion', *Travel*, July 1944, 17

'*with housing in The Hague*' Van der Boom, op. cit., 290–91

'*The revised collection*' *Encyclopedia of the Holocaust*, op. cit., 5 '*by year's end*' Reitlinger, op. cit., 335

'*in the increasingly*' Mak, op. cit., 268

'*On Christmas Day*' Mak, op. cit., 269

'*It was just girlfriends visiting each other*' Interview with Jeanne Houtepen, June, 2003

8 My Name is Toni Muller

'*Tension in the Netherlands*' *The New York Times*, 3 March 1943

'*writers such as Hanson Baldwin*', Hanson Baldwin, *Battles Lost and Won*, New York, 1966

'*Another Dutchman*' Van der Boom, op. cit., 291

'*In July, 1942*', Louis de Jong, *The Netherlands and Nazi Germany*, New Haven, 1990, 32

'*It took nearly a month*' *The Holocaust Encyclopedia*, op. cit., 434

'*pronounced himself "inspired"*' Moore, op. cit., 101

'*In February*' Bart Van der Boom, 'The Deportation of the Jewish Community of the The Hague', conference paper (unpub.), 4

'*According to the Germans' meticulous*' Martin Gilbert, *Atlas of the Holocaust*, London, 1988, 148

'*further, on 9 February*' ibid.

'*the end point for Dutch Jews*', ibid.

'*between March and July 1943*' *The Holocaust Encyclopedia*, op. cit.

'*Rauter was demonstrably*' *The Holocaust*, op. cit., 6

'*The Jews*' ibid.

'*The onderduiker war*' ibid.

'*The largest part of them*' ibid.

'*The police chief noted*' ibid.

'*a small amount of film*' 'The World at War', op. cit.

'*On 2 April 1943*' *Het 40–45 Boek*, op. cit.

'*For the vast majority*' Moore, op. cit., 156

'*Corrie ten Boom writes*' Corrie ten Boom, *The Hiding Place*, New York, 1992, 107

'*Years later*' Interview with J. Guthschmidt

'*few illusions*' Moore, op. cit., 159

'*I think that the Dutch*' Interview with Ernst Sittig, April 2002

'*Both groups*' ibid.

'*The native good ones*' ibid.

'*Annie and her sisters*' ibid.

'*No, no . . . how can*' Ten Boom, op. cit., 94

'On 4 April' *The New York Times*, 4 April 1943

'There is no animosity' 'The World at War', op. cit.

'the response' *Dutch Resistance Museum*, op. cit., 68–73

'then in a particularly' Werner Warmbrunn, *The Dutch Under German Occupation 1940–45*, Stanford, 1963, 106–11

'The strike was suppressed' *Dutch Resistance Museum*, op. cit., 83

'a national organisation' ibid., 45

'It was getting harder' Ten Boom, op. cit., 92

'I confess that' ibid., 93–4

'The members' De Jong, op. cit.

'Panic broke out' Mak, op. cit., 261

'On 6 April' Gilbert, *Atlas* op. cit., 157

'May was even better' ibid., 160

'foremost amongst these' Moore, op. cit., 119–24

'The deportations' Gilbert, *Atlas* op. cit., 161

'July 1943' ibid.

9 The Girl Next Door

'In Berlin' *The New York Times*, 4 April 1943

'As John Keegan notes' John Keegan, *Six Armies in Normandy*, London, 1990, 75–86

'for some, the stress' Moore, op. cit., 158

'apparently this is' Ten Boom, op. cit., 112

'a major point of irritation' Frank, op. cit.

'On 29 September' Reitlinger, op. cit., 335

'a photo taken' *Het 40–45 Boek*, op. cit., 327

'But still the trains' Gilbert, *Atlas*, op. cit., 171

'Rauter had fulfilled' Reitlinger, op. cit., 336–338

'In neighbouring Belgium' Werner Warmbrunn, *The German Occupation of Belgium 1940–45*, New York, 1993, 163

'In November 1943' Martin Gilbert, *The Righteous: The Unsung Heroes of the Holocaust*, New York, 2004, 256–9

'As the Dutch journalist' Mak, op. cit., 267

'In the Beethovenstraat', Mak, ibid.

'however, as his aide' De Jong, op. cit., 27

'The Dutch Prime Minister' ibid.

'Everyone knew that' ibid.

'Amongst the more graphic' *Het 40–45 Boek*, op. cit., 159

'Who exactly was a collaborator' *The Times*, 10 May 1944

'*Some civil servants*' ibid.

'*The Dutch Prime Minister*' De Jong, op. cit.

'*Several weeks later*' Moore, op. cit., 199–200

'*a photo of his visit*' *Het 40–45 Boek*, op. cit.

'*In March 1944*' Gilbert, op. cit., 181

'*On 3 March*' Gilbert, *Atlas*, 181

'*Bounties were raised*' Moore, op. cit., 207

10 The Raid

'*[we must] demonstrate*' Warmbrunn, op. cit, 60

'*The weeks before*' Henri van der Zee, *The Hunger Winter: Occupied Holland 1944–45*, London, 1982, 33

'*Take heart, downhearted*', *Never Give In!: The Best of Winston Churchill's Speeches*, New York, 2003, 302

'*Invasion fever*' Frank, op. cit., 124

'*There is a revolution*' Ten Boom, op. cit., 164

'*All those parts*' *Travel*, June 1944, 34

'*In the Hague*' Van der Zee, op. cit.

'*He reached the dead*' Cornelius Ryan, *The Longest Day*, New York, 1959, 186

'*Hitler was also sceptical*' John Keegan, *Six Armies in Normandy* op. cit., 84–90

'*Under the command*' Ryan, op. cit., 210

'*On 10 June*' *The New York Times*, 12 June 1944

'*On 7 July*', 9 July 1944 ibid.

'*The Gerbrandy Government*' Dienke Hondius, *The Return*, Princeton, 2004, 56

'*In London, Wilhelmina*' Van der Zee, op. cit., 111

'*Now that the Allied*' ibid., 18

'*These heady proclamations*' ibid., 21

'*The entire country*' Edith Velmans, *Edith's Book*, London, 1998, 85

'*Seyss-Inquart*' Van der Zee, op. cit., 130–134

'*The NSB*' ibid., 23

'*On 2 September*' Gilbert, op cit., 208

'*The hour for which*' Van der Zee, 29–33

'*Now we are over Holland*' Edward Murrow, *In Search of Light*, New York, 1967, 83–5

'*On account*' Van der Zee, op. cit., 25

'*The Railways*' ibid, 20

'*Ten Boom chillingly*' Ten Boom, op. cit., 116

'*Maastricht is a sea*' Van der Zee, op. cit, 25

'*there are no signs*' *The New York Times*, 30 September 1944

'*some rockets blew up*' V-2 website, www.v2rocket.com/start/deploy-ment/denhagg/html

'*Rockets were firing*' ibid., Van der Zee, 29–33

'*Summoning the*' ibid., 32

'*declaring "biological war"*' ibid., 33

'*All told*' Reitlinger, op. cit., 341

'*We failed*' 'The World at War,' op. cit.

'*An article published*' *Nieuwe Drentsche Courant*, 19, 22 May 1945

'*The Dutch Bureau*' ibid.

'*Bob Moore describes*' Moore, op. cit., 262

'*According to*' Bert Jan Flim, 'opportunities for Dutch Jews to hide from the Nazis', *Dutch Jews as Perceived by themselves and By others*, Chaya Brasz, Yosef Kaplan, ed., Leiden, 2002

'*We Dutch now have*' Van der Zee, op. cit., 43

'*That day*' ibid., 43

'*The Putteners*' ibid., 45

'*On 1 October*' ibid., 48

'*As a result*' *The Times*, 7 October 1944

'*The curtains have*' Van der Zee, op. cit., 39

'*Several weeks later*' Norbert Buchsbaum, *Fotograaf Zonder Camera*, Amsterdam, 1972, 56

11 Holland SOS

'*It seems that something*' Van der Zee, op. cit., 189

'*The expression "starved to death"*' ibid., 190

'*To the general misery*' Robert Fruin (tr. E. Trevelyan), *The Siege and Relief of Leyden in 1574*, The Hague, 1927, 52

'*The Siege and Relief of Leiden*' ibid.

'*Following the siege*' *Encyclopaedia Britannica*, *Volume X*, 'Leiden', 640

'*In 1943*' *Annals of the American Academy of Political Science*, op. cit., 73–95

'*the bespectacled Nazi*' Van der Zee, op. cit.

'*when Hitler had once*' ibid.

'*Wilhelmina broadcast*' *The New York Times*, 26 December 1944

'*On New Year's Eve*' Van der Zee, op. cit., 420

'*Although Eisenhower*' Baldwin, op. cit., 84–86

'All around Holland' Van der Zee, op. cit.

'In early December' ibid.

'Weekly food rations' ibid.

'the canals' ibid.

'Technically, the winter' Records of the Royal Netherlands Meteorological Society, Amsterdam.

'Early in the morning' Van der Zee, op. cit., 146–148

'In the all' ibid.

'Throughout the winter' Annals of the American Academy, op. cit., 93–109

'The Hague' ibid.

'The worsening food situation' ibid.

'For every mouth' Fruin, op. cit.

'The death of an' Van der Zee., op. cit., 52

'On 25 November' V-2 website, op. cit.

'After the war' National Geographic, September 1946

'There continued to be' V-2 website, op. cit.

'On 4 February' ibid.

'On 9 December' Van der Zee, op. cit.

'One of the most' ibid., illustrations

'On 6 January, Gerbrandy' Van der Zee, op. cit., 41

'Six weeks later' ibid., 174

'the hitherto lowest' ibid., 147

'We cannot resist' ibid., 146

'To the general misery' Fruin, op. cit., 32

'The people of the Netherlands' Van der Zee, 190

'I am trying to have' Van der Zee, ibid.

'Law' The Times, 15 February 1945

'But he continued' ibid.

'But it was a chivalrous' The Times, 15 February 1945

'February did bring' Records of the Royal Dutch Meteorological Society, op. cit.

'CUTTING DOWN TREES FORBIDDEN!' Display, Dutch Resistance Museum, Amsterdam, op. cit., 108

'A special plunder commando' Annals of the American Academy of Political Science, February, 1946, op. cit., 53

'I am a thief' Van der Boom, op. cit., 228

'More than 20,000' Dutch Resistance Museum, 108–109

'In the last weeks' Ernst Schnabel, 'The Last Days of Anne Frank', *Life Magazine*, July 1957, 82–85

'*a car carrying Rauter*' Van der Zee, op. cit., 181

'*Himmler's revenge*' ibid., 182

'*On the morning of*' ibid.

'*It was as the*' The Times, 12 March 1945

'*Four days later*' Van der Zee, op. cit., 183

'*For the people*' ibid., 185–8

'*the result of the botched*' ibid.

'*Churchill was outraged*' Martin Gilbert, *Churchill*, London, 1995, 324

'*Famine in Holland*' The Times, 5 March 1945

'*A representative*' Van der Zee, op. cit., 233

'*the three western*' ibid., 190

'*On 12 March*' 36th Division History, New York, 1946, 65

'*On the night before*' Van der Zee, op. cit., 206

'*No admirer of the*' Van der Zee, op. cit., 231

'*In streets half ripped*' ibid.

'*It's going well*' ibid.

'*Hunger, hunger,*' ibid.

'*On 10 April*' ibid., 230

'*In any case*' ibid., 232–3

'*As the frightened*' ibid., 211

'*For three long years*' The New York Times, 3 April 1945

'*Buchenwald*' Murrow, op. cit., 91–5

'*it appeared*' ibid.

'*On 22 April*' Van der Zee, ibid., 221

'*Operation Manna*' ibid., 247

'*On that glorious*' ibid., 256

12 To See the Sky

'*It is not possible*' The New York Times, 5 March 1945

'*The Netherlands News Agency*' ibid.

'*The day before*' ibid., 10 May 1945

'*Death sentences*' ibid., 22 August 1945

'*Now look here*' Van der Zee, op. cit., 265

'*The Germans have*' ibid., 275

'*Van der Zee*' ibid.

'*the joyous reception*' Official History of the Canadian First Army, Montreal, 1984

'*But they waved*' The New York Times, 5 March 1945

'*In the worst*' ibid., 9 May 1945

'*All told*' Raul Hilberg, *Perpetrators, Victims, Bystanders*, New York, 1992, 209

'*In August the*' *The New York Times*, 12 February 1946

'*As van Beinum*' ibid.

'*Their treatment*' Hondius., op cit., 75–80

'*There was no one to*' *Dutch Resistance Museum*, op. cit., 120

'*The once thriving*' *The New York Times*, 6 July 1945

'*By far the more*' ibid.

'*The correspondent*' ibid.

'*One of the disappointed*' Melissa Muller, *Anne Frank: The Biography*, New York, 1998

'*Of those a little over*' *Dutch Resistance Museum*, 119–122

'*It was no surprise*' *The New York Times*, 5 September 1945

'*On 27 November*' Albert van der Heide, 'Chronology of Dutch wartime history', *The Windmill Herald*, 23 March 1995

'*the following*' *The New York Times*, 12 February 1945

'*the Dutch found that*' ibid.

'*In June, a deadly*' ibid.

'*David Anderson*' ibid.

'*The time has come*' ibid.

'*Diminutive Anton*' *The New York Times*, 7 May 1946

'*Regarding the Anschluss*' ibid., 19 November 1945

'*Seyss-Inquart did not disappoint*' ibid., 16 November 1945

'*leaders of the resistance*' ibid.

'*He said that he was*' G. M. Gilbert, *Nuremberg Diary*, New York, 1947, 48

'*several months later*' *The New York Times*, 16 March 1948

'*A representative*' ibid.

'*Gustave Steinbauer*' ibid.

'*In late May*' ibid., 23 May 1947

'*After the end*' ibid.

'*Upon Britain*' ibid.

'*When Frank Sinatra*' *Newsweek*, 18 August 1947, 10

'*Over the past year*', ibid., 10 August 1947, 10

'*Shortly before May*' Melissa Muller, *Anne Frank: The Biography*, New York, 1998, 275

'*In spite of everything*' Frank, op. cit.

'*Shining towers*' Jan Morris, *Manhattan '45*, New York, 1987, 47

'*This was the wonder city*' ibid., 50

Epilogue

'According to Martin Gilbert', Martin Gilbert, *The Righteous: The Unsung Heroes of the Holocaust*, London, 2003, 320

Bibliography

Anne Frank Foundation., *Anne Frank 1929–1945*, Amsterdam, 1979
——, *Anne Frank: A History for Today*, Amsterdam, 1996
Baedeker, K., *Baedeker's Rhine*, Leipzig, 1878
——, *Baedeker's Berlin*, Leipzig, 1905
Baldwin, H., *Battles Lost and Won*, New York, 1966
Boas, J., *Bovlevard des Misères: The Story of Transit Camp Westerbork*, New York, 1985
Boas, H.J., *Religious Resistance in Holland*, London, 1945
Boucher, H., *The Miracle of Survival*, Berkeley, 1997
Boom, C.T., et al., *The Hiding Place*, New York, 1992
Brasz, G., Kaplan, Y., *Dutch Jews as Perceived by Themselves and by Others*, Leiden, 2001
Brendon, P., *The Dark Valley – A Panorama of the 1930s*, Great Britain, 2001
Browning, C.R., *The Origins of the Final Solution*, London, 2004
Churchill, W.S. (ed)., *Never Give In!: The Best of Winston Churchill's Speeches*, New York, 2003
Churchill, W.S., *The Second World War: Their Finest Hour*, Boston, 1949
Coué, Emile, *Self Mastery Through Conscious Autosuggestion*, Montana, 1924
De Amicis, E., *Holland and Its People*, New York, 1881
Dawidowicz, L.S., *The War Against the Jews 1933–45*, London, 1987
De Jong, L., Schama, S., *The Netherlands and Nazi Germany*, New Haven, 1990
Elon, A., *The Pity of it All*, New York, 2003

Fisher, D., Read., A., *Berlin: The Biography of a City*, London, 1994

Fogelman, E., *Conscience and Courage: Rescuers of Jews During the Holocaust*, London, 1995

Foot, M.R.D., *Resistance: European Resistance to Nazism 1940–45*, London, 1976

Frank, A., *The Diary of a Young Girl*, New York, 1995

Friedlander, S., *Nazi Germany and the Jews – The Years of Persecution 1933–39*, London, 1997

Friedrich, O., *Before the Deluge*, New York, 1972

Fruin, R., *The Siege and Relief of Leyden in 1574*, The Hague, 1927

Gies, M., Gold, A.L., *Anne Frank Remembered*, New York, 1987

Gilbert, G.M., *Nuremberg Diary*, New York, 1947

Gilbert, M., *Atlas of the Holocaust*, London, 1988

——, *Churchill: A Life*, London, 1995

——, *The Holocaust: A History of the Jews of Europe During the Second World War*, London, 1985

——, *The Righteous: The Unsung Heroes of the Holocaust*, London, 2003

Gill, A., *The Journey Back From Hell: Conversations with Concentration Camp Survivors*, London, 1988

Gunther, J., *Inside Europe*, London, 1936

Haffner, S., *Defying Hitler: A Memoir*, London, 2002

Hilberg, R., *The Destruction of the European Jews*, New York, 1985

Hilberg, R., *Perpetrators, Victims, Bystanders: The Jewish Catastrophe 1933–1945*, New York, 1992

Hillesum, E., *Letters from Westerbork*, London, 1987

Hirschfeld, G., *Nazi Rule and Dutch Collaboration: The Netherlands under German Occupation 1940–45*, New York, 1988

Hondius, D., *The Return*, Princeton, 2004

Hoover, H., *The Memoirs of Herbert Hoover*, New York, 1951

Israel, J., Salverda, R., *Dutch Jewry: Its History and Secular Culture*, Leiden, 2002

Jackson, J., *France: The Dark Years 1940–1944*, New York, 2001

Johnson, P., *A History of the Jews*, London, 1993

Kennan, G., *Sketches From A Life*, New York, 1989

Kershaw, I., *Hitler: 1936–1945 Nemesis*, New York, 1989

Klemperer, V., *I Will Bear Witness: A Diary of the Nazi Years 1942–1945*, New York, 1999

LaCapra, D., *Writing History, Writing Trauma*, Baltimore, 2001

Laqueur, W., *The Holocaust Encyclopedia*, New Haven, 2001

Large, D. C., *The Perils of Prominence: Jews in Weimar Berlin*, New York, 2002

Lee, C.A., *The Biography of Anne Frank*, London, 1999

Lindwer, W., *The Last Seven Months of Anne Frank*, New York, 1991

Ludington, T., *Marsden Hartley: The Biography of an American Artist*, Ithaca, 1998

Lukacs, J., *The Last European War: September 1939–December 1942*, London, 1976

Lukacs, J., *The Duel: The Eighty-Day Struggle Between Churchill and Hitler*, London, 1990

Mak, G., *Amsterdam, Cambridge, 2000*

Marrus, M.R., *The Holocaust in History*, London, 1989

Miller, R., et al., *The Resistance*, Time-Life Books, Canada, 1979

Moore, B., *Victims and Survivors: The Nazi Persecution of the Jews in the Netherlands 1940–1945*, London, 1997

Morris J., *Manhattan '45*, New York, 1987

Mulder, D., *Kamp Westerbork*, Westerbork, 1991

Muller, M., *Anne Frank: The Biography*, New York, 1998

Murrow, E., *In Search of Light*, New York, 1967

Paldiel, M., *The Path of the Righteous: Gentile Rescuers of the Jews during the Holocaust*, New Jersey, 1993

Pomerans, A., *An Interrupted Life: The Diaries of Etty Hillesum 1941–1943*, New York, 1983

Presser, J., *Ashes in the Wind: The Destruction of Dutch Jewry*, London, 1988

Rachlis, E., et al., *The Low Countries*, New York 1963

Reitlinger, G., *The Final Solution: The Attempt to Exterminate the Jews of Europe 1939–1945*, New York, 1953

Ready, J. Lee, *World War Two: Nation by Nation*, London, 1995

Roters, E., et al., *Berlin 1910–1933*, New York, 1982

Ryan, C., *The Longest Day*, New York, 1959

Schloss, E, *Eva's Story: A Survivor's Story by the Step Sister of Anne Frank*, London, 1988

Schnabel, E., *The Footsteps of Anne Frank*, London, 1976

Shirer, W., *The Rise and Fall of the Third Reich*, New York, 1960

——, *This Is Berlin: Reporting From Nazi Germany 1938–40*, London, 1999

Somers, E., Kok, R., *Het Boek 40–45*, Zwolle, 2002

297

Spector, S. (ed.), *Encyclopedia of the Holocaust*, London, 2000

Tuchman, B., *The Guns of August*, New York, 1962

Trachtenberg, I., *So Slow the Dawning*, New York, 1973

Van der Boom, B., *Den Haag in de Tweede Wereldoorlog*, (Dutch), The Hague, 1995

Van der Zee, H., *The Hunger Winter: Occupied Holland 1944–1945*, London, 1982

Van Kleffens, E.N., *The Rape of the Netherlands*, London, 1940

Velmans, E., *Edith's Book*, London, 1998

Warmbrunn, W., *The Dutch Under German Occupation 1940–45*, New Jersey, 1963

——, *The German Occupation of Belgium 1940–1944*, New York, 1993

Wheal, E.A., et al., *Encylopedia of The Second World War*, Princeton 1989